STUDENT ACTIVITIES
ANSWER KEY
FOR

CULTURAL
GEOGRAPHY

THIRD
EDITION

BJU PRESS
Greenville, South Carolina

NOTE: The fact that materials produced by other publishers may be referred to in this volume does not constitute an endorsement of the content or theological position of materials produced by such publishers. Any references and ancillary materials are listed as an aid to the student or the teacher and in an attempt to maintain the accepted academic standards of the publishing industry.

Student Activities Answer Key for CULTURAL GEOGRAPHY
For use with the THIRD EDITION

Michael D. Matthews, M. Ed.

CONTRIBUTING AUTHORS
Lauren Kowalk
Nathan Lentfer
Dennis Peterson

EDITOR
Manda Kalagayan

COVER & BOOK DESIGN
Drew Fields
Elly Kalagayan

PAGE LAYOUT
Drew Fields
Carol Jenkins
Megan Eshleman

PROJECT MANAGERS
Elena Emelyanova
Kevin Neat
Malachy Pierre

PHOTO ACQUISITION
Joyce Landis
Rita Mitchell
Sarah Strawhorn

PHOTOGRAPH CREDITS:
Cover
www.istockphoto.com/VisualField; www.istockphoto.com/aaussi (background photos); www.istockphoto.com/ Evgeny Kuklev (tag); www.istockphoto.com/Stephen Green (circle stamp); Copyright © 2003 by Dover Publication, Inc. (luggage labels); www.istockphoto.com/Matt Knannlein (rectangular stamp)

Front Matter
www.istockphoto.com/Evgeny Kuklev (tag); www.istockphoto.com/Stephen Green (circle stamp); www.istockphoto.com/Matt Knannlein (rectangular stamp)

Chapter 5 www.istockphoto.com/David Cannings-Bushell 33; www.istockphoto.com/Falk Kienas 35
Chapter 6 Jacques Descloitres, MODIS Land Rapid Response Team, NASA/GSFC 40
Chapter 8 Rocky Mountaineer Vacations 55-58

Produced in cooperation with the Bob Jones University Departments of History and Social Studies of the College of Arts and Science, the School of Education, and Bob Jones Academy.

© 2008 BJU Press
Greenville, South Carolina 29614

First Edition © 2000

ISBN 978-1-59166-886-4

15   14   13   12   11   10   9   8   7   6   5   4

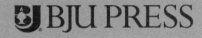

HOW TO USE THE ACTIVITIES MANUAL

These activities are designed to give you maximum flexibility. We have provided a menu of activities from which you can select the ones that will help you achieve your instructional goals. Before you begin each chapter, look over the activities and decide which ones best meet your students' needs and which ones you want to use. You do not have to use all of them. Determine how you want to assign them. The *activity* codes and *skill* codes at the bottom of each page will help you decide.

ACTIVITY CODES

Each chapter has three to seven activities. The activity code tells you which sections of the chapter each activity covers. The code also tells you whether the activity is good for reinforcement, enrichment, or review.

- *Reinforcement* activities are based solely on the information in the textbook. They help students (1) to recognize and recall major terms and concepts in the chapter and (2) to "put it all together." Some reinforcement activities cover the entire chapter. (Students can complete them as they read through the chapter or as they review for tests.) Other reinforcement activities apply to a specific section of the chapter. (Students can complete them as they read the section.)

- *Enrichment* activities go beyond the textbook. They help students (1) to apply information from the chapter, (2) to pursue subjects they find interesting, and (3) to develop special skills. Every student can benefit from these activities, but they are particularly useful for students who need a challenge. Most enrichment activities are related to a specific section in the chapter.

- *Chapter review* activities help students to prepare for the chapter test.

ALTERNATIVE USES OF THE ACTIVITIES

Activities are useful for more than just homework. You can make them an integral part of your classroom discussion. For example, you can complete many of the map activities together in class as you cover the material in the chapter. Or you can use them as a means of review after you have covered all of the material. Your students will especially appreciate your help in completing the more difficult activities.

- **Homework**—The students complete the activity at home.

- **Class activity**—The students complete the activity in class by themselves or in groups.

- **Class discussion**—You help the class complete the activity together in a classroom discussion.

- **Lecture**—You complete the activity on the chalkboard or overhead projector during your lecture, while the students take notes.

TABLE OF CONTENTS

CULTURAL GEOGRAPHY

FAMOUS MEN IN THE HISTORY OF GEOGRAPHY

Complete the following chart. Choose from the people, dates, and facts of interest listed below the chart. Then answer the questions that follow.

Person	Date	Accomplishment(s)	Significance
Alexander the Great	Reigned 336–323 BC	Conquered Persia and marched into India	Expanded Greek knowledge about world geography
Eratosthenes	ca. 276–195 BC	Calculated the circumference of the earth; wrote *Geography*	First to use the term *geography*
Hipparchus	Second century BC	Drew a map grid	Made locating places on maps easy
Ptolemy	Second century AD	1. Drew a famous ancient world map; 2. Promoted the geocentric theory	Devised a map and a theory of the universe that was unchallenged for almost fourteen centuries
Copernicus	1543	Promoted the heliocentric theory	Revolutionized scientific thought
Mercator	1569	Drew a modern world map	Set a new standard of excellence in cartography

Copernicus	1569	Promoted the geocentric theory
Eratosthenes	Drew a map grid	Promoted the heliocentric theory
ca. 276-195 BC	First to use the term *geography*	
Second century BC	Made locating places on maps easy	Set a new standard of excellence in cartography
Second century AD		

1. What empire produced the earliest surviving map (a clay tablet)? Babylonian

2. Who were the first ancient people to study the earth extensively? Greeks

3. What country calculated the meter? France

4. What sea power became the world's leading mapmaker in the eighteenth century? England

5. What military power is the world's leading mapmaker today? United States

CULTURAL GEOGRAPHY

FIND IT!

Apollo 11 has returned to earth, and you need to find it as quickly as possible. Different reports give the following different locations. With the help of an atlas, name the body of water or the continent where *Apollo 11* was sighted as it made its reentry.

1. 20° S, 140° W ___Pacific Ocean___

2. 40° S, 80° E ___Indian Ocean___

3. 20° N, 0° ___Africa___

4. 0°, 0° ___Gulf of Guinea___

5. 90° S, 180° W ___Antarctica___

Name the physical feature at each of the following locations.

6. 20° N, 90° W ___Yucatán Peninsula___

7. 40° N, 6° W ___Iberian Peninsula___

8. 40° N, 80° W ___Appalachian Mountains___

9. 70° S, 65° W ___Antarctic Peninsula___

10. 23° S, 23° E ___Kalahari Desert___

Give the approximate latitude and longitude of each of the following locations.

11. New Zealand ___40° S, 170° E___

12. Gobi Desert ___42° N, 102° E___

13. Hawaiian Islands ___20° N, 158° W___

14. Tasmania ___43° S, 146° E___

15. Lake Victoria ___3° S, 33° E___

CULTURAL GEOGRAPHY

EXPLORING MAP PROJECTIONS

Using the various map projections in this chapter, answer the following questions:

1. In what ways are directions slightly distorted on the gore map?

   East-west directions are completely accurate because they follow the straight left-right lines. The twelve

   north-south longitude lines in the middle of each gore are accurate in relationship to the east-west latitude

   lines. All other longitude lines are distorted with a slight curve.

2. What distortions does the Goode's map minimize in comparison to the gore map?

   areas and shapes

3. What distortions does the Goode's map make worse?

   distances and north-south directions

4. What is the only line of latitude on the Mercator projection that does not distort distance?

   equator

5. Are shapes distorted on the Mercator projection? Why or why not?

   No, because shapes are stretched proportionally; the shapes of the continents remain basically undistorted.

6. What advantage does each of the projections have over the Robinson projection?

   Goode's—areas at the poles; Mercator's—directions

Identify each of the following map projections by name.

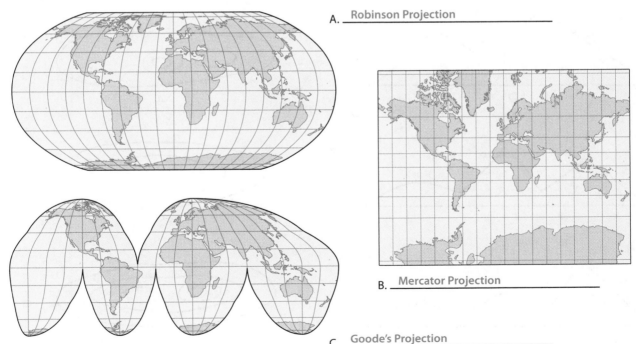

A. _Robinson Projection_

B. _Mercator Projection_

C. _Goode's Projection_

CONTOUR LINES

Using your textbook, match each of the following side views with the correct relief map on the right by connecting them with a line.

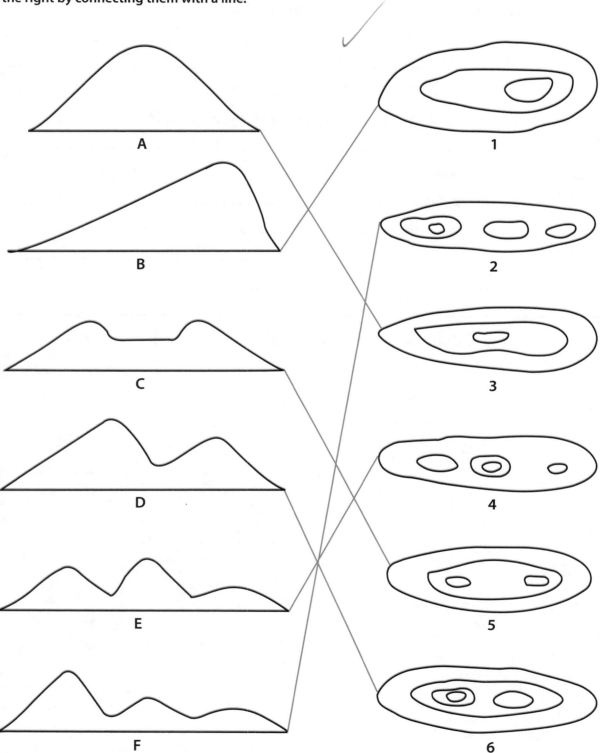

SKILL: Maps

THE RELEVANCE OF GEOGRAPHY

Read the following article, written by a professional geographer, concerning how geography is relevant to life and society today. Then answer the questions that follow.

As a discipline, geography has always dealt with analyzing spatial patterns, including both physical and human topics. Location and space are critical issues in almost every decision we make, forcing all of us to use our personal spatial analytical techniques constantly as we move about, analyze world events, invest our money, or plan our cities.

"Hasn't everything already been mapped?" is an almost comical retort about the discipline of geography. New maps of new patterns are continuously being made, as society strives to understand how the new patterns are developing and what they mean.

There are many examples of new and rapidly changing spatial patterns, some requiring quick, but very complex maps. Assessing the potential deadly impact of a hazardous waste spill, such as chloride, could keep another Bhopol, India, disaster from happening. Planning the fastest emergency vehicle routes or the most efficient school bus routes requires sophisticated mapping involving hundreds of variables.

"Location matters" is a basic tenet of geography. The discipline brings together a host of different processes and phenomena that other disciplines treat in isolation. It is not just knowing where places are located, but understanding the relationships among and between places and the external and internal influences affecting them.

Scale across both space and time is also important in geographic analysis, since many local phenomena interact with global ones over time. An example is local fossil fuel use and its cumulative effects on global change.

Geography is certainly more than making maps. While map-making, or cartography, is geography's most important tool, a host of other tools are also important, including remote sensing (aerial photography and satellite imagery), field research (sampling and interviewing) and quantitative methods (comparing and projecting patterns).

Although many Americans recognize the importance of geographic knowledge in everyday life, fewer know about opportunities available to college-educated geographers. Geographers trained in the cutting-edge, multidimensional, computerized geographic information systems (GIS) are in enormous demand across virtually all of science and society.

Examples of spatial-analytical jobs held by former students from this professor's academic department include: a Congressional redistricting analyst, an animal disease analyst with a state Department of Agriculture, a bank vice president (farmer's loan specialist), foreign area analysts with the federal agencies, airport noise analyst for Charlotte-Douglas Airport, a U.S. forest ranger, location analysts for Lowe's Companies, urban and regional planners, Enhanced E-911 mappers and tax mappers.

New technologies, combined with a very old discipline, have created a new respect among companion disciplines for the field of geography.

(Excerpt from "Hot Geography!" by Neal G. Lineback. Copyright © 2000 by maps.com. Printed by permission of the author.)

1. What is the geographer's most important tool?

   map-making, or cartography

2. What is GIS?

   computerized geographic information systems

3. List five occupations that the author lists as being represented in his academic circles.

   (any five) a Congressional redistricting analyst, an animal disease analyst with a state Department of Agriculture, a

   bank vice president (farmer's loan specialist), foreign area analysts with the federal agencies, airport noise analyst

   for Charlotte-Douglas Airport, a U.S. forest ranger, location analysts for Lowe's Companies, urban and regional

   planners, Enhanced E-911 mappers and tax mappers

4. Explain in your own words why geography is important and relevant to the average person today.

   Answers will vary but may include the following: the need to find and follow directions to get from one location

   to another; to understand one's neighbors better (both individually and nationally), to help prevent man-made

   disasters (chemical spills, etc.) or to deal with them when they do occur, to get a company's products to

   consumers quickly and efficiently, etc.

THE MAIN FEATURES OF THE EARTH

Use the glossary and the many maps in your textbook to complete the map on the other side of this page. The lists of the various geographic features are scattered throughout the chapter.

1. Label each of the five largest islands of the world: Greenland, New Guinea, Borneo, Madagascar, and Baffin.

2. Label the five longest rivers of the world.

3. Label the four principal oceans of the world.

4. Label the six largest lakes of the world.

5. Label the following mountain ranges: Appalachians, Rockies, Andes, Alps, Urals, Himalayas.

6. Label the following plains: Great Plains, Pampas, Amazon Basin.

7. Label the following plateaus: Brazilian Highlands, Deccan Plateau.

8. Label each of the seven continents.

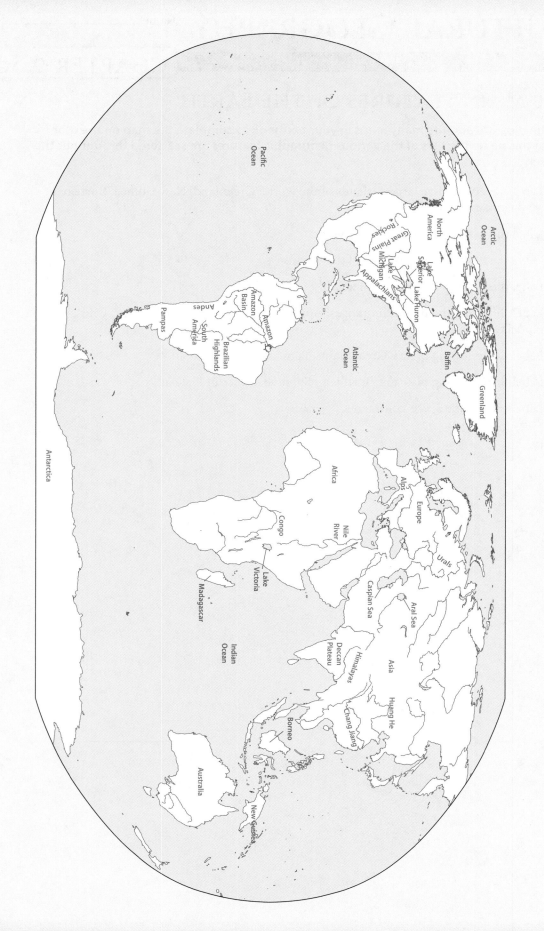

STATISTICAL AVERAGES OF THE CLIMATES

Answer the questions based on the statistical table.

Average statistics for the climates of the world					
Climate	Temperature (°F)		Precipitation (avg. in.)		
	Summer	Winter	Annual	Summer months	Winter months
TROPICAL RAINY					
Tropical wet	79	79	100	8.0	8.0
Tropical wet and dry	79	79	50	10	0.5
DRY					
Tropical and temperate dry	81	55	5	0.6	0.1
Semiarid	78	51	18	3.4	0.2
MODERATE					
Marine west coast	60	42	45	2.5	5.5
Mediterranean	72	52	23	0.4	3.8
Humid continental	66	21	27	3.2	1.6
Humid subtropical	77	47	50	6.2	2.8
COLD					
Icecap	32	−14	8	1.0	0.4
Polar	40	0	16	1.9	1.2
Subpolar	56	−8	17	1.8	1.2

1. Which climate has the highest summer temperature?

   tropical and temperate dry

2. Which two climates have the highest winter temperature?

   tropical rainy (tropical wet and tropical wet and dry)

3. Which climate has the lowest temperature?

   icecap

4. Which climate has the highest variation between summer and winter temperatures?

   subpolar

5. Which climates have no variation between summer and winter temperatures?

   tropical wet, tropical wet and dry

6. What is the only moderate climate whose average temperature dips below freezing (32°F) in winter?

humid continental

7. Which climate has the highest annual precipitation?

tropical wet

8. Which climate has the lowest annual precipitation?

tropical and temperate dry (desert)

9. Which climate has the highest variation between summer and winter precipitation?

tropical wet and dry

10. Which climate has no variation between summer and winter precipitation?

tropical wet

11. What is the monthly precipitation in the summer for a mediterranean climate?

0.4 inches

12. What is the monthly precipitation in the summer for a tropical and temperate dry climate?

0.6 inches

13. Which moderate climate gets the most winter rainfall?

marine west coast

14. What two climates have an annual precipitation about the same as a semiarid climate?

polar and subpolar

15. If a city has an average temperature of 50°F and 4.0 inches of rain in the winter months, in what climate region is it likely to be?

mediterranean

LATITUDE ZONES

Label the latitude zones on the globe below. (First, try to label each zone without looking in your book. Then check your answers using the diagram in your chapter reading.)

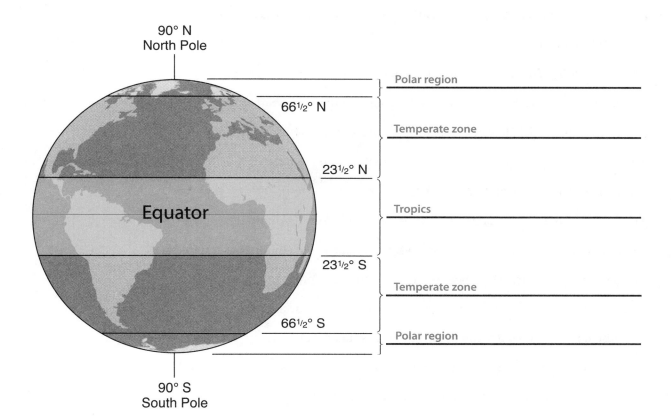

90° N
North Pole

Polar region _____

66½° N

Temperate zone _____

23½° N

Equator

Tropics _____

23½° S

Temperate zone _____

66½° S

Polar region _____

90° S
South Pole

DISTINGUISHING TERMS

Underline the word or phrase that best completes each of the following sentences.

1. According to 2 Peter 3:5, modern man is "(willingly ignorant, deceived)" about Creation and the Flood.

2. Christians believe that most of the earth's features were changed as a result of (a cataclysm, uniformitarianism).

3. The water on the earth's surface is called the (lithosphere, hydrosphere).

4. The (mantle, core) is the plastic layer of rock located under the earth's crust.

5. Some geographers debate whether (Europe, Australia) is really a continent.

6. The largest islands in the world are (continental, oceanic) islands.

7. The largest continental landmass is (Africa, Eurasia).

8. The four oceans are the Atlantic, Pacific, Indian, and (Arctic, Antarctic).

9. Some geographers contend that there is a fifth ocean around (Indonesia, Antarctica).

10. (Mount Everest, Mount McKinley) rises higher than any other mountain on earth.

11. Trees that lose their leaves every fall are called (coniferous, deciduous) trees.

12. The best agricultural land is found on the world's (plains, plateaus).

13. The Amazon River has the largest (drainage basin, volume of trade) in the world.

14. The largest lake in the world is (the Caspian Sea, Lake Baykal).

15. A (fault, depositional mountain) is an example of tectonic activity.

16. According to the (continental drift, plate tectonics) theory, the earth was once united into a supercontinent called Pangaea.

17. (Weathering, Erosion) carries away sand and soil to form sand dunes and barrier islands.

18. Decayed substances produced by living organisms are called (alluvium, humus).

19. The region between the Tropic of Cancer and the Tropic of Capricorn is called the (Temperate Zone, tropics).

20. The process of precipitation, evaporation, and transpiration is called the (hydrologic, orographic) cycle.

CULTURAL GEOGRAPHY

Name _____

CHAPTER 2 ACTIVITY 5

TINY TABLES

Complete the following "tiny tables" using information found in your chapter readings.

Phases of the earth's history	Main forces of change
1. Creation	God's miraculous intervention
2. Flood	God's miraculous intervention, floodwater, fountains of the deep, and water pressure
3. Modern world	Earthquakes, volcanic forces, weathering, erosion
4. Future world	God's miraculous intervention with fire; new heaven and earth

List the oceans by size (largest first)
1. Pacific
2. Atlantic
3. Indian
4. Arctic

List the continents by size (largest first)
1. Asia
2. Africa
3. North America
4. South America
5. Antarctica
6. Europe
7. Australia

Divisions of the earth today	Description
Atmosphere	Air that surrounds the planet
Lithosphere	Solid part of the earth
Hydrosphere	Water on the earth

Layers of the lithosphere	Depth in miles	State of matter (liquid or solid)
Crust	4.5–31	Solid rock
Mantle	1,800	Plastic (capable of being molded)
Core	2,156	Liquid outer; solid inner

Major types of landforms	Description	Advantage for man	Disadvantage for man
Mountain	Rugged land that rises high above the surrounding landscape	Mineral riches, defensible border	Hindrance to travel, poor soil
Plain	Wide, level areas	Rich soil, easy travel	Floods, no defensible borders
Plateau	Wide, level areas that rise abruptly above surrounding lands	Grass for livestock	Poor soil, few natural resources

Ways to compare rivers	Unit of measure	World leader
Length	Miles	Nile River
Discharge	Cubic feet per second	Amazon River
Drainage area	Square miles	Amazon River
Navigability	Miles	Amazon River

Types of wetlands	Distinctive characteristics
Bog	Spongy areas that look dry but are covered with wet organic materials
Marsh	Standing water where grasses and small water plants grow
Swamp	Standing water dominated by large trees

Forces of change		Manifestations	Resulting landforms
INTERNAL	Tectonic activity	Faults and folds	Deformational mountains
	Volcanic forces	Volcanoes	Depositional (volcanic) mountains
EXTERNAL	Weathering	Breakdown of rocks (by temperature changes, water, plant roots, and ice)	Unusual rock formations
	Erosion	Natural removal of weathered rock materials (by wind, waves, glaciers, and running water)	Sand dunes, terminal moraines, sea caves, sea arches, sandbars, barrier islands, gullies

SKILL: Maps

WHAT GOD SAYS ABOUT THE ENVIRONMENT AND MAN'S RESPONSIBILITY TOWARD IT

Read the following questions carefully, looking up each Bible reference cited so you can discover and communicate what God says about (1) the purpose of the environment, (2) human responsibility for the environment, and (3) mistaken views about the environment.

1. *Environmentalism* is the modern effort to protect the environment from the negative results of human industry. Typically, environmentalists reject the traditional interpretation of God's Creation Mandate, given in Genesis 1:28. A growing number of Christians advocate "Christian environmentalism," arguing that man has a duty to exercise stewardship over creation.

    a. Who owns the earth (Job 41:11; Ps. 24:1; 50:12)? _God_

    b. What is one of God's purposes for all animals and plants (Gen. 9:3)?
    to be food for mankind

    c. Has God given man dominion over all creation (Ps. 8:4–8)? _yes_

    d. Are people more valuable than animals (Matt. 10:31; 12:11–12)? _yes_

    e. When did God intervene to destroy the environment (2 Peter 3:5–6)? _at the Flood_

    f. With whom did God make a covenant not to destroy the earth again by water (Gen. 9:12–16)?
    with Noah, certainly, but also with every living creature

    g. What cataclysm will destroy the earth some day, and who will be responsible for it (2 Pet. 3:10)?
    fire; God

2. The environmentalist movement has begun to gain support in Christian circles. In 1993, the newly formed Evangelical Environmental Network (EEN) published a 1600-word document, "Evangelical Declaration on the Care of Creation," which many Christian leaders signed. It stated, "We repent of the way we have polluted, distorted, or destroyed much of the Creator's work," and it warned that "we are pressing against the finite limits God has set for creation." It called on Christians and churches to become "centers of creation's care and renewal." Interestingly, the Bible is silent concerning the government's duty to protect the environment, but it says a lot about private individuals' obligation to use private property wisely.

    a. What is our first responsibility to the environment (Gen. 1:28)?
    to subdue it

    b. What is another basic responsibility, according to the following verses: John 6:12; Proverbs 12:27; 18:9? _to be frugal, not wasteful_

    c. Of what should workers take care (Prov. 12:10)? _their beasts of burden (By extension, because modern industry generally does not use animals, this principle includes one's tools, equipment, and other machinery.)_

    d. Which trees did God forbid the Israelites to cut down during a siege (Deut. 20:19–20)? Why?
    fruit trees; because of their long-term value for man

e. What wild animals are mentioned in Deuteronomy 22:6–7? Why were the Israelites commanded not to kill them? *mother birds; apparently to ensure the survival of birds*

f. What unfair treatment of animals did God forbid in Deuteronomy 25:4?

muzzling an ox while it grinds grain (i.e., don't hinder the ox from eating while it is working)

g. What will be forgotten some day (Isa. 65:17)? *modern heaven and earth*

h. What is wrong with the EEN's proposal to make churches "centers of creation's care and renewal"?

While it is true that individual Christians have a responsibility to exercise wise stewardship over the earth, that is

not the mission of the church. See Matthew 28:19–20.

i. What is more valuable than the whole earth (Matt. 16:26)? *one human soul*

j. What should be our current attitude, now that we know the earth's future (2 Pet. 3:11)?

to be careful to live godly lives

3. Former vice president Al Gore became a leading spokesman for environmentalism after the publication of his book *Earth in the Balance* (1992). A professed Southern Baptist, he attended the launch of the Evangelical Environmental Network in 1993. His book made several controversial claims. For example, he wrote that the modern lesson of Noah and the ark is "Thou shalt preserve biodiversity." He contended that the first instance of pollution in the Bible occurred when Cain slew Abel and his blood fell on the ground, rendering the ground useless. Gore's concern was so great that he claimed, "We must make the rescue of the environment the central organizing principle for civilization."

a. According to Psalm 104:1–5, would you describe the environment as stable or unstable?

stable

b. Is it possible for human industry to disrupt the seasons (Gen. 8:22)? *no*

c. Environmentalists say that God told all mankind to "keep" the earth, but to whom was His command given, and what was to be kept (Gen. 2:15)? *Adam; the Garden of Eden*

d. Environmentalists quote a warning in Revelation 11:18 that God will "destroy them which destroy the earth." But what is God actually condemning in that verse? Who will be the one destroying the earth?

the sin that requires judgment; God

THE CHRISTIAN AND THE ENVIRONMENT

Read the following excerpts and then answer the questions that follow.

CARING AND WORKING: AN AGRARIAN PERSPECTIVE

BY: NORMAN WIRZBA

The practice of caring for the earth has traditionally fallen upon farmers. In the past the vast majority of people were directly or indirectly involved in agriculture; but in the past few centuries farms have been transformed into agribusinesses, becoming a branch of the ever-growing industrial-technological economy. Fewer and fewer people have any direct experience of food production.

How can Christians be responsible caretakers of the earth if they are not familiar with farming practices? Farming is not simply about food production. Farming is a way of being, a concrete practice in which the lessons of creatureliness can be learned. In taking care of the life that God has given us, we enter Noah's theological-agricultural laboratory [aboard the ark].

In thinking about farming there are at least two revolutions that need to be considered: the revolution of agriculture, and the more recent industrial revolution within agriculture. Wes Jackson, founder and director of the Land Institute in Salina, Kansas, says that the plow may well be the most significant and far-reaching artifact in human history. While we often think of the plow as a tool of peace and prosperity, few other instruments compare in their ability to put the long-term survival of life forms at risk. The reason is simple: tillage agriculture tears open and makes vulnerable the soft membrane that supports all life. Soil loss due to erosion (it is estimated that we lose 25 billion tons of topsoil every year, an amount that greatly outstrips nature's ability to replenish it), as well as water loss due to runoff (with cultivation the root structures that hold and absorb water are destroyed), lead to the eventual transformation of fertile ground into desert. This has been the pattern throughout history. In hardly any culture has tillage agriculture been sustainable in the long term. Such cultures eventually deplete the soil and water and start relying on imported foods.

The second agricultural revolution was the shift to using costly machinery and chemicals in farming. Because of this new approach, the energy required to grow food has risen dramatically. Some foods, it is estimated, require ten calories of fossil fuel energy (in the form of petroleum, fertilizer and pesticide production, manufacturing, transport, and meal preparation) to produce one calorie of nutrition.

Moreover, the transformation of farming into an agribusiness has brought with it a host of environmental problems, including ground water depletion and contamination, soil toxification, and contamination of food supplies. These facts surprise many of us, especially since we see the abundance of food in the supermarkets created by agribusiness. But this abundance comes at a very high cost and with a skewed accounting system. Agribusiness depends on cheap oil and an unlimited supply of water. . . . These conditions cannot last. We are transferring to future generations the problems of coping with an exhausted soil and contaminated water supply. The sins of the fathers will be visited on the children.

This brief review of farming practices suggests that we have a long way to go toward becoming responsible creatures. We have only partially succeeded or outright failed at many of our efforts at taking care of creation. Had we been in the ark instead of Noah, many species might have perished through ignorance, neglect or outright destruction. How, then, are we to honor the creator and the creation?

[W]e need to question the modern faith that teaches us to view the world as a problem to be solved through scientific knowledge and technological innovation. This idea came into its own in the modern period, when [Francis] Bacon declared the world the arena for human satisfaction and flourishing, and thus brought a missionary zeal to the program of scientific experimentation and technological innovation. But its roots extend to the ancient Greek notion of *techne*, the idea that the world can be remade or fashioned according to a human plan.

⌒

What makes modernity so striking is our sudden acquisition of the mechanical means for a rapid transformation of the earth. We no longer merely tinker with the world as the ancients did.

. . . Agrarianism has not been adequately considered by philosophers, theologians or scientists. For example, the land-grant universities that were established to promote agriculture quickly left farmers behind, and even as they advanced research programs in the service of science and technology they contributed to the demise of farming as a way of life. . . . [A]grarianism is about tending to or taking care of the world already given.

⌒

[A]t its core [are] the twin concepts of attention and responsibility. . . . [T]he trends of our economic, social and political life lead to inattention and irresponsibility. Individuals and groups often do not have to live with the consequences of their actions. For instance, corporate decision-makers frequently devise plans that damage or devastate human and nonhuman communities, without themselves having to live with the results.

⌒

Farmers have rarely been interested in "seeing the world." Their focus, if it is to be successful, must be on the local, on the needs and requirements of the specific places where they live. Would our economies better serve us if they focused more on local and less on international markets? Evidence suggests that this is the case, at least if human and environmental health, rather than corporate profits, are the issues. Increased attention to the local, combined with care and responsibility, will contribute to the growth of well-cared-for communities.

Agrarians make it clear that the scope of our care must extend beyond fellow humans to include all of creation. . . . [T]his is not to suggest that we all need to become farmers, much less farm with horses. . . . Rather, [it] promotes an alternative worldview, one that can be adopted equally by urbanites (who can take the time to garden, or learn to shop more responsibly) and by farmers.

Christians can learn from an agrarian vision to cultivate the faith. To do so is to indicate our preparedness to trust the goodness of God's Creation, and to see in our lives and in all other lives a gift from God. We will, in other words, learn to become caretakers of the earth. . . . [W]e will understand that the source of value resides not in ourselves but in a creation and creator much greater than ourselves.

⌒

I grew up in a family of farmers where it was clear that no unnecessary work was to be done on the Sabbath. This may not sound like a big deal until one realizes that the Sabbath also comes around in the midst of harvest season, when the loss of one day's work can mean the loss of thousands of dollars. I look back in astonishment at my forefathers' practice. Why not work and secure one's livelihood as best one can? Why give generously in the midst of hard economic times?

The Sabbath is a compact expression of the virtue of caretaking. The Sabbath invites us to enjoy the grace everywhere at work in creation. It calls us . . . to rest in a keeping that is not our own. . . .

(An excerpt from "Caring and Working: An Agrarian Perspective" by Norman Wirzba. Copyright © 1999 by the *Christian Century*. Reprinted by permission from the September 22, 1999, issue of the *Christian Century*.)

1. What are the two revolutions in agriculture to which the author refers?

   the revolution of agriculture begun by the plow and the industrial revolution within agriculture that led to the

   widespread use of modern machinery and chemical fertilizers

   _____

2. What conclusion does the author make concerning the effect of these revolutions on the energy required to produce food?

   He concludes that it now takes more energy to produce the food than is derived from consuming the

   products.

   _____

3. What two resources does the author contend are required for the continued success of modern agribusiness? cheap oil and an unlimited supply of water

4. Why does the author imply that farmers (agrarians) tend to be more concerned about the wise use of the environment than large corporate manufacturers?

   Farmers live on the land and realize that what they do to and with it will have consequences that will affect

   them directly, whereas the manufacturers are far removed from the land, do not see the consequences of

   their decisions and actions, and do not live where those results are felt.

   _____

5. Why do you think the author brings the Sabbath into his argument for agrarianism?

   Answers will vary, but they might include the following points. God, in His wisdom, commanded man to rest

   one day in seven. In so doing, man is giving the land a rest as well. Although this practice seems to go

   against all logic to someone who is focused only on the bottom line, it is God's way, which is always for the

   benefit of mankind.

6. Overall, do you agree or disagree with the author's premise that agrarianism promotes good environmental practices? Support your answer.

   Answers will vary.

   _____

   _____

   _____

CULTURAL GEOGRAPHY

FOREIGN PRODUCTS AT HOME

Check your home for each of the products listed below. Give the name of the manufacturer, if known, and the city or country where the company is located.

Nondurable Manufacturing		Durable Manufacturing	
peanut butter		dinner plates	
tuna		drinking glasses	
flour		clock	
leather belt		wristwatch	
aspirin		reclining chair	
book		wooden chair	
pencil		folding chair	
shirt		screwdriver	
silk tie		can opener	
pants or dress		steel knife	
woven basket		automobile	
rug		personal computer	
toy (describe)		washing machine	

List items found at your home that were manufactured in the following foreign countries. (These are the top ten trading partners of the United States.)

Canada		Taiwan	
Japan		Netherlands	
Mexico		Singapore	
United Kingdom		China	
South Korea		Other	
Germany		Other	

Mass market retailers (such as Wal-Mart) derive the vast majority of their sales from foreign-made products. Are such businesses good for America? Support your answer.

Answers will vary, but the following points might be made for each side of this question.

Yes—It means lower prices, greater variety, higher standard of living for American consumers; it's free trade

in action. No—It costs American workers' jobs; puts American manufacturers out of business; encourages

unfair trade practices by foreign companies and inhumane treatment of foreign workers; leads to dumping

of cheap goods on American markets; and makes the United States economy a vassal of foreign countries,

some of whom (notably China) have philosophies and practices that are antithetical to American freedom and

democracy

SKILLS: Analysis, Application, Evaluation

TERMS FROM INDUSTRY

Identify the terms described below.

1. Type of farmer who produces only enough for his household __subsistence__

2. Type of farmer who produces large cash crops for profit __commercial__

3. Aluminum ore __bauxite__

4. A combination of metals, such as steel __alloy__

5. Three basic fertilizers: phosphorus, nitrogen, and __potassium__

6. Gaseous fossil fuel __natural gas__

7. Liquid fossil fuel __petroleum__

8. Mineral fuel __uranium__

9. The application of science to industry __technology__

10. Basic energy and equipment needs of industries __infrastructure__

11. Any type of energy resource that will run out someday __nonrenewable__

12. Sending messages through electronic impulses __telecommunications__

13. Type of business that buys goods in large quantities from producers to sell in smaller quantities to other business __wholesale__

14. Type of business that sells goods directly to the consumer __retail__

15. Money used to build industries __capital__

16. Economic system under which the government owns the major industries __socialism__

17. Economic system under which private individuals or corporations build most industries __capitalism__

18. The people or businesses that buy products from an industry __market__

19. Goods received from other countries __imports__

20. Goods shipped to other countries __exports__

21. Taxes on imports and exports __tariffs__

22. God's command to man to subdue the earth __Creation Mandate__

23. Subsistence husbandry __nomadic herding__

24. Natural resources extracted by primary industries __raw materials__

25. The opposite of protectionism __free trade__

26. Industries that take resources from the earth to be turned into various products _primary industries_

27. Industries that change raw materials into a useful form _secondary industries_

28. Industries that provide services _tertiary industries_

29. The study of the process by which people and countries make choices _economics_

30. The value of all of the goods and services produced within a country over the course of a year
    GDP, or gross domestic product

SKILLS: Recognition, Comprehension

CULTURAL GEOGRAPHY

Name _____

A CLOSER LOOK AT THE WORLD CULTURE REGIONS

Answer the following questions about the eight world culture regions.

1. Identify the culture region for each of the following groups of subregions.

 a. Canada, United States __North America__

 b. Middle America, South America __Latin America__

 c. British Isles, Scandinavia, Continental Europe, Mediterranean Europe __Western Europe__

 d. Eastern Europe, Russia, Central Asia __Central Eurasia__

 e. South Asia, East Aasia, Southeast Asia __Asia__

 f. Persian Gulf, Eastern Mediterranean __Middle East__

 g. North Africa, West Africa, Central Africa, East Africa, Southern Africa __Africa__

 h. Australia, New Zealand, Pacific Islands __Oceania__

2. Which culture region has the most countries? __Africa__

3. Which culture region has the fewest countries? __North America__

4. What two world culture regions share part of the continent of North America?
 __North America and Latin America__

5. Which world culture region includes part of three continents? __Middle East__

6. Which continent has three world culture regions? __Asia__

7. Which world culture region is broken up into the most subregions? __Africa__

8. How many individual countries are listed as subregions? List them.
 Five: Canada, Russia, United States, Australia, and New Zealand

9. How many regions or subregions include the word *central* or *middle*?
 Five: Middle America, Central Eurasia, Central Asia, Middle East, Central Africa

10. How many regions or subregions are named after a specific body of water? List them.
 Four: Mediterranean Europe, Eastern Mediterranean, Pacific Islands, Persian Gulf

CULTURAL GEOGRAPHY

THE IMPORTANCE OF DEMOGRAPHY TO GEOGRAPHY

Using Section II of your textbook, "Demography: The Statistics of Society," answer the following questions. (Answers to some of the questions will not be stated explicitly in the text; you will have to think about them and come up with your own answers.)

1. What term means the "life signs" of a society? _vital statistics_

2. A country's crude birthrate indicates the number of children born for every how many people in the country? _1,000_

3. A country's crude death rate indicates the number of deaths for every how many people in the country?
   _1,000_

4. Subtracting a country's crude death rate from its crude birthrate gives what important statistic of the country? _rate of natural increase_

5. What do a country's life expectancy and infant mortality rates indicate about a country?
   the country's standard of living, especially the health of its people and the quality of its medical care,
   sanitation, emergency services, police/fire protection, and food supply

6. Generally, what conclusions can one make about a country whose urban population is growing and whose rural population is declining? _that the country is becoming more industrialized and is able to feed its people_
   more efficiently with fewer farm workers

7. What term is used to describe a central city and all of its surrounding suburbs?
   metropolitan area

8. What term means the average number of people who live on each square mile of land?
   population density

9. What term refers to the amount of a country's land space that can be cultivated for food production?
   arable land

10. Explain why the theory of Thomas Malthus concerning overpopulation is invalid.
    Malthus believed that food supplies would never keep pace with the increasing population and that war,
    famine, disease, and self-restraint were the only checks on catastrophic population growth. He failed to take
    into consideration, however, the effects of industrialization, which made crop production more efficient, or
    the economic prosperity that accompanies a capitalistic free market system and political freedom. Although
    population increased, so did man's ability to produce not only enough food to take care of his immediate
    country but also a surplus of food to trade to other nations in return for raw materials and finished goods.
    Rather than being a burden, population is society's greatest asset if cared for properly.

SKILLS: Recognition, Evaluation

POLITICS: THE GOVERNANCE OF SOCIETY

Complete the following chart, which classifies the basic types of government. Then answer the questions beneath the chart.

Type of government	Definition/description
1. Anarchy	No government
2. Authoritarian government	A government that holds power by claiming an authority higher than the people it governs
a. Absolute monarchy	Rule by a king or queen who receives his or her power by birth and rules as he or she pleases
b. Dictatorship	Rule by a person who is backed by the authority of the military
c. Totalitarian government	Rule by leaders who believe they should make decisions about every detail of their people's lives for the good of the whole
3. Elected government	A government that relies on the consent of the people to keep its position
a. Direct (pure) democracy	A government in which the whole population rules, voting on every issue, large and small
b. Indirect (representative) democracy	A government that gives the people an opportunity to vote for politicians of their choice, to voice their opinions, and to run for office
(1) Constitutional monarchy	A government whose monarch's power is limited by law and whose real power belongs to an elected legislature; the leader of the legislature heads the bureaucracy
(2) Republic	A government that elects both a legislature and a separate national leader (president) who supervises the bureaucracy

1. What are the two ways by which countries may resolve disputes between themselves?
   war and negotiation

2. What are the two types of international treaties? peace and military alliance treaties

3. What is the name of the international organization that tries to ensure peace and understanding among the nations of the world? United Nations

4. Name the five permanent members of the Security Council.
   United States, United Kingdom, France, China, Russia

5. What are the two basic functions of government? defense and justice

6. What term means the principles or agenda by which a country deals with other countries?
   foreign policy

7. Which country has the largest military in the world today? China

8. Which country expends the greatest dollar amount on its military forces? United States

9. Which country spends the greatest percentage of its gross domestic product on its military?
   Jordan

10. What term refers to countries that reject democracy and capitalism, oppose the countries that support
    those principles, and ignore the fundamental principles of international relations?
    rogue nations

11. What term means the art of negotiating agreements between nations? diplomacy

12. What advice did Thomas Jefferson offer concerning relations with other countries?
    to pursue "peace, commerce, and honest friendship with all nations—entangling alliances with none."

13. Define *self-determination*. the principle that all peoples have a right to vote for the type of government they
    will have

14. What treaty established basic rules for how nations are to treat wounded soldiers and prisoners of war?
    Geneva Convention

15. What is the largest volunteer organization seeking to relieve the sufferings of people who have experienced
    hardships because of war or natural disasters? Red Cross

SKILL: Charts, Comprehension

THE IMPORTANCE OF THE OBVIOUS

Americans sometimes have difficulty understanding the U.S. political and economic systems. The confusing explanations by "experts" make some people wonder if even those experts know what they mean. Why is America so successful? Calvin Coolidge said, "If all the folks . . . would do the few simple things they know they ought to do, most of our big problems would take care of themselves." This bit of practical wisdom can be applied to the principles of economic and political freedom so that average people can understand what makes America successful. The six principles in the following essay will help you gain such an understanding. Read the selection carefully, and then answer the questions at the end.

MORE FREEDOM, LESS GOVERNMENT

First, the free market philosophy increases the freedom of the individual and limits the role of government.

Socialists look upon society as a herd to be directed by governmental herdsmen with no consideration of the individual. They think society produces and consumes goods. In reality, there is no economic activity of masses but only of individuals.

The freedom philosophy permits the maximum activity of the individual. It allows him to make choices and take risks. It does not promise stability, as does collectivism. Instead, it gives uncertainty, challenge, and opportunity. It permits one to dream and then to attempt making those dreams reality. And, in order to allow this activity, it permits failure as well as success. The dreams which are considered worthwhile become successful in the market; those which are deemed worthless or too costly fail.

Socialism promises what unthinking men desire: equality. But in providing a false equality, it takes away the freedom of the individual. Truly free men are not equal, and equal men are never truly free.

There can be no mixture of these two systems, individualism and collectivism. One cannot be an individualist in one area and a collectivist in another. He is either completely one or completely the other in every aspect.

The free market is social cooperation entered into freely without coercion, i.e., social contract. The freedom philosophy, therefore, necessarily must restrict government to the protection of the life, liberty, and property of the individuals comprising society. Government is to act only as an umpire in the interrelationships of individuals, punishing those who harm or threaten to harm the rights or property of others. It is to insure an atmosphere in which the individual is free to pursue his own desired self-advancement provided he does not in the process harm others.

Henry David Thoreau accented this dual action of the freedom philosophy when he wrote in *Civil Disobedience*, "There will never be a really free and enlightened State until the State comes to recognize the individual as a higher and independent power, from which all its own power and authority are derived, and treats him accordingly."

Whenever government steps beyond this, its legitimate responsibility, it damages the economic and moral well-being of the individual and of the nation. It can do this in a variety of ways, including excessive taxation, restriction of personal freedoms, or regulation of the economy. The best government is the one that does not go beyond its protective duties or unduly limit the individual. It teaches the individual to govern himself so that government intervention becomes not only undesirable but also unnecessary.

REWARD FOR ACHIEVEMENT

Second, the free market philosophy rewards the work ethic.

In Bible times, the apostle Paul commanded that "if any would not work, neither should he eat" (2 Thess. 3:10). This principle was transplanted to America and applied by John Smith in Jamestown. As a result, the colony overcame its difficult first years and prospered.

The free enterprise philosophy offers the prospect of economic success for those who are willing to toil and exert themselves in lawful pursuits. They are free to attempt putting their dreams and ideas into practice and to succeed or fail. Opportunity, not special privilege, is the watchword of the entire system.

Workers in a planned economy, however, are mere cogs in the inter-meshing of governmental gears, striving for a bureaucratic utopia without the incentives of freedom or personal advancement of self-satisfaction.

Free enterprise rewards the worker who exhibits initiative and industry. Workers who give a good day's work are rewarded with a mutually acceptable day's wages. Those who shirk or loaf are soon forced out of their jobs by the more enthusiastic workers. The hard workers are further rewarded with bonuses, promotions, and raises to the degree they excel or produce. As one wise person put it, the worker who never does more than he is paid for never gets paid for more than he does.

In a truly free market, unemployment is strictly a voluntary condition. Those who want employment can have it—provided they are willing to work for the wages the market is willing to pay and provided they can supply the goods and/or services the market demands. There is always a job for one who is willing to work for what the market determines he and his product or services are worth.

THRIFT ENCOURAGED

Third, the free market philosophy encourages thrift.

The door of economic success swings on the hinges of thrift, the wise use of capital. The individual who is master of his money and resources succeeds; he who is mastered by them fails.

Andrew Carnegie, one of the wealthiest capitalists of the late nineteenth and early twentieth centuries, said, "The man should always be the master. He should keep money in the position of a useful servant; he must never let it be his master and make a miser of him."

Thrift may be simply summarized by five imperatives.

1. *Spend less than you receive.* Calvin Coolidge once said, "There is no dignity quite so impressive, and no independence quite so important, as living within your means." Much of the poverty and economic difficulty of our time could be alleviated if individuals and governments had the courage to say, "No, I can't afford it."

2. *Stay out of debt.* First, one should try not to run up bills. Second, if one cannot avoid debt, he should get out of it again as quickly as possible. A man in debt is not his own master; he is at the mercy of his creditors until his debts are paid in full.

3. *Never spend anticipated income before it is actually received.* In more quaint terms, "Don't count your chickens before they're hatched!"

4. *Keep a regular and accurate account of all receipts and expenditures.* Such record-keeping readily reveals unwise or unprofitable spending. It also shows the importance of little expenditures to the whole. It ensures wise and orderly expenditures and produces a visible and encouraging record of income. The record-keeping should in time develop into a wise budgeting system.

5. *Make every effort to save some of every amount received.* "I should say to young men," Carnegie advised, "no matter how little it may be possible to save, save that little." It is from such savings that investment is possible for the development of businesses which produce the goods and services needed and desired in the marketplace. It is from such savings that charity is possible for the assistance of those less fortunate than ourselves.

PHILANTHROPY INCREASED

Fourth, the free market philosophy encourages philanthropy, the caring for the less fortunate and the rewarding of worthy causes by those who are successful. Charity is the giving of one's own goods to another in need out of the generous desire of one's own heart, i.e., by voluntary contribution. It is not government-coerced funding for the support of others.

To the extent that freedom is permitted in the marketplace, philanthropy increases, for greater successes in the marketplace mean more help for those who are unable to help themselves. Contrariwise, to the extent that government restricts freedom in the market, philanthropy decreases, and those unfortunate, needy others suffer.

Charity and philanthropy are the duties of private individuals, groups, and churches, not of government. The Bible commands families to care for their own needs and for the churches to care for those who have no families. "But if any provide not for his own, and specially for those of his own house, he hath denied the faith, and is worse than an infidel" (1 Tim. 5:8).

A list of the world's great philanthropists sounds like a list from *Who's Who in Capitalism*: Philip Armour of the meat industry; Andrew Carnegie, steel magnate; E. I. DuPont de Nemours, chemical manufacturer; Henry Ford, automobile manufacturer; J. P. Morgan, financier; John Wanamaker, department store pioneer. The list could go on and on. These men were able to give vast sums to worthy causes only because the free market permitted them to earn even greater sums. Each of them forgot himself for a while in order to remember others, and practically everyone in the nation now remembers their generosity.

In the area of social welfare, as in all other areas of the free market, government only assumes this familial and religious duty in direct proportion to the degree this obligation is first abdicated by those to whom it legitimately belongs.

MORAL ATTITUDES

Fifth, the free market philosophy thrives or founders according to the moral and spiritual condition of the individuals comprising that market. Their moral and spiritual outlook determines the nation's economic outlook. As the evangelist D. L. Moody once said, "Nations are only collections of individuals, and what is true in regard to the character is always true of the whole."

Free enterprise encourages, in fact demands, adherence to the Golden Rule: "Whatsoever ye would that men should do to you, do ye even so to them" (Matt. 7:12). So long as men follow this simple but profound truth, freedom, peace, and prosperity abound. Only when some attempt to force, by government authority, their own desires on the rest do slavery and turmoil occur. When men are bad, society is bad. With such disruption of the market comes economic decline.

Alexis de Tocqueville tried to find the secret of America's greatness, searching diligently in the fields, in the schools, and in the halls of government. But he concluded those places, though great, did not hold the key to America's greatness. Not until he observed the moral strength of her citizens, derived from their religious principles, did he understand fully the cause of the nation's greatness. "America is great because America is good," he said. "When America ceases to be good, America will cease to be great."

Part of a nation's moral standing is determined by whether its citizens have the courage to do what is right regardless of the trends around them. The people with a sound moral condition will have an indestructible confidence in the ability of truth to triumph over error, good over evil. When men lose this faith in God, they inevitably lose their liberty, for God is the Author of liberty.

"Americans," Calvin Coolidge reminded us, "have not fully realized their ideals. There are imperfections. But the ideal is right. It is everlastingly right. What our country needs is the moral power to hold to it."

ABIDING PRINCIPLES OF SUCCESS IN THE FREE MARKET

Finally, the principles of economic success in the free market are the same regardless of the size of the operation, be it an individual, a family, a multinational corporation, or an entire nation. Statistics and conditions may frequently change, but principles remain forever the same.

Collectivist bureaucrats would have us believe that economics is a field larger than the common man, an area into which only the experts dare enter. With their array of charts, graphs, and frightening terms and statistics, they quickly convince many that this is exactly the case. What they themselves fail to understand, however, is that economics is, at the lowest level, merely individual human actions, choices and decisions made in the marketplace of goods, services, and ideas.

The common man is deeply involved in the economy on a daily basis. He decides to work or not to work. He chooses to buy or sell or not to buy or sell. He makes trade-offs based on his own needs, wants, and resources. He takes risks. He succeeds or fails. Multiplied several million times all across the nation, this makes up the bulk of economic action in our country. Granted, much influence is exerted on the economy by large corporations, wealthy capitalists, special interest groups, and even governments. But the principles of the free market are always the same regardless of who is involved.

If the free market philosophy was successful, correct, and good in the developmental stages of our nation's history, it remains so even today. If it has worked for America, it will also be practical and successful when applied to other nations.

The free market philosophy, regardless of where applied, is successful because of simple, obvious principles like the ones briefly examined above. The greatest complexities occur whenever these principles are ignored or forgotten. One cannot overemphasize the importance of the obvious.

(Dennis L. Peterson, "The Importance of the Obvious," *The Freeman*, August 1983.)

1. What does socialism promise that it cannot deliver? __equality__

2. In interpersonal dealings, to what role is the government restricted? __umpire__

3. What is the watchword of the free enterprise system of economics? __opportunity__

4. What are the five principles of the wise use of capital?

   Spend less than you receive, stay out of debt, don't spend money before it's earned, keep records of receipts

   and expenditures, and save part of everything received.

5. What is a philanthropist? __someone (usually one who is considered wealthy) who uses part of his or her__

   income for charitable purposes

6. Why can it be said that the economic and political outlook of a country is determined by its moral and spiritual attitudes?

   A nation is nothing more than the collective individuals within it; if those individuals are generally immoral

   and spiritually weak, the nation will be also; and that condition will be reflected in the nation's economic and

   political condition.

A MAP OF WESTERN EUROPE

Locate and label on the map the following places and geographic features.

Each country and its capital	Danube River
Atlantic Ocean	Apennine Mountains
Baltic Sea	River Thames
Corsica	Massif Central
Sardinia	Mediterranean Sea
English Channel	Mount Vesuvius
Scandinavian Peninsula	Pennine Mountains
Black Forest	Rhine River
Sicily	Iberian Peninsula
Strait of Dover	Peloponnesus
Jutland Peninsula	Ireland
Alps	Pyrenees Mountains
Po River	Strait of Gibraltar
North Sea	Crete
Seine River	

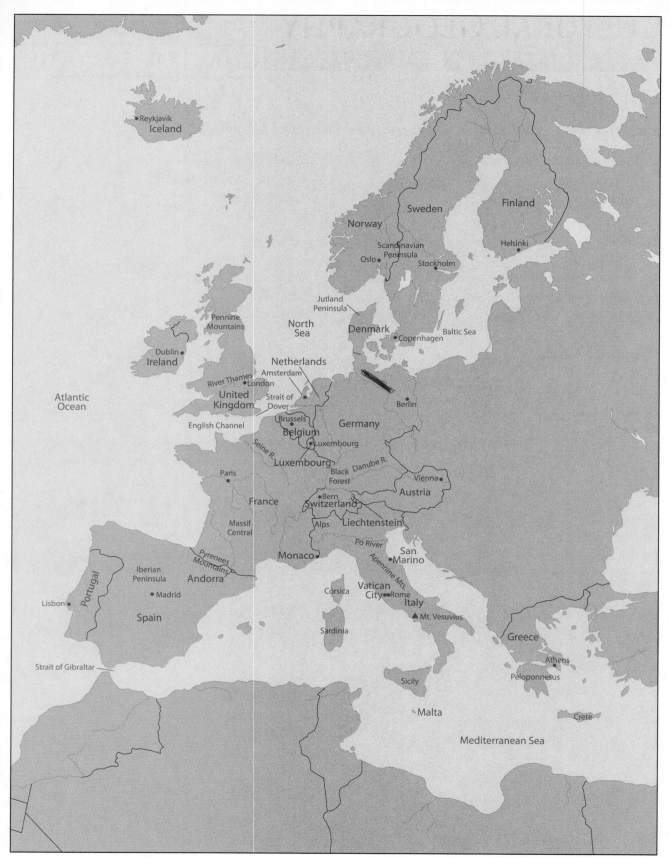

Reykjavik
Iceland

Norway
Sweden
Finland

Scandinavian
Peninsula

Oslo
Stockholm
Helsinki

Jutland
Peninsula

North
Sea

Denmark

Copenhagen
Baltic Sea

Pennine
Mountains

Dublin
Ireland

Netherlands

Amsterdam

River Thames
London

Strait of
Dover

United
Kingdom

Berlin

Atlantic
Ocean

Brussels

English Channel

Belgium

Germany

Luxembourg

Seine R.

Luxembourg

Black
Forest

Danube R.

Vienna

Paris

France

Austria

Massif
Central

Bern
Switzerland

Liechtenstein

Alps

Pyrenees
Mountains

Po River

San
Marino

Apennine Mts.

Monaco

Iberian
Peninsula

Andorra

Corsica

Vatican
City
Rome
Italy

Madrid

Lisbon

Portugal

Spain

Sardinia

Mt. Vesuvius

Greece

Athens

Strait of Gibraltar

Peloponnesus

Sicily

Crete

Malta

Mediterranean Sea

SKILLS: Maps, Recognition

THE EUROTUNNEL

Read the following excerpt and answer the questions at the end of the reading.

Matt Webb swam as hard as he could. Night had fallen, and he could not see land. Storms threatened. Large waves blocked his view and choked his breathing with salt sprays. Tiredness spread across his mind and body. His arms ached from twenty hours of swimming, and his thoughts drifted from lack of sleep. He jerked alert at the sight of a shark passing nearby.

Matt Webb had begun his swim August 24, 1875, near Calais, France. He hoped to be the first to swim across the English Channel, but he did not think it would take this long. Lights. Yes, he could see lights in the distance. Success was in sight, and he stayed alert for the last leg. When he finally reached land near the white cliffs of Dover, it was August 25, and he had been swimming twenty-one hours and forty-five minutes.

This section of the Eurotunnel route runs parallel to a roadway in Kent, England.

The English Channel stood as a great barrier. It protected England from land attacks and forced her to become a great sea power. Albert Matthieu, a French engineer, first proposed a tunnel in 1802. A tunnel linking France and England would greatly aid land transportation, but both governments rejected all proposals as impractical until 1986.

Work began December 1, 1987. The tunnel structure and machinery form a unique transportation system combining civil, mechanical, and electrical engineering. As a transportation system, the tunnel links the British, French, and Belgian railway systems. There are actually three parallel tunnels, two wide ones and a narrow one, each 131 feet beneath the bottom of the English Channel. The three tunnels are each thirty-one miles long, and twenty-four of those miles pass beneath the sea floor. Although Japan's Seikan Tunnel is a little longer (33.5 miles), only 14.5 miles of the Seikan pass under the sea to link Honshu with Hokkaido. Since the English Channel Tunnel is only 2.5 miles shorter but mostly underwater (the world's longest underwater tunnel), it was selected unanimously as a wonder of the world by the international panel of engineers.

Each of the twenty-five-foot-diameter tunnels contains a fourteen-foot-wide train. The 7,600 horsepower engines enable these trains to reach speeds of 87 mph. Each train is half a mile long and can carry 130 cars and buses. Motorists drive their cars right onto the shuttle and remain in their cars for the hourlong ride, which means that most shuttles carry about eight hundred passengers. In addition, the freight shuttle carries up to twenty-eight trucks.

Though underwater and under the sea floor, the train ride is quite comfortable and safe. The twenty-four shuttle carriages, half of which are double-deckers, are brightly lit, soundproof, and even air-conditioned. The smaller 16-foot diameter service tunnel between the large train tunnels provides for maintenance and emergencies. At almost quarter-mile intervals, cross passages eleven feet in diameter connect the service tunnel with the main tunnels. Sliding doors seal off cross passages when they are not in use. Similar steel doors can seal off the main tunnels into equal thirds. Siphons remove rainwater and condensation, and fans circulate air. Three hundred miles of pipes cool the tracks with water, and pistons open and close ducts to relieve pressure that builds up in front of the train. Fiber-optic cables relay information between controllers and engineers.

Queen Elizabeth II of England and President François Mitterrand of France presided at the opening dedication on May 6, 1994. The fifteen thousand workers completed the tunnel in six-and-a-half-years, one year behind schedule. Expenses mounted to 15 billion, twice the amount budgeted, and it also cost the lives of nine workers.

[Ron Tagliapietra, *The Seven Wonders of the World* (Greenville, SC: Bob Jones University Press, 1999), 57-60.]

The Channel Tunnel (or Chunnel)

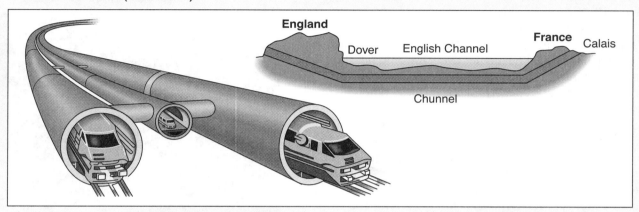

1. How many tunnels are there, and for what are they used?

   There are three tunnels. Two tunnels are used for trains, and one smaller tunnel is used as a service route.

2. How far under the English Channel is the Eurotunnel? 131 feet

3. Why is the Eurotunnel considered a wonder of the world even though the Seikan Tunnel is longer?

   Though the Seikan Tunnel is longer, less than half of it is underwater. The Eurotunnel is a little shorter, but most of it is

   underwater.

💡 How do you think the Eurotunnel has affected the United Kingdom's relations with the rest of Europe?

   Answers may include the following: It has brought the United Kingdom into a closer relationship with the rest of

   Europe because of increased trade and ease of traveling back and forth from the Continent to the United Kingdom.

SKILL: Analysis

CLIMBING THE ALPS

Read the following excerpt and answer the questions at the end of the reading.

Reinhold Messner clung to the sides of the icy cliffs called the Grandes Jorasses. The Walker Spur on these cliffs led to Walker Point, a 13,805-foot pinnacle among the various subpeaks of the massif forming Mont Blanc. Messner climbed with three friends in August of 1966. Roped in pairs—Messner with Fritz Zambra, and Sepp Mayerl with Peter Habeler—they used their crampons, ice axes, and ice pitons even though it was summer. At the top, Messner rejoiced at his personal victory: his first climb of the hardest of the three famous climbs in the Alps.

Messner's personal victories had accumulated for about twenty years. His first climb—at the age of five in 1949—had been with his father up the Sass Rigais. Five years later, on the East Face of the Kleine Fermeda, his father had first permitted him to lead the way up a Class 3 pitch. In 1960, on the North Face of the Sass Rigais with his brother Günther, he had pounded in his first pitons. Three years later, he had climbed his first Class 6 face, the Tissi Route on the first Sella Tower. The same summer, he had climbed his first ice face, the North Face of Similaun. In the summer of 1965, Messner had set his first record. With Günther and two other men, he had made the first-ever ascent of the Class 5+ route up the North Face of the Grosse Fermeda. In 1966, he soloed the Class 6 Solda route on the South Face of the Piz-de-Ciavàces.

⁓

On January 29, 1968, Messner climbed another step up a narrow snow-choked fissure. He pounded in a piton for stability. He and two friends had spent two nights wet and shivering in small overhang caves on the face of Monte Agnér. The peak rises in the Dolomites, a range of the Alps in the South Tirol region of Italy. Born at Bressanone, Messner grew up in this German-speaking region ceded from Austria to Italy in 1919. Now, as the sun set on their third day, they made the last scramble to the summit. This climb was more than a personal victory. It was the first-ever winter climb of Monte Agnér.

Messner also developed his style in the Alps. On the Dirupi di Larsec in May of 1967, Messner and his brother decided that technical aids could take the sport out of climbing. Even an amateur could succeed on difficult climbs with rope ladders, bolts, and drills. One might as well land on the summit with a helicopter.

On the other hand, Messner did not ignore safety. Messner and his companions often admitted defeat on a given day due to weather or weariness. Knowing when to turn back is part of safety, and Messner had never fallen in his climbing career. He also would not ignore the most advanced clothing or flashlights. Messner decided he would use ropes and pitons to limit the length of potential falls but would use as few pitons as possible. Messner was a free climber. His challenge was to find the best natural route up the rock face.

Climbers classify pitches much as rafters classify rapids. Climbers do not rate stretches of easy walking or impossible smooth rock faces. Everything in between gets classified from 1 to 6. Class 1 involves steep scrambles, and Class 2 adds the use of hands. Climbers rope together for safety at Class 3 and they belay one another with ropes for Class 4 pitches. Class 5 designates the most difficult technical pitches, sub-classified from 5.1 to 5.9 and now up to 5.14. Climbers also use grades to rate routes based on the toughest pitch, length of technical portions, and difficulty of retreat in case of blizzards or injury. Grades 1 through 6 range from technical portions of a few hours with easy retreats to multiple days of extreme climbing, which may be fatal even for experts. By 1969, at the age of twenty-five. Messner had achieved fifty first-ascents in the Alps and twenty solo ascents. What would be next?

Lightning sliced the sky. Messner and Peter Habeler waited for the thunder and rain of stones from the lightning-struck summit of the Matterhorn. They huddled on the difficult North Face of the 14,690-foot peak at the end of July in 1974. The ledges could not hold the large amounts of falling snow, and the sliding drifts poured over them. Pulling themselves onto the summit, they had achieved another of the three classic ascents of the Alps—and in very difficult conditions. They descended quickly because of lightning danger.

Distress signals flashed from the Eigerwand, a sheer wall of rock almost six thousand feet high from base to summit. Messner and Habeler, in spite of bad weather, set off at 5:00 AM on August 14, 1974, to see whether they could help. Rain-swollen waterfalls poured over ledges and drenched them as they ascended the Class 5 pitch called the Difficult Crack. Roped together and taking turns at the lead, they soon reached the distressed party. One of the pair had fallen forty meters and broken a leg. As they spoke, a helicopter hovered while a rescuer jumped out on a rope. He splinted the broken leg, and the helicopter hauled up each man on the rope. Messner and Habeler, their help unneeded, continued up more Class 5 pitches: the Ramp, the Spider, and the Exit Cracks. In their haste to help the injured man and to avoid afternoon rockslides, they passed parties that had been climbing for several days. They reached the top at 3:00 PM, setting a record of ten hours for the climb.

Eiger, which means Ogre, towers over 13,000 feet.

Messner had now scaled all three of the classic big walls: the Matterhorn North Face, the Grandes Jorasses, and the Eiger North Face (Eigerwand). These are considered the classic climbs because they lead to major Alpine peaks, combine high-elevation climbing with extreme technical difficulty, include both rock and ice climbing, and lack easy escape routes if the climber gets in trouble.

[Ron Tagliapietra, *Great Adventurers of the Twentieth Century* (Greenville, SC: Bob Jones University Press, 1998),179-82.]

1. How did Messner begin climbing?

   He started climbing with his father when he was five. He led his first climb at the age of ten and began to use pitons about the age of eleven.

2. What equipment did Messner use to climb the mountains described in the reading?

   the most advanced clothing, flashlights, ropes, and pitons

3. With what criteria do mountain climbers grade routes?

   how technical the pitch is, toughest pitch, length of technical portions, and difficulty of retreat in case of blizzards or injury

SKILL: Analysis

CHAPTER REVIEW

Using what you have learned from reading and studying this chapter, answer the following questions.

1. What countries are in Scandinavia?

   Iceland, Denmark, Sweden, Norway, and Finland

2. What countries are on the Iberian Peninsula?

   Spain, Portugal, and Andorra

3. What ministates are near Italy?

   Monaco, San Marino, Vatican City, and Malta

4. What are the two largest cities in Western Europe, and on what rivers are they located?

   London—River Thames, Paris—Seine River

5. What religion has its headquarters in Vatican City? Roman Catholicism

6. What is the largest mountain range in Europe? the Alps

7. Of what two major organizations are many countries in Europe members?

   European Union and North Atlantic Treaty Organization

8. What is the major mountain range of the United Kingdom? Pennine Mountains

9. What is the major mountain range of Italy? Apennine Mountains

10. On which peninsula is Denmark situated? Jutland Peninsula

11. What is the largest city in Scandinavia? Stockholm

12. What is the best-known feature in southwestern Germany? Black Forest

13. What is the lowest major pass through the Central Alps? Brenner Pass

14. What is the Meseta? a plateau across most of interior Spain

15. What nations share the Scandinavian Peninsula? Norway and Sweden

16. What mountain is famous for its triple cirque peak? the Matterhorn

17. What are the longest rivers in Italy, France, Spain, and the United Kingdom?

   Italy—Po River, France—Loire River, Spain—Tagus River, United Kingdom—River Thames

18. What are polders? parcels of land reclaimed from the sea

19. What country includes the island of Crete? Greece

20. What are the two districts of Belgium? Flanders and Wallonia

21. What country is known for dikes? __the Netherlands__

22. What mountain range forms the border of Spain and France?
__Pyrenees Mountains__

23. What is the highest mountain in the Alps? __Mont Blanc__

24. What is an imaginary line in the Pacific Ocean that separates days?
__International Date Line__

25. What is the highest mountain in the British Isles? __Ben Nevis__

SKILL: Recognition

CULTURAL GEOGRAPHY

A MAP OF EASTERN EUROPE

Locate and label on the map the following places and geographic features.

Vistula River	Dnieper River	Great Hungarian Plain
Dinaric Alps	Black Sea	Transylvanian Alps
Great European Plain	Adriatic Sea	Pinsk Marshes
Chernobyl	Balkan Mountains	Danube River
Carpathian Mountains	Crimean Peninsula	Each country and its capital
Dalmatia	Baltic Sea	

© 2008 Map Resources. All Rights Reserved.

A SATELLITE MAP OF EASTERN EUROPE

The map below is a satellite image focusing on the Eastern Balkans. Use your textbook to locate and label on the map the following countries and geographic features.

Aegean Sea	Great Hungarian Plain	Serbia
Black Sea	Greece	Transylvanian Alps
Bulgaria	Hungary	Turkey
Carpathian Mountains	Moldova	Ukraine
Danube River	Romania	

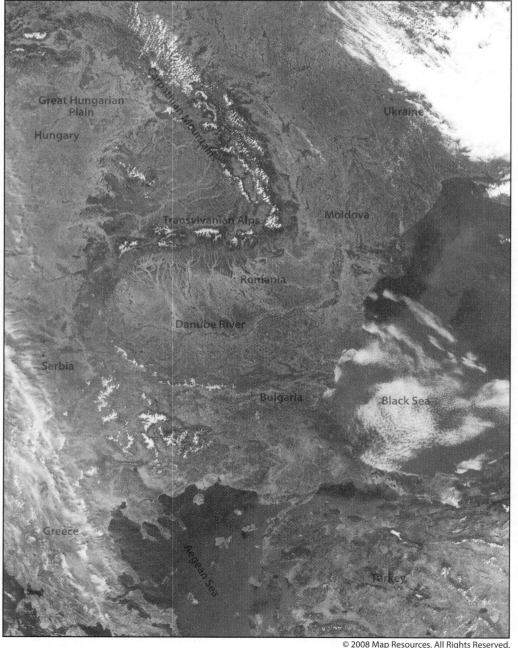

© 2008 Map Resources. All Rights Reserved.

SKILLS: Maps, Recognition

Name _____

HUMAN RIGHTS IN THE BALKANS

Read the following and answer the questions at the end of the reading.

Bosnia and Herzegovina lies on the historic divide between the Eastern and Western Roman Empires. Since the fall of the Roman Empire, the people in Bosnia have been caught between invading tribes and competing empires. After the invasion of the Ottoman Turks in the late 1300s, the Serbs in the east developed a strong allegiance to the Orthodox Church, and the Croats in the west developed a strong allegiance to Catholicism. Meanwhile, the Slavs in the center, where loyalties were weakest, converted to Islam. Serb and Croat nationalists despised these Muslim Slavs, who had adopted the faith of the conquerors.

The problems of the former country of Yugoslavia deepened with the rise of violent, opposing political parties in the 1920s and 1930s that backed either Germany or Russia. When Serb nationalists refused to bend to Hitler's will, he invaded in 1941 and dismembered the country. Hitler gave control of Croatia and Bosnia to the Ustashi, who vowed to wipe out the two million Serbs living in their lands. These Croatian fascists demanded that the Serbs convert to Roman Catholicism or die. Hundreds of thousands of Serbs were placed in death camps, tortured, and murdered. The Serb response was just as grim. A resistance army arose, led by Draza Mihajlovic. In 1942 Mihajlovic proposed that the Serbs create "a great Serbia which is to be ethnically clean . . . of all national minorities and non-national elements." Over one million people died in Yugoslavia during the war, most by the hands of their own countrymen.

During the Communist era, the Serbian and Croatian nationalists were held in check by the secret police. However hard the Communists tried, the bitterness of centuries would not go away. With the collapse of communism, old grudges returned. Between 1992 and 1995, Europe experienced its worst fighting since World War II. Serbs, Croats, and Muslims fought a three-way war, which one correspondent described as "free-lance ethnic cleansing."

Mass murders in Bosnia and Herzegovina have raised new questions about the best way to protect human rights in the world today. Human rights refers to the right of each individual to life, liberty, and property. The United Nations, founded after World War II, passed several resolutions, including the "Universal Declaration of Human Rights," defining and guaranteeing a long list of human rights. One of the UN's first actions in 1945 was to hold trials for Nazis accused of "crimes against humanity." In 1993, for the second time in its history, the UN created an eleven-man tribunal to try leaders in former Yugoslavia.

The UN actions have awakened old questions about human rights. Who picks the judges? Who issues the warrants for arrest? Is it possible for an international court to oversee a fair and speedy trial? In the recent trials, high-ranking officials were not called into account, and the UN tribunal allowed witnesses to give secret testimony without cross-examination. (This is illegal in the United States.)

1. What are the religious differences between the three major groups in Bosnia? <u>The Serbs adhere to the</u>
   <u>Orthodox Church, the Croats hold to the Roman Catholic Church, and the Slavs practice Islam.</u>

2. What are human rights? <u>the right of every person to life, liberty, and property</u>

3. How might the efforts of the United Nations affect human rights violations in the future?
   <u>Answers will vary.</u>
   _____

CHAPTER REVIEW

Using what you have learned from reading and studying this chapter, answer the following questions.

1. What city has the most people in Eastern Europe (also give the country)? __Kyiv, Ukraine__

2. What is the name of the organization founded by the former Soviet republics after the collapse of the Soviet Union? __Commonwealth of Independent States__

3. What is the name for an area where the borders are continually changing? __shatter belt__

4. What is the largest marshland in Europe? __Pinsk Marshes__

5. List the countries that make up the Baltic States. __Lithuania, Latvia, Estonia__

6. List the countries in Eastern Europe that belonged to the Soviet Union. __Lithuania, Latvia, Estonia,__ __Moldova, Ukraine, and Belarus__

7. What term refers to exotic limestone structures? __karst__

8. What is the major plain in Slovakia called? __Little Alföld__

9. List the countries that make up the Balkans. __Slovenia, Croatia, Bosnia and Herzegovina, Serbia, Montenegro,__ __Albania, Macedonia, Bulgaria, Romania__

10. In which country is the Hill of the Crosses? __Lithuania__

11. What Ukrainian river is the third-longest river in Europe? __Dnieper River__

12. To which country did the Dayton Peace Accords bring a measure of stability? __Bosnia and Herzegovina__

13. What mountain system is the dominant system of Eastern Europe? __Carpathian Mountains__

14. What is the term for the tendency of a group of various nationalities to break up into small, hostile nations? __Balkanization__

15. What economic initiative did the Czech Republic initiate after the Velvet Divorce? __mass privatization__

16. List the three regions of Romania. __Transylvania, Wallachia, and Moldavia__

17. The Transnistria region is in what country? __Moldova__

18. What is the highest peak in the Balkans? __Mount Musala__

19. What mountain range is on the western side of the Balkan Peninsula? __Dinaric Alps__

20. Minsk is the headquarters of what organization? __Commonwealth of Independent States__

RUSSIAN FEDERAL DISTRICTS

In May 2000, Russian President Vladimir Putin established the federal districts to aid the government in Russia. He grouped these according to geography. Below is a list of the federal districts, their capitals, area, and population. Study the maps in Chapter 7 of the student text and the chart below; then answer the questions that follow.

Name of Federal District	Capital	Area (sq. mi.)	Population
CENTRAL FEDERAL DISTRICT	Moscow	252,048	37,545,831
FAR EASTERN FEDERAL DISTRICT	Khabarovsk	2,386,073	6,592,959
NORTHWESTERN FEDERAL DISTRICT	St. Petersburg	647,841	13,731,015
SIBERIAN FEDERAL DISTRICT	Novosibirsk	1,974,835	19,794,160
SOUTHERN FEDERAL DISTRICT	Rostov-on-Don	226,237	22,820,849
URALS FEDERAL DISTRICT	Yekaterinburg	690,505	12,279,234
VOLGA FEDERAL DISTRICT	Nizhniy-Novgorod	399,963	30,710,171

1. What district has the largest area?

   Far Eastern Federal District

2. What district has the smallest area? What is its capital?

   Southern Federal District; Rostov-on-Don

3. What district has the greatest population?

   Central Federal District

4. What district has the smallest population?

   Far Eastern Federal District

5. What district borders no body of water?

   Volga Federal District

6. What districts border only the Arctic Ocean?

   Urals Federal District and Siberian Federal District

RUSSIANS ABROAD

Fifteen present-day countries make up what was the Soviet Union. The Soviet government sought to strengthen their control of these areas by moving large numbers of Russians into these countries. When the Soviet government collapsed, the Russians in these countries found themselves many times in a hostile environment. Some of these ethnic Russians remained in their new countries, but others returned to Russia. The conditions of the Russians living in these countries are a top concern of the Russian government today. Sometimes, this concern has increased tensions between Russia and the former Soviet republics. The chart lists the fifteen countries that were once republics in the Soviet Union. Study this chart and the maps in Chapter 7 of the student text; then answer the questions that follow.

Countries of the Former Soviet Union	% of Ethnic Russians
Russia	79.8%
Baltic Region	
Estonia	25.6%
Latvia	29.6%
Lithuania	8.0%
Eastern Plain	
Belarus	11.4%
Moldova	5.8%
Ukraine	17.3%
Caucasus	
Armenia	0.5%
Azerbaijan	1.8%
Georgia	1.5%
Central Asia	
Kazakhstan	30.0%
Kyrgyzstan	12.5%
Tajikistan	1.1%
Turkmenistan	4.0%
Uzbekistan	5.5%

1. Which of the four regions (outside Russia) appears to have the largest percentage of Russians?
   Baltic Region

2. Which of the four regions (outside Russia) appears to have the smallest percentage of Russians?
   Caucasus

3. Which country (outside Russia) has the largest percentage of Russians? __Kazakhstan__

4. Which country (outside Russia) has the smallest percentage of Russians? __Armenia__

5. Which countries share no borders with Russia? What is the highest percentage of Russians among any of these countries? __Moldova, Armenia, Kyrgyzstan, Tajikistan, Turkmenistan,__
   __Uzbekistan; 12.5% in Kyrgyzstan__

A MAP OF RUSSIA

Locate and label on the map the following places and geographic features.

Don River	Kuril Islands
Yekaterinburg	Baltic Sea
Moscow	Black Sea
Kaliningrad	Bering Strait
Mount Elbrus	St. Petersburg
Taymyr Peninsula	Caucasus Mountains
Nizhniy Novgorod	Lake Baykal
Ural Mountains	Volga River
Novosibirsk	Rostov
Arctic Ocean	Sakhalin Island
Volgograd	Kamchatka Peninsula
Siberia	

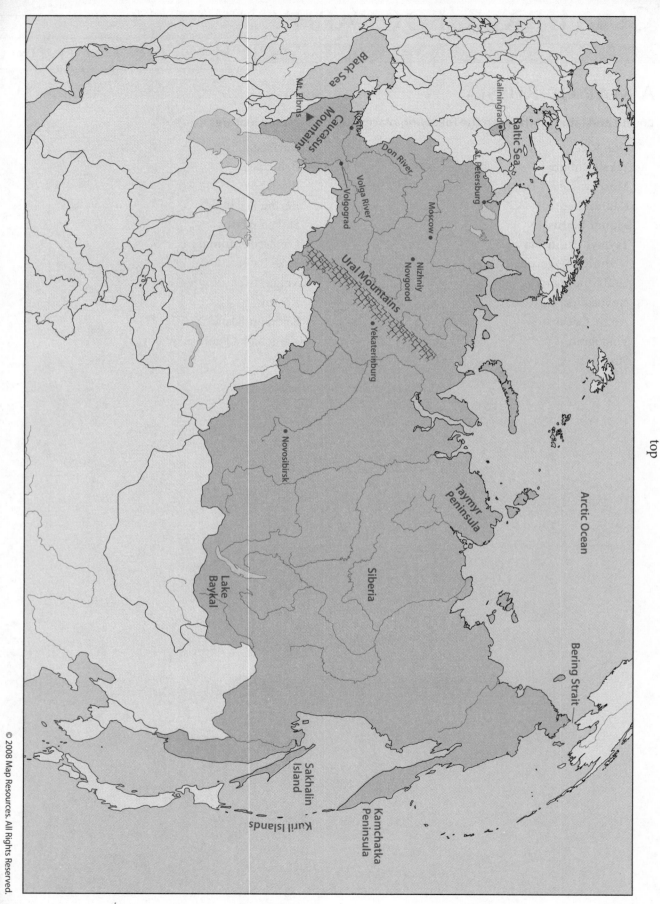

top

Arctic Ocean

Bering Strait

Black Sea

Mt. Elbrus

Caucasus Mountains

Don River

Volga River

Volgograd

Rostov

Baltic Sea

Kaliningrad

St. Petersburg

Moscow

Nizhniy Novgorod

Ural Mountains

Yekaterinburg

Novosibirsk

Taymyr Peninsula

Siberia

Lake Baykal

Sakhalin Island

Kuril Islands

Kamchatka Peninsula

A LETTER FROM RUSSIA

Grigory Shishatsky lives in Russia. He grew up in the Soviet Union and later saw the changes in Russia after the collapse of the Soviet Union. This is a letter that he wrote giving his viewpoint on what has occurred in Russia. Read the following article and then answer the questions following the article.

Hello, I am Grigory (Greg), . . .

More than ten years have already passed since the beginning of perestroika and almost seven years since the disintegration of the Union of Soviet Socialist Republics. But Russia (to say nothing of all the other republics of the former Soviet empire) is still very far from being a free country. But regardless of what the pro-communist newspapers say, it is my firm conviction that life is improving in Russia, and events are becoming more predictable.

Even with the little freedom we now have in Russia, I think the situation is great because in Soviet times I had less than I have now. As surprising as it may seem, I was not so much disappointed by the continual shortage of various consumer products as by the lack of information about what had been going on in the rest of the world. The Soviet people lived in a kind of information vacuum. All we heard and read was "the tremendous achievements of the Soviet people on the road to communism. . . ."

Nowadays I know for sure that I will not have to run all over the town and through every store in search of a package of washing powder, an electric bulb, or a pair of socks, as I used to do in Soviet times. All of these products are available at the local marketplace at reasonable prices. I will never forget how in 1982 a friend and I used to stand in line for three hours or even longer at the only milk shop in this town just to buy some milk. . . .

Since the beginning of the perestroika and glasnost of Mikhail Gorbachev, we have read a lot of materials about V. I. Lenin, Josef Stalin, Nikita Khrushchev, Kliment Voroshilov, Vyacheslav Molotov, and other creators of the first socialist state in the world. Such materials had been top secret because they depicted "the leaders of the world socialist revolution" in their true devilish nature: extremely cruel, ambitious, bloodthirsty, and power-craving. Now many young people hardly believe in socialism "with a human face," and the aged people have become disappointed and even frustrated because they have lost the ideals (and the idols) in which they truly believed.

Unfortunately, some people fail to see and enjoy the newly gained liberties, and I am inclined to think that most of these people are men and women who are fond of the bottle. They are unemployed but hardly even make an effort to find themselves jobs. They grumble about the difficulties of life and at the same time sell their own last belongings (such as chicken feed, pillowcases, or blankets) to whoever may be interested in buying them. However, they spend the money they gain not for improving their living conditions but on another couple of bottles of vodka or moonshine. Such people don't care about reading books or doing anything else that might lead to self-improvement and the acquisition of a marketable profession. I don't think that it would make any difference for them whether they lived in Russia or in America—they will never be satisfied.

Having talked to a good number of people, I've come to the conclusion that there are seven categories of people in Russia today.

1. Those who care little about which kind of regime they live under—socialism, capitalism, or totalitarianism. They hardly know or care about the difference. Such people are usually drunkards, loafers, drug users, petty criminals, or tramps.

2. Those who make every effort to improve their living conditions but are unable to adjust themselves to the current political and economic situation in Russia. Such people usually say, "We lived much better in Soviet times." They are inclined to blame the government, the reforms, and even "the hand of Washington" for all of their troubles.

3. Those who are categorically against the return to the road to communism because they realize that any such return would lead to civil war. These people fully support the reforms, in spite of the difficulties they may face, because they know how to benefit from the new liberties and the free market, not only in the political and economic sense but also in the sense of spiritual self-improvement. I believe that I am in this category.

4. Those who are known as the "New Russians," the richest people in this country. They have become rich as a result of the reforms, and they know full well that if the communists come back to power they will be deprived of their wealth very soon after and will go straight to a labor camp. Of course, they are against the communist ideals.

5. Those who are nostalgic for "the good old Soviet times" when all the Soviet people were "brothers and sisters" and unanimously supported the Communist Party, which was doing its best day and night to achieve the well-being of the whole Soviet nation. Most of these people are elderly, in their sixties and seventies. They are pensioners, veterans of World War II (who had a lot of privileges in Soviet times), and the many ordinary aged people who are lonely and frustrated. These are the only people for whom I am sorry. They had fervently believed in the "radiant future," but they gained nothing. Now they think that it is too late for them to think about the future, whatever it may be.

6. Those who are involved in organized crime. They are neither for nor against the reforms. They are accustomed to solving their "problems" with "the fists of iron." They have all the necessary means to do this, being even better equipped than the police force. They are extremely dangerous (as much as in any other country, regardless of political system), and the only "comfort," according to the opinions of some people, is that they do not physically harm the ordinary people because the ordinary people almost never stand in their way.

7. The young Russians who are in their twenties and thirties. Most of them look to the future with confidence. They are too young to remember Soviet times, having been their parents' dependents, and they have a rather vague idea of life in those days. They are not at all excited about socialist ideas. Many of them study at colleges, in technical schools, and in business schools. Many have good jobs and are even able to support their parents. For example, a 23-year-old kung-fu student of mine recently married, started his own small business, and seems to be very happy. I could say the same about many young men and women who were students of mine.

A lot of changes have occurred in Russia over the last few years, and many of them are, in my opinion, for the better. At least for now, Russia seems to be on the right way despite all the difficulties.

Your friend in Russia,

Grigory Shishatsky

(Source: Grigory Shishatsky, "A Letter from Russia," *The Freeman*, August 1998, Vol. 48, no. 8. All rights reserved.)

↜

1. What frustrated Grigory the most when the Soviets were in charge?

   lack of information of what was going on outside Russia
   _____

2. According to Grigory, why do the young people not believe "in socialism 'with a human face'"?

   The young people have learned the truth about the leaders of the Soviet Union, such as Lenin, Stalin, and Khrushchev.
   _____

3. Which of the seven groups does Grigory see himself in?

   those who think that a return to communism would lead to civil war and that the reforms are good despite the

   difficulties they bring

4. For which group does Grigory feel sorry?

   the elderly, most of whom are pensioners or veterans of World War II

5. Which group(s) is/are indifferent to the reforms?

   those who do not care about the regime that they live under and those involved in organized crime

6. Why does Grigory think that life is improving?

   He has more now than in Soviet times. He has access to more information. He sees young people being able to start

   families and businesses.
   _____

CULTURAL GEOGRAPHY

Name _____

CHAPTER REVIEW

Using what you have learned from this chapter, answer the following questions.

1. What were the autocratic rulers of Russia from the middle of the sixteenth century to the beginning of the twentieth century called? ___czars___

2. Who led the Russian Revolution in 1917? ___Vladimir Ilich Lenin___

3. What organization, comprising the former republics of the USSR, was formed after the fall of the Soviet Union? ___Commonwealth of Independent States (CIS)___

4. List five administrative divisions of the Russian government.
   ___Any five: oblast, autonomous oblast, okrug, federal city, krai, autonomous republic, or federal district___

   _____

5. What is the legislature of Russia called? ___Federation Assembly___

6. What is longest river in Russia and in Europe? ___Volga River___

7. What is the largest city in Russia? ___Moscow___

8. What is the largest port city in Russia? ___St. Petersburg___

9. What major city is in a portion of Russia that is not connected to the rest of Russia? ___Kaliningrad___

10. What river is associated with the Black Earth region of Russia? ___Don River___

11. What cultural group has a reputation for being strong military fighters? ___the Cossacks___

12. What is the highest mountain in Europe? ___Mount Elbrus___

13. What two mountain chains divide Europe and Asia? ___Caucasus and Ural mountains___

14. What is the major connection between Moscow and Vladivostok? ___Trans-Siberian Railway___

15. What is the largest city in Siberia? ___Novosibirsk___

16. What is the deepest lake in the world? ___Lake Baykal___

17. What waterway divides Russia and the United States? ___Bering Strait___

18. Russia and another nation disagree about the ownership of a group of islands off the Pacific coast of Russia. Name the other nation and the group of islands. ___Japan; Kuril Islands___

19. What is Russia's major Pacific port city? ___Vladivostok___

20. What is Siberia's highest peak? ___Mount Klyuchevskaya___

SKILL: Recognition

CULTURAL GEOGRAPHY

A MAP OF CANADA

Locate and label on the map the following places and geographic features.

Hudson Bay	London	Ottawa
Vancouver Island	Calgary	Each province/territory and its capital
Saskatoon	Labrador Sea	Each of the Great Lakes
Hamilton	Arctic Ocean	
St. Lawrence River	Vancouver	
Baffin Island	Montreal	

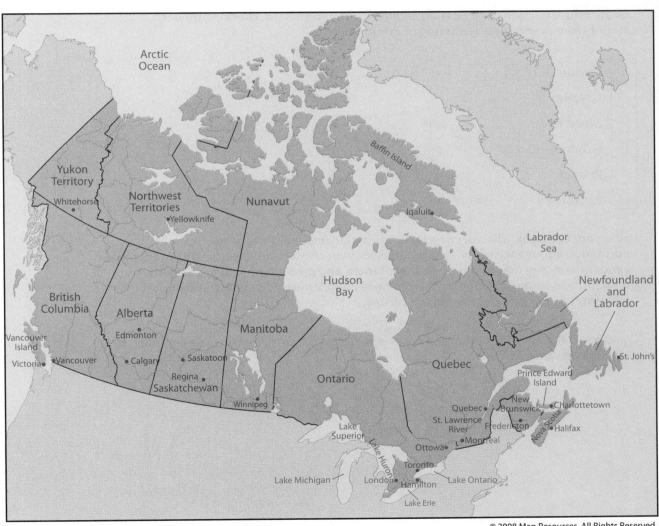

© 2008 Map Resources. All Rights Reserved.

PROVINCE PROJECT PRESENTATION

For this activity, choose one of the provinces discussed in Sections I and II of this chapter on which you will do an in-depth study. You may choose one of the following provinces:

MARITIME PROVINCES

◊ Newfoundland
◊ Nova Scotia
◊ New Brunswick
◊ Prince Edward Island

CENTRAL PROVINCES

◊ Quebec
◊ Ontario
◊ Ottawa

Conduct research into the following categories of information, checking off each category as you complete gathering of information:

☐	GEOGRAPHY
☐	HISTORY
☐	INDUSTRY
☐	GOVERNMENT
☐	PEOPLE
☐	RELIGIONS

Using your textbook, atlases, encyclopedias, almanacs, and the Internet, compile information about each of those categories for your chosen province. Find photographs of your province in magazines or on the Internet, and paste them into your report. You might include among the photos the province's flag, its varied peoples, and important buildings, tourist sites, or government offices.

Compile all of your information in a notebook, or share it with the class in a computerized visual presentation.

A BRIEF HISTORY OF THE ROYAL CANADIAN MOUNTED POLICE

The "Mounties" are the symbol of the world's most famous national police force. Read the following historical sketch of the Royal Canadian Mounted Police. Then answer the questions at the end.

It may be Canada's best-known symbol internationally: a police officer in a scarlet coat, sitting on a horse. It's been used to promote Canada abroad since 1880—and was glamorized by Hollywood in the 1920s, '30s and '40s.

Hollywood took great liberties with the Royal Canadian Mounted Police, and is usually cited as the source of the saying that the Mounties "always get their man." However, the phrase can be traced to the Fort Benton [Montana] Record in April 1877, four years after the formation of the North-West Mounted Police.

The force was created after Prime Minister John A. Macdonald declared that the Prairies needed a strong police force. The force's job would be to solidify Canada's claim to the West, improve relations with First Nations and wipe out the illegal whiskey trade.

This police force was initially only meant to be temporary; it was to see the West through its transition period and then be disbanded.

Macdonald modeled the Mounties on the Royal Irish Constabulary, one of the world's first national police forces.

The recruitment of officers for the new force started in September of 1873. On July 8, 1874, 275 mounted police officers set out from Dufferin, Man[itoba]. They covered [932 miles] over the next three months, arriving in what is now southern Alberta. They set up camp and started to build Fort Macleod—and began the work of enforcing Canadian law in the West.

Over the next few years, the NWMP set up several outposts in Alberta—and by 1885, 1,000 Mounties were in uniform.

The whiskey trade was in check and Canadian law was being enforced—as effectively as 1,000 men could enforce it across Alberta and Saskatchewan, and into what is now the Northwest Territories. Relations with most First Nations were also improving.

But on March 26, 1885, a force of North-West Mounted Police and civilian volunteers was defeated by a group of Métis [people of mixed Native American and French-Canadian ancestry] at Duck Lake, Sask[atchewan]. The NWMP abandoned its largest post in the area, Fort Carlton, and retreated to Prince Albert.

The battle stood as the single biggest loss of life in the history of the Mounties. The federal government sent in troops and by July, the Northwest Rebellion was over.

In 1896, the future of the NWMP seemed in doubt. The prime minister, Sir Wilfrid Laurier, wanted to reduce the size of the force and eventually disband it. He argued it had served its purpose: Canada's claim to the West was well entrenched.

But Laurier didn't get his way. Support for the force in the West was strong, and getting stronger as it built on its reputation by policing the Klondike Gold Rush.

By 1903, the NWMP's jurisdiction had been extended to the Yukon and the Arctic coast. In June 1904, King Edward VII signed a document turning the North West Mounted Police into the Royal North West Mounted Police. The next year, the RNWMP became the official police force of the new provinces of Alberta and Saskatchewan.

In 1920, the RNWMP became a national force when it absorbed the eastern-based Dominion Police and became the Royal Canadian Mounted Police. The new body was responsible for enforcing federal laws in all provinces and territories.

The RCMP underwent several changes, taking on new responsibilities over the next few decades, including:

- Development of "national police services" in the 1930s, including fingerprints, crime index, firearms registration, photo section, forensic laboratory.

- The RCMP supply vessel, *St. Roch*, makes its historic voyage through the Northwest Passage, 1940–1942.

- Expansion and evolution of RCMP security operations: Special Branch, 1950; Directorate of Security and Intelligence, 1962; Security Service, 1970.

- Expansion of duties and responsibilities in the 1970s: airport policing, VIP security, drug enforcement, economic crime.

- In 1974: women are recruited as RCMP officers for the first time.

- The RCMP gets out of security and intelligence when the Canadian Security Intelligence Service is created in 1984.

- International policing efforts are expanded in the 1990s with stints in Namibia, Yugoslavia, Haiti, Kosovo, Bosnia/Herzegovina, East Timor, Guatemala, Croatia, Western Sahara.

Currently, the RCMP acts as the provincial police force in all provinces except Ontario, Quebec, and Newfoundland and Labrador. While larger cities usually have their own police forces, the RCMP provides policing services to about 200 municipalities across Canada.

In Newfoundland and Labrador, the Royal Newfoundland Constabulary [RNC] polices Labrador West, Corner Brook and certain areas on the Avalon Peninsula, including St. John's, accounting for about 40 per cent of the province's population. The RCMP has responsibility in areas outside the RNC's jurisdiction. The Mounties are also the police force in nearly 200 First Nations communities.

("RCMP: A brief history," CBC News Online, June 22, 2005. Used by permission of cbc.ca.)

1. What saying was applied to the Mounties and then glamorized and embellished by Hollywood?

   that the Mounties "always get their man," meaning that they always catch the bad guys or the criminals

2. What were the three original goals of the Mounties when they were founded?

   to bring law and order to the Canadian West, to improve relations with First Nations, and to wipe out the trade of

   illegal whiskey

3. What event in 1885 resulted in the greatest loss of life in the history of the Mounties?

   the defeat of the Mounties by a group of Métis at Duck Lake, Saskatchewan, during the Northwest Rebellion

4. How did the responsibilities of the RCMP change dramatically in the 1990s?

   They were employed as peacekeeping troops in foreign countries in Eastern Europe, Africa, the Caribbean, and

   Central America.

SKILL: Analysis

Name _____

TOURING CANADA ON THE ROCKY MOUNTAINEER

Read the following description of the experience of touring western Canada aboard the premier tourist railroad of that nation. Then answer the questions at the end.

A TRANSPORTATION EXPERIENCE OF A LIFETIME: ROCKY MOUNTAINEER RAILTOURS BY LOUIS CHARLES

Lovers of intrepid travel owe many thanks to William Van Horne. As President of the Canadian Pacific Railway, he was responsible (some would even argue single-handedly) for opening up the abundant wildlife, snowy mountain peaks, glacier lakes and towering trees of the Canadian West to tourists. His greatest lifetime achievement: In 1886, he oversaw the first scheduled transcontinental trip across Canada, from Montreal to Port Moody, BC. His greatest legacy: Rocky Mountaineer Railtours, a company that unites Van Horne's passion for rail adventure with the spirit of 19th century train travel and brings it into the new millennium.

The Rocky Mountaineer gives vistors to the Canadian West an unforgetable experience.

Day 1

The Rocky Mountaineer offers two main itineraries: the Yellowhead Route (Vancouver-Kamloops-Jasper) and the Kicking Horse Route (Vancouver-Kamloops-Banff-Calgary). Both journeys can be taken from east to west or west to east. We recommend starting in the west, so that you can experience the dramatic build-up of scenery as you coast toward the Rocky Mountains. We also recommend the Banff route, as it delivers you to the awe-inspiring Banff/Lake Louise region via a fascinating passage through the Spiral Tunnels and the larger-than-life Yoho National Wilderness.

Following a stay at the Fairmont Waterfront, we boarded the Rocky Mountaineer at its terminal near Vancouver's Pacific Central Station. You know it's time to board when the uniformed staff lines up to announce in song, complete with whistle-blowing, the train's departure. Of the service levels available, we chose the GoldLeaf Service for its double-decker train cars with full-length dome-window observation decks. Chairs on these decks rotate and recline, and views are unobstructed—essential in this part of the world and decidedly the whole point of the trip.

As the train crosses the plains through the Fraser River Valley, breakfast is served onboard. There is a maximum of 70 passengers per car; half remain upstairs on the observation deck, while the other half are hosted in the downstairs dining car, complete with picture windows. All meals are freshly cooked under the guidance of executive chef Mark Jorundson. When our turn came, we ordered the GoldLeaf Breakfast, which features wild British Columbia smoked salmon. On a journey through the Canadian wilderness, BC salmon is a natural choice, and we weren't disappointed.

As the day progressed and the train traveled on through the Coast Mountains and into Fraser Canyon, passengers enjoyed the service of Onboard Attendants. Not only are the attendants available to serve beverages and snacks (. . . hors d'oeuvres, Canadian cheeses and local sweets are complimentary all day long), they act as guides, offering interpretive commentary on history, local culture and points of interest. They also teach you games to help you spot wildlife. At times the train stops so that you can linger over a view, although passengers are not allowed off. (Keep in mind that the train also stops occasionally at points not so interesting, in order to load and unload cargo.)

Lunch is served onboard, and the day progresses against the backdrop of the thundering waters of Hell's Gate. This is one of the stops that delivers an amazing show of nature during the salmon runs. There is actually a tram that brings people from the highway above to watch the fish make their final journey to give life in the Shuswap Lake four hundred miles inland. It is said that the fish are so tightly packed that you can walk across the river.

Comfortable seating and large windows provide for an enjoyable ride and view.

A change of scenery occurs as the train veers off to follow the Thompson River. The dryer conditions through White Canyon, also known as Avalanche Alley, necessitate travel through a series of tunnels to protect the train from the chasm's constantly crumbling edges. This desert-like landscape stretches from the upper reaches of Canada all the way through Washington, Oregon and California to Arizona.

Then comes the plateau with pristine, serene and undeveloped Lake Kamloops, which ushers the train into the historic city of Kamloops, gateway to the interior of British Columbia. This will be your overnight. Since your luggage actually rides on trucks, it will be waiting for you at your lodging. Rocky Mountaineer Railtours has selected several Kamloops accommodation options. Most of the train's guests stay in town and enjoy the Two River Junction and Musical Review. We chose the outlying rustic South Thompson Inn, where we dined in Madisens restaurant overlooking the river. Because these journeys take place only during daylight hours—for maximum rubber-necking—there is time when you arrive in Kamloops to enjoy a horseback ride, play nine holes of golf or take a walk along the river.

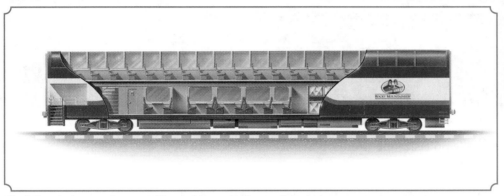

The bilevel observation car offers panoramic views of the scenery.

DAY 2

An early departure assures the now train-legged voyageurs another full day of adventure, with anticipation building to conquer the Rockies. You can sense the excitement on the train and the feeling of possible reward—not unlike climbers going for the summit. Breakfast is once again served on board, as the train travels through ranchland along the South Thompson River, gaining altitude as it nears meandering Shuswap Lake (with more than 1,000 miles of lakeshore). This is also the start of serious wild animal territory, and the sighting games rehearsed the day before begin to pay off.

The search for wildlife is ongoing and it takes three passengers to confirm a sighting for it to count. Those in the rear cars have the advantage of front car passengers, who initiate the sightings, to prepare them to see a bear on the left or a moose on the right.

To complement the commentary from the attendants, who are available at all times to answer questions, are copies of *The Rocky Mountaineer*. This gazette includes a detailed description of your journey along with historical articles, interesting trivia and lots of great old photos, as well as suggestions for prime photo-ops. The route is divided into subdivisions with each subdivision broken down with a series of mile markers. Using the guide and the mile markers, you can learn about the Great (and least successful) Train Robbery of the Bill Miner Gang, the unique clay formations called Hoodoos and the site of the world's largest salmon run. No detail is too small, and all come together to create a larger picture of one of the greatest manmade undertakings through one of the most beautiful and rugged natural regions in the world. But while the facts and figures are interesting, it is the actual scenery that is the star of

The Rocky Mountaineer is an excellent way to see the beauty of Canada's western provinces.

this trip. . . . Once again, we must emphasize the GoldLeaf Service dome cars for best enjoying the views.

After the train passes Craigellachie, where the last spike of the Canadian Pacific Railway was driven, it enters the tunnels, snow sheds and glaciers of Rogers Pass. The journey follows Kicking Horse River to Kicking Horse Pass. By the time it travels beyond the village of Field and reaches the Spiral Tunnels—a marvel of engineering that inspired several books—the views are astounding. This is a good part of what the trip is all about: the Rocky Mountains. Following the dizzying ascent through the tunnels, dominated by glaciers and cathedral-shaped Jurassic formations, you have a chance to stare at the Yoho glacial valley. All of a sudden you realize how small you are and how big this transcontinental achievement was.

Soon comes another highlight as you pass over the Continental Divide (more than once), defined geologically as the highest point on the trip. It is exhilarating and a letdown at the same time: exhilarating because it's so beautiful, big, crisp and magical, and a letdown because you're nearing the end of the fantastic journey. From here the train enters Banff National Park and crosses over to Alberta. The ride from this point on to Banff takes place in an awe-inspiring glacial valley surrounded by a multitude of varied rock formations—we were particularly struck by "Castle Mountain."

First Nations people enjoyed this scenery in peace for centuries and lived in perfect harmony with nature. Today, the Canadian government has done its best to preserve this landscape and its wildlife. Also in this magical setting, you will find the luxurious accommodations of The Fairmont Banff Springs and The Fairmont Chateau Lake Louise. We chose to stay in Banff, but for travelers who have a few extra days, we recommend driving on to Jasper to take in even more pristine lake, glacier and mountain.

Thanks to the early rail pioneers and the hard work of the Rocky Mountaineer staff, we were transported both physically and spiritually through this vast geological domain. We will never forget the grand vistas, fabulous animals and fresh air. We agree with Rocky Mountaineer Railtours: this is a truly spectacular rail journey. We look forward to returning.

(Reprinted from gayot.com by permission of Gayot Publications.)

1. Which cities are the departure and terminal points of the Rocky Mountaineer Railtour (going in either direction)? __Vancouver and Jasper or Calgary, depending on which tour route one chooses__

2. Who was responsible for sharing with millions of people the beauty of the Canadian Rockies by organizing the Rocky Mountaineer rail tours? __William Van Horne, president of Canadian Pacific Railway__

3. Why is the tour's "GoldLeaf Service" the preferred method of travel aboard the Rocky Mountaineer?
   __GoldLeaf Service features double-decker, full-length dome cars and premier food services.__

4. What interesting attraction occurs once a year along "the thundering waters of Hell's Gate"?
   __the annual salmon run__

5. Which city along the way boasts of being the "gateway to the interior of British Columbia"?
   __Kamloops__

6. Through which Canadian national park does the Rocky Mountaineer pass, offering views of awesome rock formations? __Banff National Park__

7. Is the Rocky Mountaineer tour a genuine and harmless (to the environment) effort to introduce tourists to the natural beauty of the Canadian Rockies or merely a for-profit business venture that endangers the environment of the region? (Support your opinion.)
   __Answers will vary, but some points that might be made include the following: It is a for-profit business—as the__
   __prices of the service (more than $1000 per person) and the sumptuous GoldLeaf Service reveal—but no evidence__
   __exists of negative effects of the train on the flora or fauna; it has allowed thousands of people to enjoy nature from__
   __a respectful distance and has opened the eyes of many people to the need to be good stewards of this part of God's__
   __creation.__

8. Who were the "First Nations people"? Do you agree with the author that they "lived in perfect harmony with nature"? Why or why not?
   __natives who lived in Canada long before the Europeans came to the New World; answers to the second__
   __question will vary.__

OVERVIEW OF CANADA

Using your textbook, provide the following information about Canada.

CLIMATE	Generally moderate to cold, especially the farther north one goes; has no desert, mediterranean, or tropical climates
AREA	3,855,174 sq. mi.
MAIN MOUNTAIN RANGES	Appalachians, Pacific Mountain System (including Rockies and Coastal Mountains)
MAIN LAKES	Great Lakes (except for Lake Michigan, which is US), Great Slave Lake, Great Bear Lake
LONGEST RIVER	Mackenzie
PER CAPITA GDP	$31,500 ($US)
POPULATION	32.3 million
LIFE EXPECTANCY	80.1 years
LARGEST METROPOLITAN AREA	Toronto
NUMBER OF PROVINCES/ TERRITORIES (LIST THEM)	13—Newfoundland/Labrador, Nova Scotia, Prince Edward Island, New Brunswick, Quebec, Ontario, Manitoba, Saskatchewan, Alberta, British Columbia, Yukon Territory, Northwest Territories, Nunavut
NEWEST PROVINCE	Nunavut
MAJOR PRODUCTS	Fish, wheat, barley, dairy, gold, silver, iron, copper, zinc, nickel, potash, uranium, automobiles, computers
FORM OF GOVERNMENT	Federated parliamentary democracy
MAIN LANGUAGE(S)	English, French
MAIN MINORITIES	French, Indian, Inuit
MAIN SPORTS	Hockey, baseball, rodeo

MAP OF THE UNITED STATES

Locate and label the following places and features on the map of the United States.

Each state and its capital	Pittsburgh
Appalachian Mountains	Seattle
Houston	Missouri River
Each of the Great Lakes	Washington, D.C.
Rocky Mountains	Anchorage
St. Louis	Rio Grande
Hudson River	Charleston
New York City	Mexico
San Diego	Colorado River
Tennessee River	Miami
Philadelphia	Canada
Los Angeles	Atlantic Ocean
Ohio River	New Orleans
Baltimore	Gulf of Mexico
San Francisco	Pacific Ocean
Mississippi River	

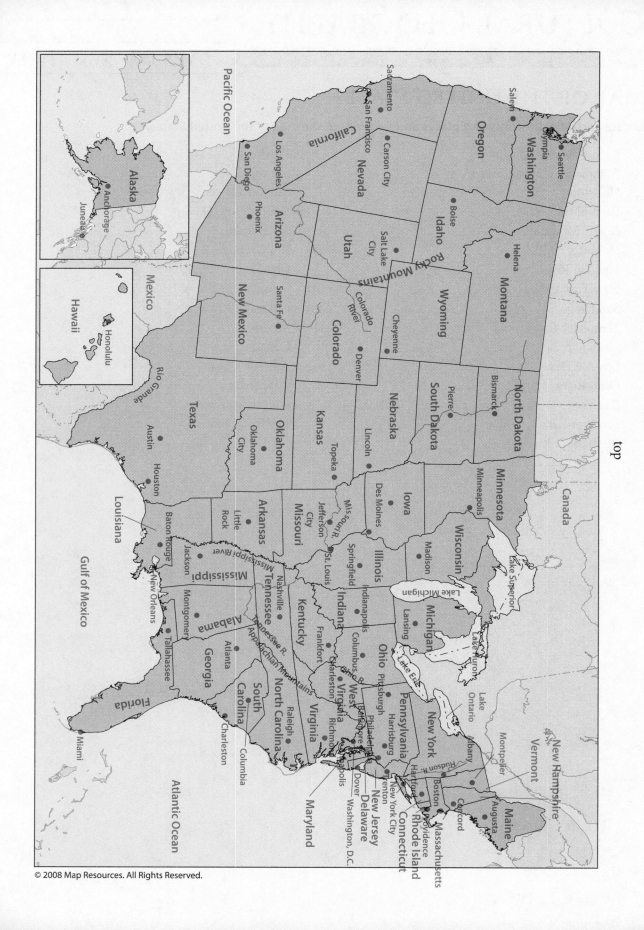

top

SKILL: Maps

U.S. IMMIGRATION POLICY: WHERE DO YOU STAND?

Read the following brief paragraph about the pros and cons of current U.S. immigration policy. Then read and think about the questions at the end. Formulate what you believe and answer the questions, offering support for each of your opinions.

As more and more people of different races and cultures enter the United States and the ethnic composition of the country changes, immigration becomes a more intensely debated issue. Some Americans favor tighter immigration restrictions and argue that immigrants take jobs away from U.S. citizens, drain social services, and resist learning English. Others, however, point to America's historic commitment to immigration and believe that immigrants keep the nation strong, economically competitive, and culturally rich. The question of whether America's doors should be open or closed will continue to be intensely debated in the courts, in Congress, and in communities where immigrants settle.

Source: http://www.closeup.org/immigrat.htm#conclusion
Copyright © 2005 Close Up Foundation

1. Should the United States restrict the number of immigrants allowed into the country? Should the government limit the number of refugees who become residents of the United States?

   Answers will vary. _____

   _____

   _____

   _____

2. Is illegal immigration hurting the U.S. economy? Does the average American benefit from having immigrants as a source of cheap labor? Do illegal immigrants have a right to education and medical services?

   Answers will vary. _____

   _____

   _____

   _____

3. Do highly skilled illegal immigrants benefit the U.S. economy, or do they harm it by taking jobs from American citizens? Answers will vary. _____

   _____

   _____

   _____

4. Should English be the official language of the United States? Should all government business be conducted in English? Answers will vary. _____

   _____

   _____

   _____

5. If you could make one change in current U.S. immigration policy, what would it be and why?

Answers will vary.

_____

_____

_____

_____

_____

_____

6. How can the United States ensure that its borders are secure from would-be terrorists, criminals, and drug smugglers without preventing legal entry by people who are persecuted in their native countries or who want to improve their economic conditions?

Answers will vary.

_____

_____

_____

_____

_____

_____

_____

7. Optional activity:
Research current information on the immigration issue, focusing especially on the security problems involved, and then write a positon paper addressing those problems and how you think the U.S. government should address it. Consider writing a letter to your senator or representative expressing your views.

Skills: Analysis, Evaluation

THE STATUE OF LIBERTY AND ELLIS ISLAND

In New York Harbor stand two symbols of America's historic welcome of immigrants: the Statue of Liberty and Ellis Island, which was once the main clearinghouse for immigrants. On the pedestal of the Statue of Liberty is a poem, "The New Colossus," written in 1883 by Emma Lazarus. Read the poem carefully. Then read the article about the Statue of Liberty and Ellis Island and answer the questions following the article.

Not like the brazen giant of Greek fame
With conquering limbs astride from land to land;
Here at our sea-washed, sunset gates shall stand
A mighty woman with a torch, whose flame
Is the imprisoned lightning, and her name
Mother of Exiles. From her beacon-hand
Glows world-wide welcome; her mild eyes command
The air-bridged harbor that twin cities frame,
"Keep, ancient lands, your storied pomp!" cries she
With silent lips. "Give me your tired, your poor,
Your huddled masses yearning to breathe free,
The wretched refuse of your teeming shore,
Send these, the homeless, tempest-tossed to me,
I lift my lamp beside the golden door!"

"GIVE ME YOUR TIRED, YOUR POOR" By: NEAL G. LINEBACK

Kosovo refugees entering the United States seeking protection from a war-torn homeland join millions of our ancestors who also were persecuted and sought refuge here.

For most of the world's oppressed peoples, the United States offers hopes of freedom and opportunity, as symbolized by the Statue of Liberty. Standing in New York Bay, it was a breathtaking sight for the millions of immigrants who entered the United States through Ellis Island.

Although many more tourists visit the statue, the Statue of Liberty National Monument also includes a museum on Ellis Island, slightly more than a mile away. Seventy percent of the 12 million immigrant arrivals to the United States between 1892 and 1924 came through Ellis Island. An average of 5,000 hopeful immigrants a day were medically screened there before entering the United States. Nearly half of all Americans today can claim an ancestor who entered through Ellis Island, according to a recent Scripts (sic) Howard News Service article.

Ellis Island was the busiest of 30 scattered U.S. immigration centers. When new immigrants arrived, their ships docked at the Hudson River pier and the immigrant passengers were ferried to Ellis Island, which they called the "Island of Hope, Island of Tears."

Many arrived totally destitute, having spent every cent on passage in steerage. Steerage accommodations were dank and noisy group quarters in the stifling holds of ships, where passengers saw no daylight during the one- to three-week passage. Because this was many passengers' first trip on a ship, seasickness made life a torment for the sick and the well alike.

It generally took immigrants less than 12 hours to be processed through the Ellis Island. Luggage was left on the ground floor of the building, before immigrants proceeded up a great staircase, dubbed the Stairs of Separation, for their examinations.

Although only about 2 percent of the immigrants were rejected during Ellis Island's operation, it was a traumatic ordeal for large families, fearful that a family member would be rejected.

When immigrants cleared Ellis Island, they were essentially on their own. However, a process known as networking often eased the transition for immigrants.

Networking occurs when potential migrants communicate with former migrants. Sometimes this occurs between family members or others within a common culture, such as religious, village, or tribal groups. Such transfer of information to new immigrants through the networking process is common the world over.

Thus, most Ellis Island immigrants moved directly to areas where their own culture prevailed. Immigrants from Ireland moved to Irish neighborhoods, Germans to German areas, and Italians to Italian sections. This eased the immigrant assimilation process.

Between 1820 and 1940, Europe was by far the leading source area for U.S. immigrants. Germanic states, including Austria, provided the largest numbers at 8.5, followed by Italy (4.7), Ireland (4.6), United Kingdom (4.3), former USSR republics (3.3) and Canada (3.0 million).

Only 56,787 emigrants from the former Yugoslav states arrived in the United States during this same period. Between 1941 and 1996, however, 100,000 more arrived.

Now, as more than one million new homeless refugees flee persecution in Kosovo, some are becoming U.S. immigrants. They represent the most recent wave of ". . .those huddled masses yearning to breathe free."

The Statue of Liberty National Monument is the 10th most visited National Park site in the United States, established purposefully to remind us of our own immigrant ancestry.

(An excerpt from "Give Me Your Tired, Your Poor" by Neal G. Lineback. Copyright © 2000 by maps.com. Printed by permission of the author.)

1. Which place is visited more, the Statue of Liberty or Ellis Island? __the Statue of Liberty__

2. Between 1892 and 1924, what percentage of immigrants were processed at Ellis Island? __70 percent__

3. How many per day were screened for medical problems? __an average of 5,000/day__

4. Approximately what fraction of Americans' ancestors came through Ellis Island? __nearly half__

5. How many immigration centers did the United States operate in 1892–1924? __thirty__

6. What type of accommodations did many immigrants have on their voyage to the United States?
   __steerage__

7. How long did it generally take to process each immigrant (assuming no problems occurred)?
   __twelve hours__

8. What percentage of immigrants were rejected during the Ellis Island screening process? __2 percent__

9. Which area was the greatest source of immigrants during 1820–1940? __Europe__

Optional in-depth study: Conduct research on the screening process at Ellis Island. Based on your findings, do you think the process was effective, too restrictive, or ineffective? Why? __Answers will vary__

_____

_____

_____

SKILLS: Analysis, Synthesis, Evaluation

THE 21ST-CENTURY AMERICAN ECONOMY

Read the following summary of the economy of the United States. Read and think carefully about each of the quotations that follow the summary. Then select one and write an essay explaining how the principle stated in the quotation helps explain both the strengths and the problems of the twenty-first-century American economy.

AN OVERVIEW OF THE AMERICAN ECONOMY TODAY

The United States has the largest and most technologically powerful economy in the world, with a per capita GDP of $40,100. In this market-oriented economy, private individuals and business firms make most of the decisions, and the federal and state governments buy needed goods and services predominantly in the private market-place. U.S. business firms enjoy considerably greater flexibility than their counterparts in Western Europe and Japan in decisions to expand capital plant, to lay off surplus workers, and to develop new products. At the same time, they face higher barriers to entry in their rivals' home markets than the barriers to entry of foreign firms in U.S. markets. U.S. firms are at or near the forefront in technological advances, especially in computers and in medical, aerospace, and military equipment; their advantage has narrowed since the end of World War II. The onrush of technology largely explains the gradual development of a "two-tier labor market" in which those at the bottom lack the education and the professional/technical skills of those at the top and, more and more, fail to get comparable pay raises, health insurance coverage, and other benefits. Since 1975, practically all the gains in household income have gone to the top 20 percent of households. The response to the terrorist attacks of September 11, 2001, showed the remarkable resilience of the economy. The war in March/April 2003 between a U.S.-led coalition and Iraq, and the subsequent occupation of Iraq, required major shifts in national resources to the military. The rise in GDP in 2004 was under-girded by substantial gains in labor productivity. The economy suffered from a sharp increase in energy prices in the second half of 2004. Long-term problems include inadequate investment in economic infrastructure, rapidly rising medical and pension costs of an aging population, sizable trade and budget deficits, and stagnation of family income in the lower economic groups.
(Source: CIA, The World Factbook 2005)

THOUGHT-PROVOKING QUOTATIONS

1. "Force cannot change right."
   (Thomas Jefferson, U.S. president and author, Declaration of Independence)

2. "Freedom does not make people strong; rather, it makes strength possible."
   (Leonard E. Read, founder, Foundation for Economic Education)

3. "Liberty is not the power of doing what we like, but the right of being able to do what we ought."
   (Lord Acton, 19th-century English historian)

4. "Free enterprise is possible only within a framework of law and order and morality."
   (Henry Hazlitt, 20th-century American economist)

5. "Competition is merely the absence of oppression."
   (Frédéric Bastiat, 19th-century French economist)

6. "The more the state 'plans,' the more difficult planning becomes for the individual."
   (F.A. Hayek, economist)

7. "The end [purpose, goal] of law is not to abolish or restrain, but to preserve and enlarge freedom."
   (John Locke, philosopher)

8. "Progress is precisely that which the rules and regulations did not foresee."
   (Ludwig von Mises, 20th-century Austrian economist)

Answers given in the students' essays will vary.

SKILLS: Writing, Analysis

CHAPTER REVIEW

Using what you have learned from reading and studying this chapter, answer the following questions.

GEOGRAPHY:

1. List the outer boundaries of the United States, including neighboring countries and bodies of water.

   North—Canada, St. Lawrence River, Great Lakes; East—Atlantic Ocean; South—Gulf of Mexico, Mexico, Rio Grande;

   West—Pacific Ocean

2. Name the generally flat topographic feature that is prominent inland along both the eastern border and roughly half of the southeastern border. **Coastal Plain**

3. If one is traveling from east to west across the continent, which mountains will he or she encounter first?

   Appalachian Mountains

4. What is the name given to the gently undulating hills between the areas in questions 2 and 3?

   Piedmont

5. Which river system drains most of the land in the central portion of the United States?

   Mississippi River system

6. What is the largest mountain system in the United States? **Rocky Mountains**

7. Which two states are not part of the forty-eight contiguous states?

   Alaska and Hawaii

8. List, from largest to smallest, the three largest states by area.

   Alaska, Texas, California

PEOPLE:

9. List, from largest to smallest, the three largest broad religious groups in the United States.

   Protestants, Roman Catholics, Jews

10. How did John Winthrop characterize the role of his colony? **as being "a city upon a hill"**

11. What is the American national motto? *E pluribus unum*

12. From which country did most immigrants come in 1850? From which country do most of them come today? Ireland; Mexico

13. What term means the study of the characteristics of people in a particular place or segment of the population? **demographics**

14. What percentage of America's approximately 296 million people now live in urban and suburban areas?

    79 percent

15. What does one mean by the "graying" of America?

    An increasing percentage of the American population is now classified as senior citizens, and they are living longer.

16. What term is used to describe the southern one-third of the nation where the greatest growth has occurred in recent years and where the greatest number of senior citizens tends to retire?

    the Sun Belt

17. Which state has the highest percentage of black population? Mississippi

18. Which state has the highest percentage of Hispanic population? New Mexico

19. What term is used to describe the form of government of the United States?

    federal republic

20. Which region of the country includes the greatest amount of federally owned land and what is the percentage? West; 55 percent

SKILL: Recognition

THE REGIONS OF THE UNITED STATES

For each of the following maps, locate and label the places and geographic features indicated for that specific region. Have the students complete each map as they finish reading/studying about each region.

I. THE NORTHEAST

Northeast states and capitals	Plymouth	Lake Champlain
Great Lakes shown	Erie	Allegheny River
Philadelphia	New Brunswick	Atlantic Ocean
Delmarva Peninsula	Burlington	Hudson River
Pittsburgh	Niagara River/Falls	Baltimore
Quebec	New York City	Delaware Bay
Cape Cod	Finger Lakes	Newark
Buffalo	Long Island	Washington, D.C.
Ontario	Delaware River	Chesapeake Bay

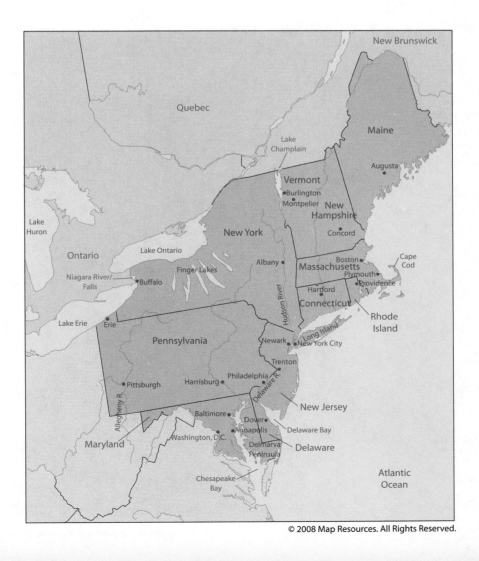

© 2008 Map Resources. All Rights Reserved.

II. The South

Southern states and capitals
Wilmington
New Orleans
Tennessee River
Charleston
Dallas/Fort Worth
Mississippi River

Savannah
El Paso
Ohio River
Miami
Memphis
Cumberland River
Key West

Gulf of Mexico
Rio Grande
Tampa
Atlantic Ocean
Charlotte
Pensacola
Mexico

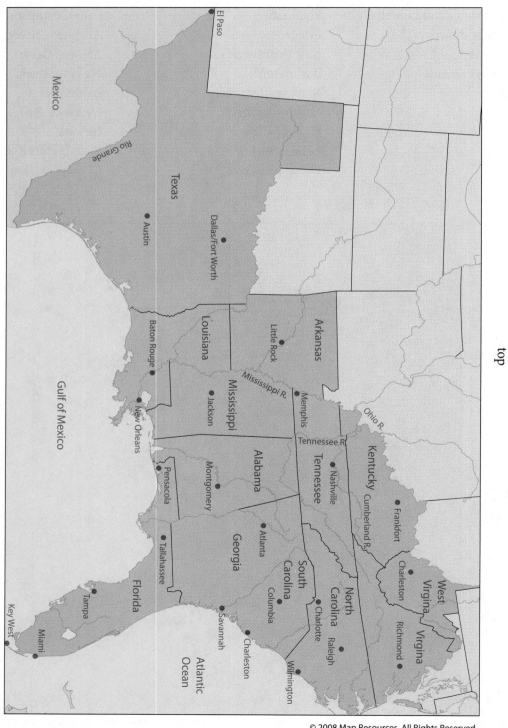

top

III. The Midwest

Midwest states and capitals
Toledo
Milwaukee
Great Lakes shown
Akron
Chicago
Ohio River
Dayton

St. Louis
Mississippi River
Cincinnati
Kansas City (2)
Missouri River
Detroit
Minneapolis
Illinois River

Grand Rapids
International Falls
Wabash River
Sault Sainte Marie
Canada
Cleveland
Green Bay

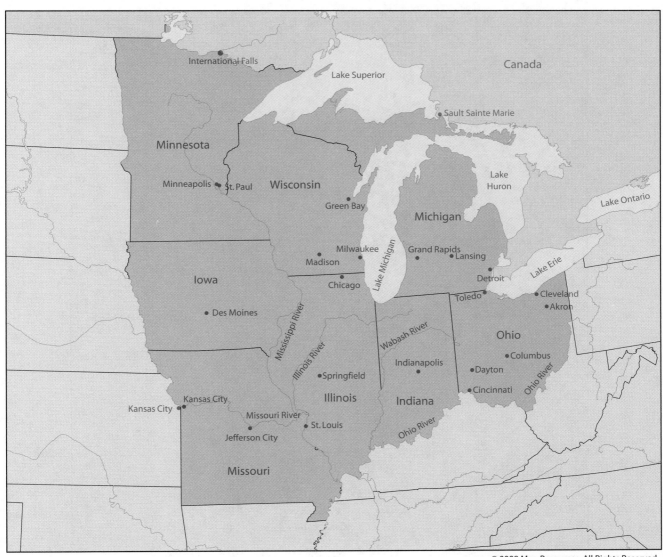

IV. The Plains

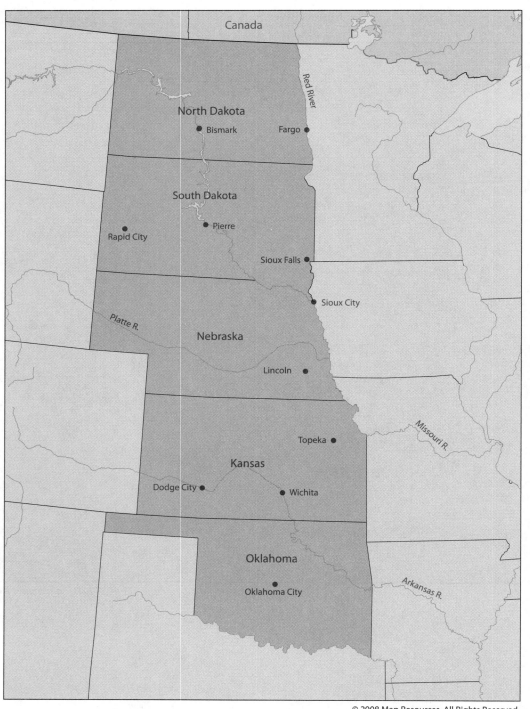

Canada

North Dakota
● Bismark   Fargo ●

Red River

South Dakota
● Pierre

Rapid City ●

Sioux Falls ●

Sioux City ●

Platte R.

Nebraska

Lincoln ●

Topeka ●

Kansas

Dodge City ●   ● Wichita

Oklahoma

Oklahoma City ●

Missouri R.

Arkansas R.

V. The West

Western states and capitals

Yuma	Boulder
San Diego	Spokane
Pacific Ocean	Snake River
Billings	Yukon River
Flagstaff	Colorado Springs
Missouri River	Portland
Gulf of California	Columbia River
Bozeman	Russia
Provo	Pueblo
Yellowstone River	Eugene
Fairbanks	Great Salt Lake
Casper	Bering Strait
Ogden	Albuquerque
Rio Grande	San Francisco
Anchorage	Canada
Jackson	Gulf of Alaska
Seattle	Tucson
Colorado River	Los Angeles
Nome	Mexico
	Hilo

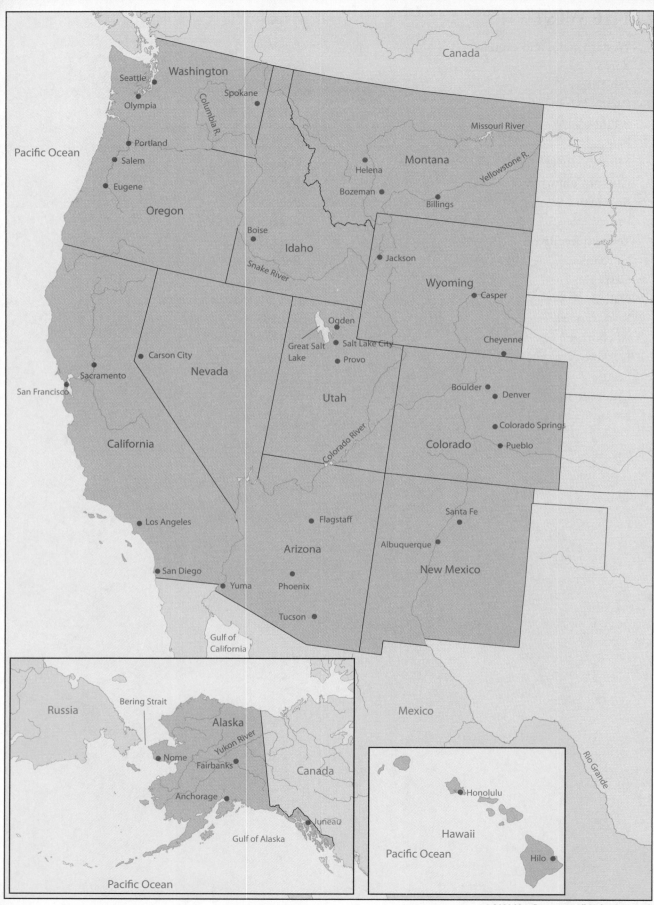

Seattle
Washington
Olympia
Spokane
Columbia R.
Portland
Pacific Ocean
Salem
Eugene
Oregon
Boise
Idaho
Snake River

Missouri River
Montana
Helena
Yellowstone R.
Bozeman
Billings

Jackson
Wyoming
Casper

Canada

Ogden
Great Salt Lake
Salt Lake City
Provo
Cheyenne

Carson City
Sacramento
San Francisco
Nevada
Utah
Colorado River

Boulder
Denver
Colorado Springs
Colorado
Pueblo

California

Los Angeles

San Diego
Yuma
Phoenix
Tucson
Arizona
Flagstaff

Santa Fe
Albuquerque
New Mexico

Gulf of California

Russia
Bering Strait
Nome
Alaska
Yukon River
Fairbanks
Canada
Anchorage
Juneau
Gulf of Alaska
Pacific Ocean

Mexico

Honolulu

Hawaii
Pacific Ocean
Hilo

Rio Grande

SKILL: Maps

THE APPALACHIAN TRAIL

The Appalachian Mountains extend fifteen hundred miles from Birmingham, Alabama, to Quebec, Canada. The Appalachian Trail runs the length of those mountains, from northern Georgia to north central Maine. From April 4 to August 5, 1948, Earl Shaffer hiked the entire trail. Read the account of the southern portion of his trek; then answer the questions.

EARL SHAFFER: HIKING THE APPALACHIAN TRAIL BY RON TAGLIAPIETRA

A shrill scream broke the steady patter of raindrops. Earl Shaffer dropped his ax and listened through the gloomy twilight. He turned slowly, peering through the gloom. Was a mountain lion stalking him, or was a lady in distress? He shivered and drew near the fire. As he grew calmer, he recognized the scream of a wildcat. Wildcats, called bobcats in some regions, do not attack adults unless cornered—unlike mountain lions.

Shaffer crossed the wide summit of Blood Mountain (4,461 ft.) the next day. The view surpassed the previous sights of his trip, which included the start of the trail on Mount Oglethorpe, the tallest waterfall in the Appalachians, Amicalola Falls, Springer Mountain, and Long Creek Falls. He enjoyed the view but not the rain, which had drenched him daily these first few days of his hike. He had started on April 4, 1948, having decided to hike the entire Appalachian Trail.

Although trail planners had laid out and hiked most of the route, no one had yet journeyed from end to end in one trip. Shaffer, born on November 8, 1918, in York, Pennsylvania, had recently returned from World War II at the age of twenty-nine. He had decided to combine the solace of the wilderness with the challenge of the first through-hike.

Shaffer flopped onto the ground. He felt dizzy, and his legs were sore and wobbly. He had walked twenty-five miles, and the last few miles of steep climbing had brought him close to collapse. He had found his challenge but still hoped to reach the rustic shelter on Tray Mountain (4,430 ft.) for the evening. Rising, he hauled himself up the last steep grade to the summit. He was so weary, he hardly noticed the spectacular panoramic view, but he instantly noted that no shelter could fit on this craggy pinnacle. His last reserves were exhausted. Cold from the chilly mountain night, he removed his backpack, put on all his clothes, and slept on the ground.

Shaffer had not covered even one hundred miles yet, and he must travel more than two thousand total. He was still in Georgia, only the first of fourteen states on the route. Nevertheless, by morning he felt refreshed. He found the missing shelter only half a mile farther on a ridge below the summit crags. This experience taught him not to give up too quickly. He had been on the trail one week when he crossed the state line into North Carolina.

North Carolina, however, turned out to be rugged country. The Nantahala Mountains stretch all the way to the Great Smoky Mountains. Several of the summits—Standing Indian, Mount Albert, Wayah Bald, and Cheoah Bald—offered beautiful views across the wilderness. Standing Indian was Shaffer's first five-thousand-foot peak, of which there are 195 in the South. The view from Standing Indian has earned it the nickname "Grandstand of the Southern Appalachians."

Shaffer hummed "On Top of Old Smoky" as he climbed Parsons Bald (4,948 ft.), where the Cherokees say the bears gather to hibernate, into the Great Smoky Mountains. . . . The "Old Smoky" of the song refers to Clingman's Dome, the highest peak in the range and formerly called Smoky Dome. In fact, Clingman's Dome is the highest peak on the entire Appalachian Trail and third highest east of the Mississippi.

The Smokies contain the greatest remaining deciduous forest in the world. The ruggedness of the range provided natural protection to the virgin forest on its slopes. Of the forty-one peaks that exceed six thousand feet in elevation east of the Mississippi, the Smokies contain a dozen, making this the most rugged of the Eastern ranges. The Appalachian Trail passes in sight of all twelve of these Sixers [a mountain exceeding six thousand feet in elevation], including Mount Le Conte, the highest from its base, and remote Mount Guyot. The trail follows the North Carolina–Tennessee state line along this chain of high peaks.

Beyond the Smokies, Shaffer followed the trail along the state line through Hot Springs into the Bald Mountains. Balds are mountains with no trees. The grassy balds have great views, and the heath balds, such as Roan Mountain, have beautiful displays of rhododendron. Soon Shaffer crossed the Nolichucky River, where he listened to the whippoorwills most of the night.

Shaffer spent a month hiking across Virginia, which boasts five hundred miles of trail. Fully a quarter of the entire trail lies in this one state. Following the trail, he climbed Virginia's highest mountain, Mount Rogers, and crossed its farmlands and valleys. Before he got very far through the farmlands, he bought mosquito netting. Later, he enjoyed the rugged Pinnacles of Dan and the Peaks of Otter in the famous Blue Ridge Mountains.

Shaffer stared at a sign pointing north into the brush. The trail had become faint, but now he realized that there would be no trail at all for the next seven miles. The trail was being relocated, and the new route was not completed. Shaffer got out his compass and began pushing through the dense tangles of brush. . . .

The Blue Ridge soon became a long spine of peaks across Shenandoah National Park. Shaffer took a few side trips in the park to see its highlights: Hawksbill Mountain, Dark Hollow Falls, the six waterfalls of White Oak Canyon, and Old Rag Mountain.

Soon after Shenandoah, Shaffer hiked into Harpers Ferry, West Virginia, the site of a famous Civil War battle. The Shenandoah River joins the Potomac River here as well, and when he had crossed the bridge over the Potomac, he found himself in Maryland. Soon, he had finished the twenty-three-mile walk across Maryland to the Mason-Dixon Line. He had completed his trek across Dixie.

From Ron Tagliapietra, *Great Adventurers of the Twentieth Century* (Greenville, S.C.: BJU Press, 1998), pp. 65-72.

1. What kinds of natural dangers did Shaffer encounter during his hike?
   wildcats (bobcats), rain, cold, mosquitoes, and the danger of losing the trail

2. What feat did Shaffer accomplish? hiked the entire length of the Appalachian Trail in one trip

3. What is the approximate total length of the Appalachian Trail? more than 2000 miles

4. Through how many states does the Appalachian Trail pass? 14

5. What important lesson did Shaffer learn early on his hike? not to give up too quickly

6. To what feature in the Great Smoky Mountains National Park does the song "On Top of Old Smoky" refer?
   Clingman's Dome, the highest peak in the range and the third highest east of the Mississippi River

7. What is a "bald"? a mountaintop that has no trees but only grasses

8. Along the boundaries between which two states does the Appalachian Trail run? Tennessee and North
   Carolina

9. Through which West Virginia city, the site of a Civil War battle, does the Appalachian Trail pass?
   Harpers Ferry

10. What point marks the end of the southern portion of the Appalachian Trail and the border between
    Maryland and Pennsylvania? Mason-Dixon Line

SKILL: Using Resources

CULTURAL GEOGRAPHY

WHERE AM I?

Based on your readings about the states of each region of the United States, write the name of each place or feature.

THE NORTHEAST

1. Low, rocky plateau between the New England coast and the Appalachians __New England uplands__

2. Potato-producing valley in Maine __Aroostook Valley__

3. The megalopolis of the Northeast __New York City__

4. The Constitution State __Connecticut__

5. A border state on the Chesapeake Bay __Maryland__

6. Mountains of Massachusetts __Berkshire Hills__

7. Mountains of Vermont __Green Mountains__

8. Mountains of New Hampshire __White Mountains__

9. State known for its lobsters __Maine__

10. State known for its steel and anthracite production __Pennsylvania__

11. State with the lowest population in the Northeast __Vermont__

12. State where the textile industry began __Rhode Island__

13. River that divides Pennsylvania and New Jersey __Delaware River__

14. Lakes in New York's Allegheny Plateau __Finger Lakes__

15. Wooded wilderness in New Jersey __Pine Barrens__

16. State of the Pilgrims __Massachusetts__

17. State of Roger Williams __Rhode Island__

18. State in which Jonathan Edwards was born __Connecticut__

19. Home of many Amish __Pennsylvania__

20. Home of the most famous waterfall in the world __New York__

THE SOUTH

1. Four Southern states that were among the original thirteen colonies __Virginia, North Carolina,__
   __South Carolina, Georgia__

2. Formed during the Civil War as a Union state __West Virginia__

3. Historically the poorest state in the United States Mississippi

4. Southern state with the lowest population West Virginia

5. Southern state with the highest population Texas

6. Four Southern states without a coastline Arkansas, Kentucky, Tennessee, West Virginia

7. Southern state with coasts on both the Atlantic Ocean and the Gulf of Mexico Florida

8. The five Southern states of the Atlantic Coastal Plain Florida, Georgia, South Carolina, North Carolina, Virginia

9. The Bluegrass State Kentucky

10. State that includes the Everglades Florida

11. Two Southern states that share the Great Smoky Mountains National Park North Carolina, Tennessee

12. State that includes the "Atomic City" Tennessee

13. State that holds the Mississippi Delta Louisiana

14. State of the Outer Banks North Carolina

15. State that contains the Shenandoah Valley Virginia

THE MIDWEST

1. Most populous state in the Midwest Illinois

2. The three Great Lakes that touch Michigan Lake Michigan, Lake Huron, Lake Erie

3. Area of rich soil left by glaciers that covers much of the southern Midwest till plains

4. Name given to a region of the Midwest that is home to many declining steel industries rust belt

5. Area of rolling plains covered with high grasses prairie

6. City that is nicknamed the "Motor City" Detroit

7. "America's Dairyland" Wisconsin

8. The "Twin Cities" Minneapolis and St. Paul, Minnesota

9. The "Gateway to the West" Missouri (especially the city of St. Louis)

10. Original name for the area that became the states of the Midwest Northwest Territory

11. The "Buckeye State" Ohio

12. The two rivers that join at the city of St. Louis Mississippi River and Missouri River

13. The name of the westward route that began in Independence, Missouri Oregon Trail

14. The site of the nation's richest iron ore-producing mines Mesabi Range

THE PLAINS

1. What early pioneers called the region of the Great Plains __"the Great American Desert"__

2. The area in southwest South Dakota that is remote, rugged, and covered with knobs, spires, rock pinnacles, isolated buttes, and windswept ridges __the Badlands__

3. The four presidents whose heads are carved on Mount Rushmore __George Washington, Thomas Jefferson, Theodore Roosevelt, Abraham Lincoln__

4. The only state with a unicameral legislature __Nebraska__

5. What the name Oklahoma means __"red man" (okla, "red"; homa, "man")__

6. Names of the Five Civilized Tribes whose members the United States government forced to move from the Southeast to Oklahoma __Cherokee, Chickasaw, Choctaw, Creek, Seminole__

7. The most important nonagricultural products of Oklahoma __oil and helium__

8. The "Sunflower State" __Kansas__

9. The two agricultural "belts" included in the Plains states __corn belt and wheat belt__

10. The least populous of the Plains states __North Dakota__

THE WEST

1. "Big Sky Country" __Montana__

2. The most famous attraction in Yellowstone National Park __the geyser "Old Faithful"__

3. The major crop of Idaho __potatoes__

4. What the letters "GSP" signify __gross state product__

5. The "mile-high city" __Denver, Colorado__

6. The bowl-shaped area of low, rugged land immediately west of the Rocky Mountains __Great Basin__

7. Religion headquartered in Salt Lake City, Utah __Church of Jesus Christ of Latter-Day Saints (Mormons)__

8. The founder of that religion __Joseph Smith__

9. Site of completion of the first American transcontinental railroad __Promontory Point, Utah__

10. The three largest cities of New Mexico __Santa Fe, Albuquerque, Las Cruces__

11. Two Indian groups whose reservations take up most of the eastern half of Arizona __Navajo and Hopi__

12. Site where Utah, Colorado, Arizona, and New Mexico meet __Four Corners__

13. Name given to the area of California that concentrates on the development of computer technology __"Silicon Valley"__

14. The three metals which Nevada leads the nation in producing __silver, gold, mercury__

15. The arm of the Pacific Ocean that juts into western Washington __Puget Sound__

Name _____

DISTINCTIVES OF U.S. CULTURAL SUBREGIONS

Multidisciplinary studies (history, physical geography, cultural geography, etc.) help one distinguish distinctive traits of different peoples. Consider, for example, the distinctives of the subregions within the United States that you have studied during this and the previous chapter. For each of the following words, phrases, or places, identify the specific subregion with which it is associated. Indicate your answers using the following abbreviations. (Some items might require more than one letter.)

N for Northeast	P for Plains
S for South	W for West
M for Midwest	

1. Great Smoky Mountains __S__

2. Mount Rushmore __P__

3. Mormon headquarters __W__

4. Rocky coastline, little beach, lobsters __N__

5. Humid subtropical climate __S__

6. Atlanta __S__

7. New York City __N__

8. Chicago __M__

9. Jonathan Edwards __N__

10. Universal manhood suffrage __M__

11. Wheat, corn __M/P__

12. Automobiles __M__

13. Cotton, tobacco __S__

SKILL: Recognition

CULTURAL GEOGRAPHY

Name _____

MEXICO MAP

Locate and label the following places and features on the map of Mexico. Using the key, indicate Mexico's cultural subregions.

Tijuana	Sonoran Desert	Baja California
Tampico	Matamoros	Isthmus of Tehuantepec
Bay of Campeche	Acapulco	Guadalajara
Mexicali	Sierra Madre Occidental	Gulf of California
Mexico City	Chihuahua	Yucatán Peninsula
Pacific Ocean	Cancún	San Luis Potosí
Ciudad Juarez	Sierra Madre Oriental	Gulf of Mexico
Veracruz	Monterrey	

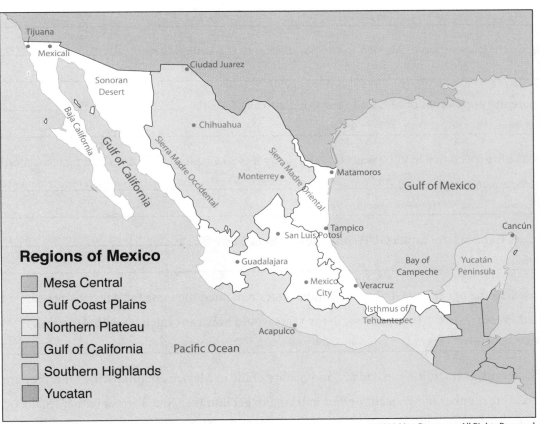

Regions of Mexico

- Mesa Central
- Gulf Coast Plains
- Northern Plateau
- Gulf of California
- Southern Highlands
- Yucatan

CULTURAL GEOGRAPHY

Name _____

COMPARATIVE STATISTICS

Complete the following table of statistics using the charts in the student book.
(Some data are already provided.) Then answer the questions below the chart.

Measurement	United States	Canada	Mexico
AREA (SQ. MI.)	3,718,711	3,855,174	761,601
POPULATION (M)	295.73	32.3	106.67
POPULATION DENSITY	31	10.6	139
LIFE EXPECTANCY	77.7	80.1	75.2
LITERACY RATE (%)	97	97	92
PER CAPITA GDP ($US)	40,100	31,500	9,600

1. Compare the area of Mexico to the area of the next largest country in North America. __Mexico's area is__
   __less than one-fourth the area of the United States.__

2. Compare the population of Mexico to the population of the United States. __Mexico's population is__
   __about one-third that of the United States.__

3. Compare the population of Mexico to the population of Canada. __Mexico's population is__
   __almost three times larger than that of Canada.__

4. Mexico's life expectancy in 2000 was 66 years; today it is 75.2 years. What does that fact say about Mexico's
   progress as a country? __Its economy is progressing to the point that the average person is able to eat better and get__
   __better medical care and therefore is more likely to live longer.__

5. How does Canada's per capita GDP compare to that of Mexico? __It is more than three times larger than that__
   __of Mexico.__

6. Suppose that the per capita GDP of the United States remained the same but Mexico's per capita GDP
   doubled every ten years. In about how many years would Mexicans catch up with Americans?
   __In a little more than twenty years ($19,200 in ten years, $38,400 in twenty years)__

7. If the economy, literacy, life expectancy, and quality of life in Mexico are improving (and they are), why do
   an increasing number of Mexicans persist in trying to get into the United States (either legally or illegally)?
   __Answers will vary. Possible points might include that the increases and improvements are not occurring as quickly as__
   __Mexicans want or think they should or that the Mexicans think that they can make more money faster in the United__
   __States and return portions of it to relatives in Mexico so that they can see a more immediate improvement in their__
   __quality of life.__

SKILL: Analysis

CHICHÉN ITZÁ

Read the following selection about Chichén Itzá on the Yucatan Peninsula of Mexico. Then answer the questions that follow.

CHICHÉN ITZÁ, YUCATAN, MEXICO   By Ron Tagliapietra

David Kelley sounded out the symbols on the ancient stone building, "Kakupakal." It stunned him; the translation really worked! Kelley knew that records from the Spanish colonial era stated that Kakupakal, meaning "Fiery Serpent," had been the name of a great Maya leader and the founder of an important city. Now he had found that leader's name inscribed at a Maya city, Chichén Itzá.

Kelley had read the old works about Mayan inscriptions, but this new work of Yuri Knorosov in 1952 had broken the code for the first time. Kelley reviewed the history. When Cortés conquered the Aztecs at Tenochtitlán in 1521, priests accompanied the conquistadors in order to convert the Indians. Soon after, when conquistador Francisco de Montejo came to Mexico's Yucatán Peninsula, Diego de Landa, a Franciscan priest, obtained what he thought was the Mayan alphabet from one of the few Aztecs who could still read the ancient writings. By 1800, both Mexicans and Europeans had lost all knowledge of reading Mayan. After 1832, Constantine Rafinesque and others began deciphering the Maya calendar and dates, but when they used de Landa's alphabet to read words, they found only nonsense. Kelley had recently read the work of Yuri Knorosov, a communist scholar in the Soviet Union. While ignoring all the communist propaganda in the work, Kelley recognized that Yuri Knorosov had corrected de Landa's error. Mayan was written, not with letter symbols but with syllable symbols. Kelley's discovery of the Maya leader's name had just proved that Knosorov's translation method was correct.

Kelley walked past the Temple of the Warriors and its rows of pillars decorated with eagles, jaguars, and Toltec warriors. Apparently, the Toltec Indians of Central Mexico had traded with or perhaps conquered the Mayas of Chichén Itzá at one time. This also explained the similarity of their main gods, which Mayas called Kukulcan and Toltecs called Quetzalcoatl.

Kelley climbed the north stairs of the nine-tiered pyramid now called the El Castillo ("the castle"). The seventy-five-foot-high pyramid had four sides perfectly aligned with the compass points. The staircase on each side split the nine tiers into eighteen halves, one for each Maya month. Each of the four staircases had ninety-one steps, which together with the top platform totaled the 365 days of the Maya year. Artistic panels surrounded the tiers, one for each of the fifty-two years in the Maya cycle (like a century). Kelley entered the pyramid through a passage on the north side, where narrow steps led to two small chambers. One chamber had an idol of Chac Mool, a god carved in a reclining position with his knees and head up and an altar on his belly. As Kelley entered the other chamber, a huge red jaguar looked at him through eyes of green jade. In the gloom, it looked eerie, though he knew that it was just an ornate throne.

While admiring the architectural beauty, Kelley cringed at the evidence of bloody pagan rituals. At the seventy-five-foot-deep Well of Sacrifice, he reflected on the fact that skeletons found show that living persons, many of them children, had been thrown into the well to appease the rain gods during famines.

The walls of the Maya ball court stood ninety feet apart, rising twenty-seven feet high and extending for 272 feet, almost as long as a football field. The ball court was the largest in Central America. The artwork on the sides of the court showed that players had to get a ball through rings at the ends of the court without using their hands, similar to soccer. The artwork also proved that the games involved a life and death struggle—decapitation for the losers.

Nearby stood the most gruesome structures: the Platform of the Jaguars, Skull Rack, and the Platform of the Eagles. Carvings at these platforms showed rows of human skulls on stakes and eagles ripping out human hearts. Kelley knew that these carvings reflected Maya rituals to placate the gods. In some artwork, the heads of victims were raised on stakes or the still-throbbing hearts of others were sacrificed on their bloody altars. Another temple depicted Kukulcan with a human heart in its mouth.

Maya civilization in Mexico, Belize, Guatemala, Honduras, and El Salvador traces back to about 1000 B.C. The linguistic breakthroughs have made much Mayan readable, but the language is not fully deciphered even today. Chichén Itzá seems to date from about A.D. 435, but the oldest known specific Maya date translates into A.D. 879, which suggests that the city reached its peak even later. About 1224, another city, Mayapan, conquered Chichén Itzá and caused its decline. Perhaps the idolatry and cruelty explain its decline. God is patient, but He eventually destroys the cruel as He did when He destroyed the Assyrians for their cruelty (Isa. 14:25).

Tourists from all over the world flock to Chichén Itzá, the most famous Maya ruin, in the state of Yucatán, Mexico. Every evening, popular multimedia sound-and-light shows are presented in English and Spanish. The most popular times to visit are on the spring and fall equinoxes. The Mayas built the pyramid so that shadows cast by the north terrace look like a snake. The shadow aligns with a sculpture of a serpent's head to complete the illusion.

Ron Tagliapietra, *The Seven Wonders of the World* (Greenville, SC: BJU Press, 1999), pp. 108–12.

1. Who broke the code of the Mayan writings and when? __Soviet scholar Yuri Knorosov in 1952__

2. What did that person discover that permitted the breaking of the code? __that Mayan was written with__ __syllable symbols, not letter symbols__

3. Whom did Cortés bring to the New World with him and why? __Roman Catholic priests; to convert the__ __Indians to Catholicism__

4. What names did the Mayas and Toltecs give their main god? __Mayas—Kukulcan;__ __Toltecs—Quetzalcoatl__

5. What was the nine-tiered pyramid called? __El Castillo, "the castle"__

6. Where (two places) did Kelley find evidence of human sacrifice, and what were the worshipers' motives for performing such gruesome practices? __in the well (to appease the rain gods during famines) and at the__ __Platform of the Jaguars, Skull Rack, and the Platform of the Eagles (to placate the gods)__

7. What was the consequence of losing a soccer match in Mayan religious practice? __decapitation for the__ __losers__

8. In what countries have Mayan ruins been found, indicating the extent of the Mayan Empire? __Mexico, Belize, Guatemala, Honduras, El Salvador__

9. What two possible reasons does the author give for the decline of the Mayas? __idolatry and cruelty__

10. What three evidences of Mayan sophistication and learning do the ruins present? __fine masonry (architecture and craftsmanship), precise astronomical alignments, 365-day calendar__

SKILLS: Analysis, Evaluation

MAP OF CENTRAL AMERICA AND THE WEST INDIES

Locate and label each of the following places and/or features.

Nicaragua	Curaçao
St. Lucia	Santo Domingo
Panama City	Atlantic Ocean
Mexico	Dominican Republic
Costa Rica	Belmopan
Barbados	Nassau
Havana	Pacific Ocean
Colombia	Puerto Rico
Panama	Guatemala City
San José	St. Croix
Guantánamo	Guatemala
Venezuela	Bahamas
Panama Canal	San Salvador
Grenada	Anguilla
Kingston	Belize
Guyana	Antigua & Barbuda
Cuba	Managua
Trinidad & Tobago	Guadaloupe
Port-au-Prince	El Salvador
Gulf of Mexico	St. Kitts & Nevis
Jamaica	Martinique
Aruba	Honduras
Tegucigalpa	Dominica
Caribbean Sea	St. Vincent & the Grenadines
Haiti	

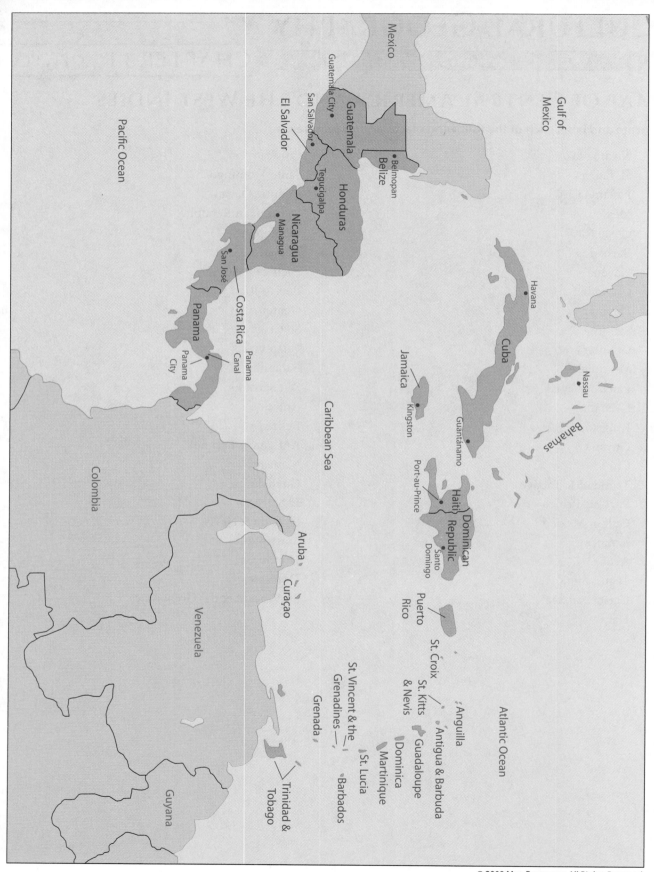

top

SKILL: Maps

CULTURAL GEOGRAPHY

Name _____

MAP OF SOUTH AMERICA

Locate and label on the map each of the places or features in the following list.

Each country and its capital	Trujillo	Amazon River	Rio de Janeiro
Cali	Atacama Desert	Atlantic Ocean	Strait of Magellan
Andes Mountains	Rio de la Plata	Recife	Pampas
Cape Horn	Caribbean Sea	Tierra del Fuego	Medellin
Pacific Ocean	Valparaíso	Patagonia	São Paulo
	Lake Titicaca	Maracaibo	Falkland Islands

© 2008 Map Resources. All Rights Reserved.

WHO'S WHO IN THE COLOMBIAN DRUG WARS?

Read the following synopsis of the drug wars in Colombia. Then answer the questions.

It is often difficult to determine who is who in the violence and civil and political unrest that have plagued Colombia for decades. Most of it stems from the drug trade: the cultivation, transportation, and sale of illicit drugs and the drug lords' efforts to protect their "business." Three types of groups are involved in this war, and all of them have been accused of human rights violations.

Leftist guerrilla groups include the *Revolutionary Armed Forces of Colombia* (FARC); the *National Liberation Army* (ELN); and three smaller groups, all of which are communistic in their political views.

The FARC was organized in 1964. It operates freely over 40–60 percent of the country (usually in rural, sparsely populated areas) but is strongest to the east and south of the Andes. The FARC boasts about 18,000 troops. It was financed early on by the Soviet Union, but today its money comes primarily from drugs, extortion, and kidnapping for ransom. Drugs account for half of its income ($100 million to $1 billion a year). It is responsible for most of the kidnappings that occur in the country. Most of its targets are government officials and political candidates who have taken a stand against the leftists and drug lords and civilian contractors, but many innocent civilians have also suffered at their hands. Most of Colombia's drugs are grown in FARC-controlled areas.

The ELN was organized in 1964 by Cuban-trained students, and they launched their first attacks in 1965. They were able to recruit a lot of students and priests, who preached something called "liberation theology" rather than the gospel. They have about 3,500 members today, down from a high of about 5,000 in the early 1990s. Their violence targets primarily the oil industry and its pipelines and other infrastructure.

Paramilitary groups are the privately financed armies of the drug lords. They fight not only against government forces but also often against each other in competition for the drug trade. The largest such groups are *Muerte a Secuestradores* (MAS), which is strongest in the north-central region, and the *United Self-Defense Groups of Colombia* (AUC), which is strongest in the north and northwest. Evidence exists that in some cases these groups and government forces have collaborated in protecting the drug fields and conspiring not to capture or imprison drug lords.

Colombian government security forces have a reputation for corruption, human rights abuses, and poor fighting, whether through lack of ability, lack of sufficient equipment, or collaboration with the paramilitary groups. Government forces have received much financial, military, and diplomatic support from the United States. Unfortunately, they have been implicated in 5–7 percent of the killings and kidnappings.

1. Using an atlas, study a map of Colombia, noting the areas dominated by each group named in this reading. How much of the country is actually controlled by the government forces? __Very little. Although most of__ __their control is in urban areas, even that control is questionable.__

2. With the drug trade so profitable and so much of the country controlled by drug lords and leftist guerrillas, how do you think the government can win the drug war? __Answers will vary.__

3. What do you think would be the wisest action for the United States in this war? __Answers will vary.__

THE LOST CITY OF THE INCAS

American explorer Hiram Bingham was born in Honolulu, Hawaii, in 1875 and attended Yale, the University of California, and Harvard. In 1907, he began teaching Latin American history at Yale. Eventually, he was elected the governor of Connecticut and then later a U.S. senator. He is best remembered, however, for his 1911 expedition to Peru, where he discovered Machu Picchu, the magnificent Inca ruins high in the Andes. Read the following excerpts from his book *Lost City of the Incas.* **Then answer the questions that follow the selections.**

People often say to me: "How did you happen to discover Machu Picchu?" The answer is, I was looking for the last Inca capital [Vilcabamba, the last refuge of the Incas who fled from Spanish adventurer Francisco Pizarro in the sixteenth century]. Its ruins were believed to be in the Cordillera Vilcabamba. . . . Those snow-capped peaks in an unknown and unexplored part of Peru fascinated me greatly. They tempted me to go and see what lay beyond. In the ever famous words of Rudyard Kipling there was "Something hidden! Go and find it! Go and look behind the ranges—Something lost behind the Ranges. Lost and waiting for you. Go! . . ."

[T]he Yale Peruvian Expedition of 1911 was organized in the hope that we might climb the highest mountain in America, collect a lot of geological and biological data and above all try to find the last capital of the Incas. . . .

[**THE FOLLOWING EXCERPTS RECORD BINGHAM'S FIRST VIEWS OF MACHU PICCHU.**]

The morning of July 24 dawned in a cold drizzle. Arteaga [a local farmer] shivered and seemed inclined to stay in his hut. I offered to pay him well if he would show me the ruins. He demurred [objected] and said it was too hard a climb for such a wet day. But when he found that I was willing to pay him a *sol* (a Peruvian silver dollar, fifty cents, gold), three or four times the ordinary daily wage in this vicinity, he finally agreed to go. When asked just where the ruins were, he pointed straight up to the top of the mountain. No one supposed that they would be particularly interesting. And no one cared to go with me. The Naturalist said there were "more butterflies near the river!" and he was reasonably certain he could collect some new varieties. The Surgeon said he had to wash his clothes and mend them. Anyhow it was my job to investigate all reports of ruins and try to find the Inca capital.

So, accompanied by Sergeant Carrasco [the party's armed escort] I left camp at ten o'clock. Arteaga took us some distance upstream. On the road we passed a snake which had only just been killed. He said the region was the favorite haunt of "vipers." . . .

[W]e now struggled up the bank through dense jungle, and in a few minutes reached the bottom of a very precipitous slope. For an hour and twenty minutes we had a hard climb. A good part of the distance we went on all fours, sometimes holding on by our fingernails. Here and there, a primitive ladder made from the roughly notched trunk of a small tree was placed in such a way as to help one over what might otherwise have proved to be an impassable cliff. In another place the slope was covered with slippery grass where it was hard to find either handholds or footholds. Arteaga groaned and said that there were lots of snakes here. Sergeant Carrasco said nothing but was glad he had good military shoes. The humidity was great. We were in the belt of maximum precipitation in Eastern Peru. The heat was excessive; and I was not in training! There were no ruins or *andenes* [terraces] of any kind in sight. I began to think my companions had chosen the better part.

Shortly after noon, just as we were completely exhausted, we reached a little grass-covered hut 2,000 feet above the river where several good-natured Indians, pleasantly surprised at our unexpected arrival, welcomed us with dripping gourds full of cool, delicious water. . . .

Through Sergeant Carrasco I learned that the ruins were "a little further along." In this country one never can tell whether such a report is worthy of credence. "He may have been lying" is a good footnote to affix to all hearsay evidence. Accordingly, I was not unduly excited, nor in a great hurry to move. . . . The view was simply enchanting. Tremendous green precipices fell away to the white rapids of the Urubamba below. Immediately in front, on the north side of the valley, was a great granite cliff rising 2,000 feet sheer. To the left was the solitary peak of Huayna Picchu, surrounded by seemingly inaccessible precipices. On all sides were rocky cliffs. Beyond them cloud-capped snow-covered mountains rose thousands of feet above us.

We continued to enjoy the wonderful view of the canyon, but all the ruins we could see from our cool shelter were a few terraces.

Without the slightest expectation of finding anything more interesting than the ruins of two or three stone houses such as we had encountered at various places on the road [already], I finally left the cool shade of the pleasant little hut and climbed farther up the ridge and around a slight promontory [a protruding crest of rock]. Melchor Arteaga had "been there once before," so he decided to rest and gossip with Richarte and Alvarez (the Indian farmers who gave the party water). They sent a small boy with me as a "guide." The Sergeant was in duty bound to follow, but I think he may have been a little curious to see what there was to see.

Hardly had we left the hut and rounded the promontory than we were confronted with an unexpected sight, a great flight of beautifully constructed stone-faced terraces, perhaps a hundred of them, each hundreds of feet long and ten feet high. They had been recently rescued from the jungle by the Indians [Richarte and Alvarez]. A veritable forest of large trees which had been growing on them for centuries had been chopped down and partly burned to make a clearing for agricultural purposes. The task was too great for the two Indians so the tree trunks had been allowed to lie as they fell and only the smaller branches removed. But the ancient soil, carefully put in place by the Incas, was still capable of producing rich crops of maize and potatoes. . . .

[W]e patiently followed the little guide along one of the widest terraces where there had once been a small conduit [channel for transporting water] and made our way into an untouched forest beyond. Suddenly I found myself confronted with the walls of ruined houses built of the finest quality of Inca stone work. It was hard to see them for they were partly covered with trees and moss, the growth of centuries, but in the dense shadow, hiding in bamboo thickets and tangled vines, appeared here and there walls of white granite ashlars [square blocks of building stone] carefully cut and exquisitely fitted together. . . .

[Bingham then discovered two temples, described in the following excerpt.]
The flowing lines, the symmetrical arrangement of the ashlars, and the gradual gradation of the courses, combined to produce a wonderful effect, softer and more pleasing than that of the marble temples of the Old World. Owing to the absence of mortar, there were not ugly spaces between the rocks. They might have grown together. On account of the beauty of the white granite this structure surpassed in attractiveness the best Inca walls in Cuzco [ancient Inca capital] which had caused visitors to marvel for four centuries. It seemed like an unbelievable dream. Dimly, I began to realize that this wall and its adjoining semicircular temple over the cave were as fine as the finest stone-work in the world.

It fairly took my breath away. What could this place be? Why had no one given us any idea of it? Even Melchor Arteaga was only moderately interested and had no appreciation of the importance of the ruins which Richarte and Alvarez had adopted for their little farm. Perhaps after all this was an isolated small place which had escaped notice because it was inaccessible.

Then the little boy urged us to climb up a steep hill over what seemed to be a flight of stone steps. Surprise followed surprise in bewildering succession. We came to a great stairway of large granite blocks. Then we walked along a path to a clearing where the Indians had planted a small vegetable garden. Suddenly we found ourselves standing in front of the ruins of two of the finest and most interesting structures in ancient America [two temples]. Made of beautiful white granite, the walls contained blocks of Cyclopean size, higher than a man. The sight held me spellbound. . . .

I could scarcely believe my senses as I examined the larger blocks in the lower course and estimated that they must weight from ten to fifteen tons each. Would anyone believe what I had found? Fortunately, in this land where accuracy in reporting what one has seen is not a prevailing characteristic of travelers, I had a good camera and the sun was shining. . . .

In view of the probable importance of the ancient Inca city which we had found on top of the ridge between the peaks of Machu Picchu and Huayna Picchu, our first task was to make a map of the ruins. On account of the forest and the dense undergrowth this proved to be a difficult task, but it was finally accomplished. . . . After the map was completed everyone was amazed at the remarkable extent of the area which had once been the site of an important city.

1. What was the purpose of the Yale Peruvian Expedition of 1911? to "climb the highest mountain in America, collect a lot of geological and biological data and . . . try to find the last capital of the Incas"

2. What qualification seemed to fit Bingham to gather information about the Incas? He was educated and taught Latin American history at Yale.

3. The words of which British writer inspired Bingham to go exploring in South America, and what was the quotation? Rudyard Kipling; "Something hidden! Go and find it! Go and look behind the ranges–Something lost behind the Ranges. Lost and waiting for you. Go! . . ."

4. What other two types of scientists were on the trip with Bingham but did not join him in his search for the ruins at the top of the mountain? a naturalist and a surgeon

5. List the hardships that Bingham faced on his search for the ruins. heat/humidity, rain, snakes, a difficult and dangerous climb

6. What features described in his account show that the expedition took place in a tropical rainforest? rain, humidity, large trees, dense jungles and vines, snakes, rapids

7. What was the attitude of the locals toward the ruins? They were not impressed and saw no great importance attached to them.

8. What was Bingham's expectation of the ruins before he actually saw them? He was not expecting to be so impressed.

9. Why was Bingham impressed by the Inca masonry work? The stones were huge (10–15 tons each) and cut to fit together perfectly—without benefit of mortar.

10. What precaution did Bingham take to ensure that others would believe his report of finding such an archeological wonder? He took photographs of the ruins using a camera he had taken with him.

11. What general principles about archeology do you learn from this account?

   Answers will vary but might include the following points: archeologists must be physically fit (having to go into

   dangerous and physically taxing environments and conditions); they must rely on native guides or assistants to get

   to their destination safely; they should take the proper equipment for the environment in which they will be working;

   they should be prepared to document what they see (whether on film, as Bingham did, or in writing or sketches);

   they should be capable of expressing themselves clearly and accurately; they should be prepared for uncooperative

   colleagues or workers, etc.

12. If you could conduct a historical expedition to any site in the world, where would it be and why? What

   types of scientists would you take with you and why? __Answers will vary.__

   _____

   _____

   _____

   _____

   _____

THE GAUCHOS: HORSEMEN OF THE PAMPAS BY SCOTT J. VAN JACOB

Read the following brief descriptions of the history and work of the gauchos. Then fill in the blanks to indicate the gauchos' unique tools and articles of clothing.

As horses and cattle escaped from the first Spanish settlers, they quickly populated the fertile pampas region. From these undomesticated [wild] resources emerged the gaucho. Relying on the horses for transportation and the cattle and wildlife for food and clothing, he wandered the vast expanses of the region working for the *estancieros* [ranch owners] when the mood struck him. . . .

The gaucho resided outside the region's growing urban centers and farming settlements. He developed a strong sense of identity and code of conduct, traveling when and where he wanted. He willingly shared his food and lodgings with fellow travelers. . . .

The gaucho was the ideal soldier during the wars of independence and the civil wars that followed. This skilled rider could survive off the land, knew the terrain intimately, and was a brave warrior. When Spanish forces threatened northwest Argentina, Martín Güemes' gaucho army harassed and slowed the Spanish advances. The *caudillos'* [boss or foreman of a ranch crew] rise in the Argentine interior derived from his ability to control the gaucho militia.

The life of the gaucho became increasingly difficult during the nineteenth century, as anti-vagrancy and passport requirement laws used to round up workers for the estancieros and soldiers for the Argentine army forced the gaucho further into the interior. Extensive portions of the pampas were settled, leaving less room for the gaucho to roam with his ponies and the wild herds of cattle he lived upon. At times, he escaped to Indian territory where he could live outside the Argentine laws.

The gaucho has come to mean many things to Latin America. He is the romantic image of the past, representing freedom from colonial control and from the urban encumbrances that have come to define the Latin American experience. He could live off of the land with no need for civilization, only his horse, knife, and lasso. Not unlike the American cowboy, the gaucho has become idealized and the stuff of myth. No one did so much to create that myth than José Hernandez with his poem *Martín Fierro* . . . , one of the finest and best-known pieces of Latin American literature.

(Included in the University of Notre Dame Department of Special Collections. Used by permission of the author.)

AN EXCERPT FROM THE EPIC POEM "MARTÍN FIERRO" BY JOSÉ HERNANDEZ

A son am I of the rolling plain,
A gaucho born and bred,
And this is my pride: to live as free
As the bird that cleaves the sky.

THE GAUCHO AND THE TOOLS OF HIS TRADE

The gaucho was unique in his dress and tools or weapons. He wore baggy pants called *bombachas* and a long-sleeved cotton shirt. Over his shoulders and down to about his waist was a square fringed cloth poncho, which had a hole in the center through which he put his head. On his head was a broad-brimmed leather hat. For footwear, he had leather legging-like boots that reached almost to his knees to protect him from the tough grasses of the pampas. On his heels he wore silver spurs to prod his *caballo* (horse).

Many of the gaucho's tools doubled as weapons. He carried one or more boleadoras, short lassoes with one or more stone or metal balls attached. One ball made a bola loca ("crazy ball"). Two balls made avestruceras ("ostriches"). And three balls, two of the same weight and one slightly lighter so they would separate when thrown, made Tres Marías ("Three Marys"). He used these boleadoras in hunting or fighting. He also had a plain rope lasso, which he used in roping animals. In his belt or attached to his saddle was his cuchillo (knife), an all-purpose tool and weapon with a long triangular blade and one sharpened side. Finally, he carried his rebenque (whip), with which he could either encourage his caballo or defend himself from an enemy.

broad-brimmed hat

long-sleeved cotton shirt

cuchillo

lasso

boleadoras

fringed poncho

bombachas

leather-legging-like boots

spurs

SKILLS: Recognition, Analysis

ITAIPU DAM—BRAZIL-PARAGUAY

Read the following description of the building of the Itaipu Dam on the border of Brazil and Paraguay. Then answer the questions that follow.

Power courses through water. The media often document fearsome destruction caused by hurricanes, floods, and tidal waves; but even normal seas claim swimmers in their powerful rip tides, shorebreaks, and undertows. White-water rafters and swimmers drown in powerful hydraulics. People build dams to harness this power. [On November 6, 1977], an earthen dam [built in 1887] in Toccoa, Georgia, broke, loosing the waters [of a fifty-five-square mile lake into] Toccoa Creek. This [otherwise] small creek tragically wiped out a college, leaving thirty-nine dead. How much more power is in the Paraná River—a river the size of the Mississippi?

The Paraná River is among the ten largest rivers in the world. At one time, as it flowed across southern Brazil, it roared over Salto das Sete Quedas or Guaíra Falls. These rapids dropped 375 feet to create the most powerful waterfall in the world. At this location, where the town of Guaíra overlooks the river border between Brazil and Paraguay, 470,000 cubic feet of water course down each second. The reservoir from the dam submerged the falls, but the volume of water still displays the size of the river.

About forty miles downstream, at the point selected for the dam, the river spreads out a quarter-mile wide and two hundred feet deep. In 1978 engineers diverted the river by digging a new channel for the river, 1.25 miles long and almost one-tenth of a mile wide (490 ft.). Changing the course of such a great river required blasting and the moving of fifty million tons of rock and dirt. The next year, when the original riverbed had dried out, they began to build the new dam. Almost five miles long, the dam required enough iron and steel to build 380 Eiffel Towers and enough concrete to build fifteen Eurotunnels [English Channel Tunnel between the United Kingdom and France].

At last, on October 13, 1982, the dam was completed at a cost of $18 billion. The twelve great gates descended in only eight minutes to seal off the new channel. The churning waters built up behind the dam for fourteen days until the waters were 328 feet above the normal water level. When water began to flow over the quarter-mile-wide spillway, the backed-up waters had already created a new lake covering 520 square miles—more than Lake Champlain. While impressive, this expansiveness is not what gives Itaipu Dam its fame since Owen Falls Dam in Uganda holds back a larger reservoir.

Itaipu Dam attains a maximum height of 738 feet. This surpasses Hoover Dam (Arizona-Nevada) by thirteen feet, a dam which held the record for the highest dam in the world in 1936. However, in 1989, Rogun Dam in Tajikistan took the record from Itaipu Dam, with its 1,099-foot height. Thus, Itaipu's impressive height is not what makes it famous either. Itaipu Dam's claim to fame is its power.

Each second, 160 tons of water pours down a thirty-five-foot-wide tube onto a turbine. This operates a fifty-three-foot-wide generator. If the size of this engine were not enough, the dam has eighteen of these, all working at once. The twelve thousand megawatts produced could supply energy for the entire states of New York and New Jersey. Itaipu Binacional, a two-nation company, owns the dam. Brazil and Paraguay split the power, but Paraguay uses only one-third of its share and sells the rest to Brazil at a reasonable rate. Not far downstream from the dam, the mighty Paraná River flows into Argentina, and all three countries plan smaller dams to harness this resource and save the costs of imported oil. Itaipu Dam supplies more hydroelectric power than any other dam in the world.

The dam generating the most power in 1942 was Grand Coulee Dam in Washington. Ranked as one of the seven wonders of the world in the 1960s, no dam surpassed its power until Itaipu Dam. For comparison, Grand Coulee Dam is about one mile long across the Columbia River and 550 feet high, required twelve million cubic yards of concrete, and produces 6,500 megawatts of electricity annually. This is enough electricity to power most of California. If Grand Coulee Dam once belonged among the wonders, then Itaipu Dam belongs in the list and has no rival today.

The town of Fox do Iguaça, twelve miles south of the dam, marks the mouth of the Iguaça River where it enters the Paraná River. Since both rivers form international boundaries, three nations meet at this point. Bridges from Brazil cross the Paraná into Paraguay and the Iguaça into Argentina. The town, therefore, provides a perfect base point for touring Itaipu Dam, its reservoir, and Iguaçu Falls. Flights arrive from major cities of all three nations: Rio de Janeiro, Brazil; Asuncíon, Paraguay; and Buenos Aires, Argentina. Buses run from two major Brazilian cities, but it is a long trip: 650 miles from São Paulo or 930 miles from Rio de Janeiro. The dam and reservoir receive about seven hundred thousand visitors annually.

(Source: Ron Tagliapietra, *The Seven Wonders of the World*, Greenville, SC: BJU Press, pp. 65–68.)

1. On the border of which two South American countries is the Itaipu Dam located?
   Brazil and Paraguay

2. On what powerful river is the dam? Paraná River

3. In what year was construction on the dam completed, and how much did it cost? 1982; $18 billion

4. Which two dams in the United States does the Itaipu Dam surpass in both size and power production?
   Hoover Dam and Grand Coulee Dam

5. How much power does the Itaipu Dam produce? 12,000 megawatts

6. That amount of electricity could produce enough power to supply the needs of which two American states combined? New York and New Jersey

7. Since the dam is located on the border between two countries, who owns it? a two-nation company called
   Itaipu Binacional

8. What third nation also benefits from the power produced by the Itaipu Dam? Argentina

9. No matter how big the dam is or how much power it produces, what is essential for such a multinational project to work efficiently? peace and good international relations

10. What practical benefits do you think the people of the two countries derive from the Itaipu Dam?
    Answers will vary but might include less expensive electricity for their homes and businesses, flood control below the
    dam, larger lake for fishing commercially or recreationally, and better relations between the two countries and their
    peoples.

SKILL: Original Sources

CULTURAL GEOGRAPHY

Name _____

COUNTRY COMPARISONS AND CONTRASTS

Using the data in the following table and your textbook readings, answer the questions.

Country	Capital	Area (sq. mi.)	Pop. (M)	Pop. Density (sq. mi.)	Per Capita GDP ($US)	Life Span
Argentina	Buenos Aires	1,068,297	39.54	37	12,400	75.9
Bolivia	La Paz & Sucre	424,162	8.86	21	2,600	65.5
Brazil	Brasilia	3,286,472	186.11	57	8,100	71.7
Chile	Santiago	292,257	15.99	55	10,700	76.6
Colombia	Bogotá	439,735	42.95	98	6,600	71.7
Ecuador	Quito	109,483	13.36	122	3,700	76.2
French Guiana	Cayenne	33,399	0.20	6	8,300	77.1
Guyana	Georgetown	83,000	0.77	9	3,800	65.5
Paraguay	Asunción	157,047	6.35	40	4,800	74.9
Peru	Lima	496,222	27.93	56	5,600	69.5
Suriname	Paramaribo	63,037	0.44	7	4,300	69.0
Uruguay	Montevideo	68,037	3.42	50	14,500	76.1
Venezuela	Caracas	352,143	25.38	72	5,800	74.3

1. According to these data, the people of which two countries possess the greatest wealth?

   Uruguay ($14,500/yr.) and Argentina ($12,400/yr.)

2. Although Brazil is the largest South American country in both area and population, what is one reason its per capita GDP is not competitive with that of the two countries in the first question?

   Much of Brazil's area is undeveloped rain forest, and many of its people live in poverty in the rain forests.

3. What is the least densely populated country?   French Guiana (6 people per square mile)

4. What is the most densely populated country?   Ecuador (122 people per square mile)

5. Which South American countries are the only ones with life expectancies of less than seventy years? Why do you think that is the case?   Bolivia (65.5), Guyana (65.5), Peru (69.5), Suriname (69.0); answers will vary but might include the relative poverty, lack of medical care, and poor economies of those countries.

6. What is the second-largest country by area? by population? __Argentina; Colombia__

7. What is the smallest country by area? by population? __French Guiana on both counts__

8. Which two countries have the lowest per capita GDP? __Bolivia ($2,600/yr.) and Ecuador ($3,700/yr.)__

9. Which country's citizens have the greatest life expectancy? __French Guiana (77.1)__

10. By adding the life expectancies of all thirteen South American countries and dividing the total, what is the average life expectancy of South Americans? __72.6__

SKILL: Charts

THE JOURNALS OF DAVID LIVINGSTONE: A LION ENCOUNTER

Born in Scotland in 1813, David Livingstone loved to read and taught himself Latin. When he was twenty-three, he entered medical school because he wanted to become a medical missionary to China. The Opium Wars, however, thwarted his plan. After he finished medical school in 1840, he went to southern Africa to minister instead. He established missions there and explored the interior of the "Dark Continent." He was the first European to see Victoria Falls and several African lakes. He faithfully recorded his observations in journals. Read the following excerpt from his *Missionary Travels and Researches in South Africa*. Then answer the questions that follow.

The Bakatla of the village Mabotsa were much troubled by lions, which leaped into the cattle-pens by night, and destroyed their cows. They even attacked the herds in open day. This was so unusual an occurrence that the people believed that they were bewitched—"given," as they said, "into the power of the lions by a neighboring tribe." They went once to attack the animals, but, being rather a cowardly people compared to Bechuanas in general on such occasions, they returned without killing any.

It is well known that if one of a troop of lions is killed, the others take the hint and leave that part of the country. So, the next time the herds were attacked, I went with the people, in order to encourage them to rid themselves of the annoyance by destroying one of the marauders. We found the lions on a small hill about a quarter of a mile in length, and covered with trees. A circle of men was formed round it, and they gradually closed up, ascending pretty near to each other. Being down below on the plain with a native schoolmaster, named Mebalwe, a most excellent man, I saw one of the lions sitting on a piece of rock within the now closed circle of men. Mebalwe fired at him before I could, and the ball struck the rock on which the animal was sitting. He bit at the spot struck, as a dog does at a stick or stone thrown at him; then leaping away, broke through the opening circle and escaped unhurt. The men were afraid to attack him, perhaps on account of their belief in witchcraft. When the circle was re-formed, we saw two other lions in it; but we were afraid to fire lest we should strike the men, and they allowed the beasts to burst through also. If the Bakatla had acted according to the custom of the country, they would have speared the lions in their attempt to get out. Seeing we could not get them to kill one of the lions, we bent our footsteps toward the village; in going round the end of the hill, however, I saw one of the beasts sitting on a piece of rock as before, but this time he had a little bush in front. Being about thirty yards off, I took a good aim at his body through the bush, and fired both barrels into it. The men then called out, "He is shot, he is shot!" Others cried, "He has been shot by another man too; let us go to him!" I did not see any one else shoot at him, but I saw the lion's tail erected in anger behind the bush, and, turning to the people, said, "Stop a little, till I load again." When in the act of ramming down the bullets, I heard a shout. Starting, and looking half round, I saw the lion just in the act of springing upon me. I was upon a little height; he caught my shoulder as he sprang, and we both came to the ground below together. Growling horribly close to my ear, he shook me as a terrier dog does a rat. The shock produced a stupor similar to that which seems to be felt by a mouse after the first shake of the cat. It caused a sort of dreaminess, in which there was no sense of pain nor feeling of terror, though quite conscious of all that was happening. It was like what patients partially under the influence of chloroform describe, who see all the operation, but feel not the knife. This singular condition was not the result of any mental process. The shake annihilated fear, and allowed no sense of horror in looking round at the beast. This peculiar state is probably produced in all animals killed by the carnivora; and if so, is a merciful provision by our benevolent Creator for lessening the pain of death. Turning round to relieve myself of the weight, as he had one paw on the back of my head, I saw his eyes directed to Mebalwe, who was trying to shoot him at a distance of ten or fifteen yards. His gun, a flint one, missed fire in both barrels; the lion immediately left me, and, attacking Mebalwe, bit his thigh. Another man, whose life I had saved before, after he had been tossed by a buffalo, attempted to spear the lion while he was biting Mebalwe. He left Mebalwe and caught this man by the shoulder, but at that moment the bullets he had received took effect, and he fell down dead. The whole was the work of a few moments, and must have been his paroxysms of dying rage. In order to take out the charm from him, the Bakatla on the following day made a huge bonfire over the carcass, which was declared to be that of the largest lion they had ever seen. Besides crunching the bone into splinters, he left eleven teeth wounds on the upper part of my arm.

A wound from this animal's tooth resembles a gun-shot wound; it is generally followed by a great deal of sloughing and discharge, and pains are felt in the part periodically ever afterward. I had on a tartan jacket on the occasion, and I believe that it wiped off all the virus from the teeth that pierced the flesh, for my two companions in this affray have both suffered from the peculiar pains, while I have escaped with only the inconvenience of a false joint in my limb. The man whose shoulder was wounded showed me his wound actually burst forth afresh on the same month of the following year. This curious point deserves the attention of inquirers.

1. Why were the Bakatla concerned about the lions? _The lions were killing their cattle._

2. Why, according to Livingstone, did the Bakatla not kill the lions? _They were a cowardly people._

3. By what logic did Livingstone conclude that they would have to kill only one lion to solve the problem?
   The understanding of the time was that whenever one lion in a "troop" of lions was killed, the others took the hint and left the area, presumably to avoid their own deaths.

4. How did the Bakatla go about trapping the lion? _The men arranged themselves in a wide circle and walked toward the center, slowly reducing the size of the circle and entrapping the lions._

5. Why did they not shoot when they had two lions trapped? _The circle was so small by that point that they were afraid they would accidentally shoot one of the men._

6. Why did the hunters think two men had shot the lion? _Livingstone's gun had two barrels, and he shot the lion with both barrels, creating two wounds._

7. What did the lion do to Livingstone once it had him in its mouth? _It shook him "as a terrier dog does a rat."_

8. What prevented the lion from killing Livingstone? _The lion's attention was distracted first by Mebalwe, whose gun had misfired, and then by another man, who was attempting to spear the beast. The lion left Livingstone to attack those men._

9. What superstitious act did the Bakatla perform after the lion was dead and why? _They built a huge bonfire over the carcass, which their superstitions stated would "take the charm from him."_

10. What did Livingstone conclude kept him from feeling pain after his wound healed whereas the lion's other victims did experience post-healing pain? _Livingstone believed that when the lion's teeth pierced the tartan jacket he was wearing at the time, it "wiped off all the virus from the teeth," whereas the native men had no such protection._

SKILLS: Analysis, Original Sources

MAP OF SOUTHERN AFRICA

Locate and label on the map each of the following places or features.

Atlantic Ocean	Mozambique	Johannesburg	Zambia
Tanzania	Lesotho	Angola	Namibia
Malawi	Mozambique Channel	Botswana	Comoros
South Africa	Cabinda (Angola)	Madagascar	Capital cities of all
Indian Ocean	Zimbabwe	Democratic Republic	southern African
Cape of Good Hope	Swaziland	of the Congo	countries

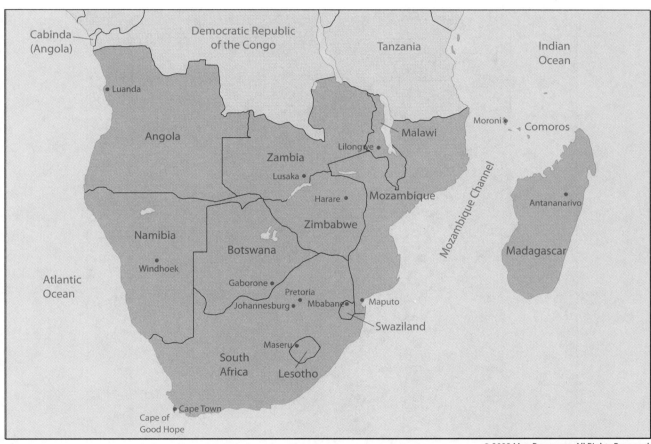

Name _____

MAP OF EASTERN AFRICA

Locate and label on the map each of the following places or features.

Sudan	Rwanda	Red Sea	Kenya
Uganda	Lake Victoria	Bab al-Mandeb	Djibouti
Gulf of Aden	Indian Ocean	Somalia	Horn of Africa
Serengeti Plain	Ethiopia	Burundi	Capitals of all eastern
Eritrea	Tanzania	Mount Kilimanjaro	African countries

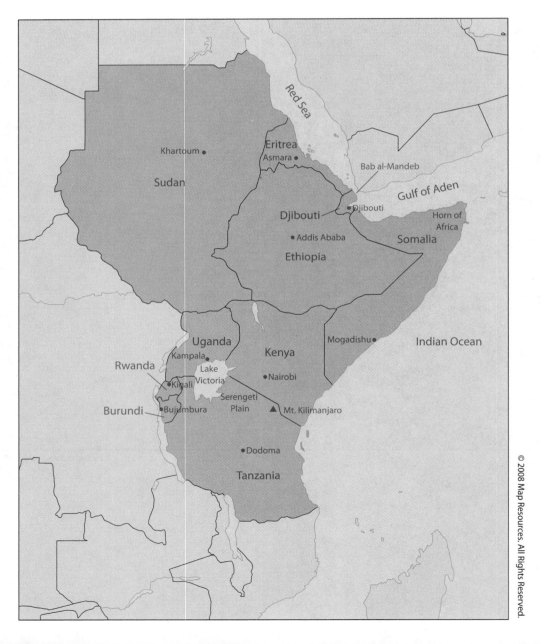

SKILL: Maps

CHAPTER REVIEW

Answer the following questions in preparation for the chapter test.

1. What name is given to all lands below the Sahara Desert? __Sub-Saharan Africa__

2. Which famous British missionary devoted his life to ministry in eastern and southern Africa?
   David Livingstone

3. What is the extreme southern tip of the African continent called? __Cape of Good Hope__

4. What city of more than 3.3 million people is located there? __Cape Town__

5. What term is applied to people in South Africa who are of mixed European and African descent?
   Coloureds

6. What were the Dutch farmers who settled beyond Cape Town called? __Boers__

7. What nation did the Dutch establish after they fled British control? __Orange Free State__

8. What language did those Dutch settlers speak? __Afrikaans__

9. What term is used for the policy of strict racial segregation practiced in South Africa until the 1990s?
   apartheid

10. Which three countries lie on the plateau in southwest Africa? __Botswana, Namibia, and Angola__

11. Which African country has the highest incidence of AIDS among the adult population? __Swaziland__

12. What large desert covers more than half of Botswana? __Kalahari Desert__

13. What geographic feature did David Livingstone describe as "the most wonderful sight I had witnessed in Africa"? __Victoria Falls__

14. What island—the fourth largest in the world—is off the southeast coast of Africa? __Madagascar__

15. What is the name of the group of 115 islands located northeast of the island in question 14?
    the Seychelles

16. What geographic feature is like a large gash in the earth stretching from the Middle East southward through East Africa? __Great Rift Valley__

17. What is the *lingua franca* of East Africa? __Swahili__

18. Which country is the key to East Africa, and what is its capital?
    Kenya; Nairobi

19. The country in question 18 is home to which tribe of nomads known for their skills as warriors?
    Masai

20. What is the highest mountain in Africa? Mount Kilimanjaro

21. What countries make up the Horn of Africa? Ethiopia, Eritrea, Djibouti, and Somalia

22. What are the vast grasslands, or savannas, that stretch over much of southern Africa called?
veldt

23. What word was applied to both the region across the Vaal River and the second independent Boer state?
Transvaal

24. What people group includes hundreds of tribes in Sub-Saharan Africa? Bantu

25. Which black leader, perhaps more than any other, helped to end the policy of segregation in South Africa?
Nelson Mandela

26. Which nation in southern Africa is surrounded by South Africa, one of only a handful of countries that are surrounded by another country? Lesotho

27. What oil-rich area that is part of Angola is bordered on two sides by the Republic of the Congo, one side by the Democratic Republic of the Congo, and on one side by the Atlantic Ocean? Cabinda

28. The export of what commodity is responsible for more than half of Angola's GDP? oil

29. Which river originates in Zambia and flows across southern Africa and into the Indian Ocean?
Zambezi River

30. What two rivers join in East Africa to form the Nile River? Blue Nile and White Nile

31. Which island off the coast of eastern Africa once produced 80 percent of the world's cloves?
Zanzibar

32. In what area are more forms of large wildlife found than in any other part of Africa?
Serengeti Plain

33. What two Rwandan tribes make up most of the population of that country and have periodically warred against each other? Hutus and Tutsis

34. What is the major export for both Rwanda and Burundi? coffee

35. Which eastern African country is one of only two African countries that no foreign power has ever successfully colonized? Ethiopia

SKILL: Recognition

MAP OF CENTRAL AFRICA

Locate and label on the map each of the places or features in the following list.

Cameroon	São Tomé and Príncipe	Chad	Congo River
Central African Republic	Equatorial Guinea	Sudan	Ubangi River
Republic of the Congo	Gulf of Guinea	Angola	All capital cities of Central African countries
Gabon	Atlantic Ocean	Zambia	
Democratic Republic of the Congo	Nigeria	Burundi	
		Rwanda	

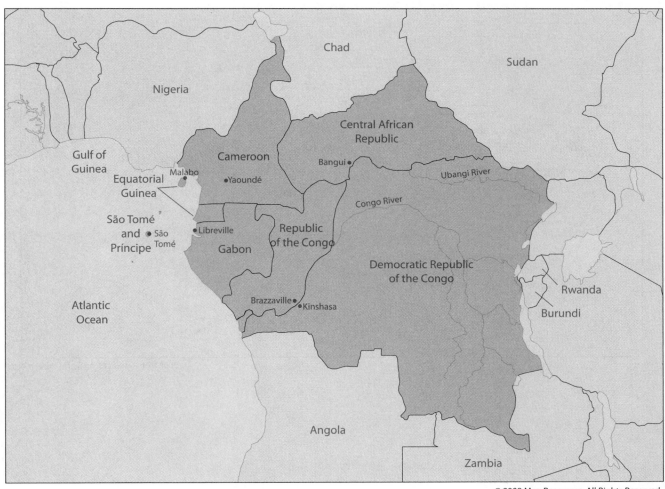

© 2008 Map Resources. All Rights Reserved.

MAP OF WESTERN AFRICA

Locate and label on the map each of the places or features in the following list.

Benin	Guinea	Togo	Atlantic Ocean
Burkina Faso	Guinea-Bissau	Cameroon	Capital cities of all
Cape Verde	Liberia	Mali	Western African
Côte d'Ivoire	Nigeria	Mauritania	countries
Gambia	Senegal	Niger	
Ghana	Sierra Leone	Gulf of Guinea	

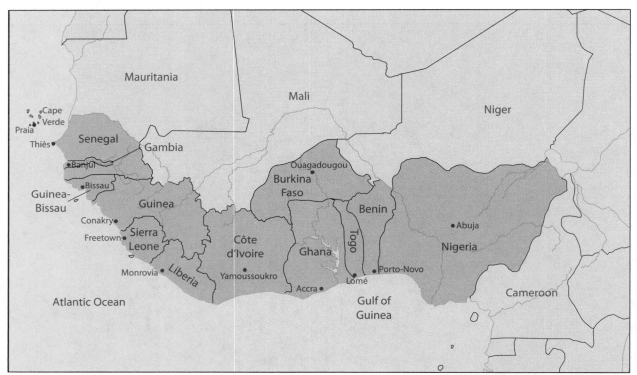

© 2008 Map Resources. All Rights Reserved.

BLOOD OF BAT AND TOE OF FROG BY STEPHEN DAVIES

Stephen Davies is a British missionary living among the Fulani people of Burkina Faso. The following anecdote reveals the superstition and unbelief that often frustrate missionaries as they seek to share the gospel with such people. Yet Davies was able to turn their superstition into an object lesson to show the power of God and the powerlessness of superstition. Read the anecdote and then answer the questions that follow.

MARCH 04, 2005

In Djibo market sits Al Hadji Amadou, the medicine-man. There are various different sorts of medicine-men in Djibo. There are Western-style doctors in Western-style clinics, including the great Australian surgeon Ken Elliot, famous throughout West Africa for his philanthropy and skill. There are also hawkers of "street-medicine," mostly young men with sacks of colored pills in unmarked sachets—they are the reluctant subjects of a current radio and billboard campaign "Medicaments de la rue—ça tue!" And there is Al Hadji Amadou, who does a roaring trade in blood of bat and toe of frog and skin of spitting cobra. His products are interesting, expensive and occultic.

In the market on Wednesday Al Hadji called me over and engaged me in a debate about his wares. I said we shouldn't need a snake skin in our pocket to protect us and solve our financial worries—that we should trust in God, who knows what we need even before we ask it. Al Hadji countered that it was God who had helped him to catch and kill the snake, so that people could buy bits of its skin. I said that God doesn't like us putting our hope in bits of wood and cloth and bone and skin. He said, "This stuff is powerful—whose power is it, if not God's?"

"What are the most powerful things here?"

"This falcon foot here and that bush-rat skin over there."

"What would happen to me if I burned the bush-rat skin?"

"If you burned the bush-rat skin, you would not be able to find your way home—you'd just wander around the market here for ever and ever."

"What would happen to me if I burned the falcon foot?"

"You'd turn into a falcon and fly away."

"Do you have fire?"

"Are you serious?"

"I want to show you that God's power is greater than the power of these things."

"I refuse to be responsible for what happens to you if you burn them."

"You are not responsible."

"Okay (turning to a child nearby). Bring me some hot coals from the brazier."

By this time quite a crowd had gathered around for the show, some laughing, some visibly frightened, all craning their necks to see what would happen to me. The child returned with the coals. I burned the falcon foot and the bush-rat skin (what a smell!) and said briefly to the people gathered that God's power is greater than all other powers in heaven and on earth. After that I chatted with Al Hadji for a while, gave him some money to compensate him for the two items, and went home. Carl and Shar prayed for me later that morning for protection from any occult power in those objects.

I have nothing against Al Hadji personally, or against traditional medicines per se (some of which are tried and tested natural products). But when it comes to the use of "power objects" (a falcon's foot in the pocket or a bush-rat skin under the hat), I am convinced that God Himself is much more worthy of our faith and trust.

Update: I went out to Monde So last night . . . and found people in the village already talking about the above incident—news here travels incredibly quickly. One child there told me that after I had left, Al Hadji rescued the remains of the falcon's foot from the fire and put it back on his stall.

(Reprinted from the online article at http://www.voiceinthedesert.org.uk. Used by permission.)

1. Why did Stephen ask the medicine man to show him his most powerful objects of superstition?

   If Stephen could discredit his most powerful objects of superstition, he could discredit all of them in the eyes of the bystanders, thereby reducing the man's powerful grip over the minds and hearts of the people.

2. Why did Stephen ask the medicine man what would happen to him if he burned those objects?

   He wanted the people to see the powerlessness of such objects over him and consequently the greater power of the true God. When they saw that he was unharmed, they too would be less likely to fear the objects.

3. Think "beyond the text." What is the symbolism of Stephen's use of fire to destroy the objects of superstition? In the Bible, fire is a symbol of God's judgment. Stephen's use of fire to destroy the objects represented God's hatred of such superstition and foreshadows His judgment on all such things that distract people from the truth of the gospel.

4. What was the significance of Stephen's chatting with the medicine man after his demonstration?

   By staying to chat with the medicine man, he was showing that he had no ill will toward the man himself but only toward his spreading of superstition among the people, which was preventing their coming to the truth.

5. Why did Stephen pay the man for the objects that he had destroyed? He had destroyed part of the man's livelihood, so to maintain good will among the people who still might not believe, he paid the man for the losses he had incurred.

6. What fact was demonstrated when the medicine man retrieved the undestroyed parts of his objects of superstition? He obviously had not believed the truth demonstrated by Stephen's object lesson and instead persisted in his superstitions.

7. Can you think of any other superstitions that might prevent people from accepting the truth of God's power? Answers will vary.

Skills: Analysis, Evaluation

CULTURAL GEOGRAPHY

CHAPTER REVIEW

Read each description or characteristic of Central African countries; then match it with the appropriate country from the list.

A. Cameroon	C. Democratic Republic of the Congo	E. Gabon
B. Central African Republic	D. Equatorial Guinea	F. Republic of the Congo
		G. São Tomé and Príncipe

___E___   1. Has a large (50–75 percent) Christian population

___A___   2. A German colony before being divided between Britain and France

___F___   3. Capital is Brazzaville

___D___   4. The only African country with Spanish as its official language

___C___   5. The third-largest country in Africa and the largest in the Congo Basin

___G___   6. Uninhabited until settled by the Portuguese

___B___   7. The only landlocked country in Central Africa; located almost exactly in the center of Africa

Read each description or characteristic of Western African countries; then match it with the appropriate country from the list.

A. Benin	F. Ghana	K. Senegal
B. Burkina Faso	G. Guinea	L. Sierra Leone
C. Cape Verde	H. Guinea-Bissau	M. Togo
D. Côte d'Ivoire	I. Liberia	
E. Gambia	J. Nigeria	

___B___   8. The French called it Upper Volta.

___I___   9. A colony for freed slaves; capital was named after a U.S. president

___L___ 10. Name is Portuguese meaning "lion mountains"; a major source of diamonds

___K___ 11. Its capital, Dakar, is the westernmost point of Africa.

___E___ 12. Africa's smallest country

___D___ 13. Its name is French for "Ivory Coast."

___A___ 14. Two-thirds of its people practice voodoo.

___J___ 15. Divided into three regions by its respective ethnic groups: Ibo, Yoruba, and Hausa

___C___ 16. Ten islands and five islets

_____M_____ 17. Its capital is its only seaport because it is a very narrow country.

_____F_____ 18. Formerly known as the Gold Coast

_____H_____ 19. A major (eighth in the world) producer of cashews

_____G_____ 20. Africa's leading (and the world's third-largest) producer of bauxite

Miscellaneous Facts and Trivia: Answer the following questions about Central and Western African countries.

21. What disease is spread by the *Aëdes aegypti* mosquito? __yellow fever_____

22. What insect spreads African sleeping sickness? __tsetse fly_____

23. The diseases mentioned in questions 21 and 22 above are traditional for the Central and Western African areas. What other disease has assumed epidemic proportions since it first appeared in the 1970s?

   __AIDS (acquired immune deficiency syndrome)_____

24. What disease is spread by the anopheles mosquito? __malaria_____

25. In addition to Christianity (both Protestant and Catholic), animism, and various tribal religions, which religion claims many adherents among the population of Central and Western Africa?

   __Islam_____

SKILL: Recognition

MAP OF NORTHERN AFRICA

Locate and label the following places and geographic features of Northern Africa. Shade the general Sahel region in brown and the Sahara region in yellow.

Mauritania	Nile River
Mali	Lake Nasser
Niger	Eastern Desert
Chad	Qattara Depression
Morocco	Sinai Peninsula
Algeria	Gulf of Suez
Tunisia	Suez Canal
Libya	Aswan High Dam
Egypt	Nouakchott
Western Sahara	Bamako
Senegal River	Niamey
Niger River	N'Djamena
Aîr Mountains	Rabat
Tibesti Mountains	Casablanca
Lake Chad	Tangier
Atlas Mountains	Algiers
Strait of Gibraltar	Tunis
Ahaggar Mountains	Tripoli
Gulf of Sidra	Cairo
Libyan Desert	Alexandria

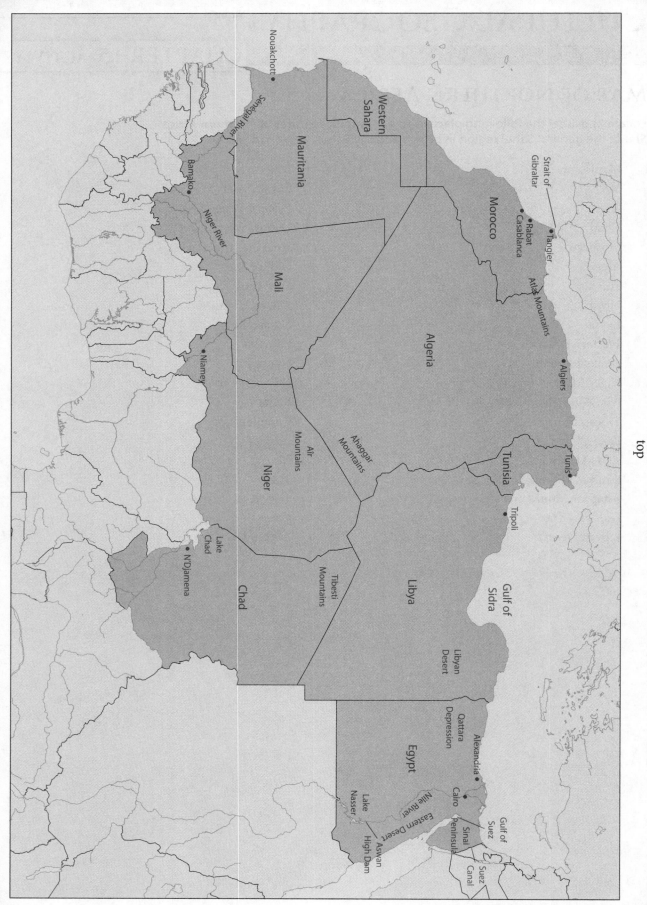

SKILL: Maps

A YOUNG EXPLORER SNEAKS A PEEK AT TIMBUKTU

Leo Africanus, whose real name was El Hasan ben Muhammed el-Wazzan-ez-Zayyati, was a Spanish Moor living during the time of Ferdinand and Isabella. When the Muslims were expelled from Spain in 1492, Leo moved to Morocco and began traveling through Africa with his diplomat uncle. He was captured and brought before Pope Leo X. The pope baptized him with the name Johannis Leo de Medici and sent him out to write a description of Africa. When the young explorer saw Timbuktu, it was beginning to decline but was still a center of learning. Read the excerpt and then answer the questions that follow.

The houses of Timbuktu are huts made of clay-covered wattles with thatched roofs. In the center of the city is a temple built of stone and mortar, built by an architect named Granata, and in addition there is a large palace, constructed by the same architect, where the king lives. The shops of the artisans, the merchants, and especially weavers of cotton cloth are very numerous. Fabrics are also imported from Europe to Timbuktu, borne by Berber merchants.

The women of the city maintain the custom of veiling their faces, except for the slaves who sell all the foodstuffs. The inhabitants are very rich, especially the strangers who have settled in the country; so much so that the current king has given two of his daughters in marriage to two brothers, both businessmen, on account of their wealth. There are many wells containing sweet water in Timbuktu; and in addition, when the Niger is in flood canals deliver the water to the city. Grain and animals are abundant, so that the consumption of milk and butter is considerable. But salt is in very short supply because it is carried here from Tegaza, some 500 miles from Timbuktu. I happened to be in this city at a time when a load of salt sold for eighty ducats. The king has a rich treasure of coins and gold ingots. One of these ingots weighs 970 pounds. The royal court is magnificent and very well organized. When the king goes from one city to another with the people of his court, he rides a camel and the horses are led by hand by servants. If fighting becomes necessary, the servants mount the camels and all the soldiers mount on horseback. When someone wishes to speak to the king, he must kneel before him and bow down; but this is only required of those who have never before spoken to the king, or of ambassadors. The king has about 3,000 horsemen and infinity of foot-soldiers armed with bows made of wild fennel . . . which they use to shoot poisoned arrows. This king makes war only upon neighboring enemies and upon those who do not want to pay him tribute. When he has gained a victory, he has all of them—even the children—sold in the market at Timbuktu.

Only small, poor horses are born in this country. The merchants use them for their voyages and the courtiers to move about the city. But the good horses come from Barbary. They arrive in a caravan and, ten or twelve days later, they are led to the ruler, who takes as many as he likes and pays appropriately for them.

The king is a declared enemy of the Jews. He will not allow any to live in the city. If he hears it said that a Berber merchant frequents them or does business with them, he confiscates his goods. There are in Timbuktu numerous judges, teachers and priests, all properly appointed by the king. He greatly honors learning. Many hand-written books imported from Barbary are also sold. There is more profit made from this commerce than from all other merchandise.

Instead of coined money, pure gold nuggets are used; and for small purchases, cowrie shells which have been carried from Persia, and of which 400 equal a ducat. Six and two-thirds of their ducats equal one Roman gold ounce.

The people of Timbuktu are of a peaceful nature. They have a custom of almost continuously walking about the city in the evening (except for those that sell gold), between 10 PM and 1 AM, playing musical instruments and dancing. The citizens have at their service many slaves, both men and women.

The city is very much endangered by fire. At the time when I was there on my second voyage, half the city burned in the space of five hours. But the wind was violent and the inhabitants of the other half of the city began to move their belongings for fear that the other half would burn.

There are no gardens or orchards in the area surrounding Timbuktu.

(Excerpt from "Leo Africanus: Description of Timbuktu" [1526] from *Reading About the World*, 3rd ed, Vol. 2, Harcourt Custom Books, 1999. Translated and edited by Paul Brians.)

1. From what you have already studied in this chapter, how do you think popular European fabrics were transported to Timbuktu? __caravan routes through the Sahara__

2. What motivated the king to marry his daughters to "strangers," or foreigners? Why is this not surprising, considering the history of Timbuktu? __The "strangers" were wealthy; the king probably wanted access to their__ __wealth because Timbuktu had a history of extreme wealth and was at the time falling into decline.__

3. Compare the food supply in Timbuktu during the writer's visit to the food supply in the modern Sahel. __He describes "grain and animals" as "abundant"; today, drought and overpopulation have caused food shortages.__

4. How did the king of Timbuktu display his absolute power after a military victory? __He sold the losing__ __people, including their children, at market.__

5. How did the king display his hatred of the Jews? From what you have read in the chapter, explain why a king in the heart of Africa might hate this faraway people. __He did not allow Jews to live in the city or do__ __business with the city's merchants; The founder of Timbuktu, Mansa Musa, traveled to Mecca and promoted the__ __Islamic religion and an Arabic education. Because the Islamic religion often does not respect Jews, kings after Mansa__ __Musa probably learned to dislike Jews.__

6. How can you tell that learning was important in Timbuktu? __He wrote that Timbuktu had many teachers and__ __that books were imported from the Barbary Coast. The book trade was more profitable than any other trade.__

7. How can you tell that gold was abundant in Timbuktu? __The king had a gold ingot weighing 970 pounds, and__ __gold nuggets were used instead of coins.__

8. Ancient Timbuktu was threatened by a fire spread by strong winds. How is wind still a problem in the Sahel region today? __Wind blows sands across the Sahel, causing storms and desertification.__

SKILLS: Analysis, Original Sources

CHRISTIANITY IN NORTHERN AFRICA

Read the following article about the difficulties facing missionaries in Northern Africa. Then answer the questions at the end of the article.

IN ISLAMIC LANDS, A SECRET LIFE By Carla Smithson

Ontarians Don and Jeanie Little arrived in North Africa in the spring of 1988, with one child in tow, another on the way and a dual agenda in mind. After three years of Arabic language studies in Europe, they were realizing a long-sought goal: to work as Christian witnesses in an Islamic nation. This would be their home over the next ten years.

To protect both Christian converts and foreign workers there, Don Little advises that the particular country not be named. It has no recognized Christian minority and, as is usual in the Muslim world, proselytizing is forbidden. Western residents are free to practise the Christian faith privately, however. Moreover, the Littles discovered, in long discussions with friends and acquaintances they could discreetly but effectively introduce them to Jesus Christ.

Don worked as an English teacher while Jeanie cared for and schooled their children. As his students came to trust and respect him they would often talk freely about faith, so he tried to make plenty of time for this. Other teachers at the language school were in North Africa for a cultural experience; the Littles also wanted to change lives.

When he addressed shopkeepers in Arabic, they would often ask if he were Muslim. His reply—"No, I'm a follower of Jesus"—frequently led to discussion, but seldom to conversion. "They would try to convert me—more or less aggressively," he recalls, "but when they realized I was set on remaining Christian, the discussions would end." This did not apply on a more personal level, however, and the Littles were able to quietly help establish a small "house church," which has grown to three houses and about 50 Christians today.

"Many young North Africans are disillusioned with Islam," he says. "They see the faltering economy and the corruption among Muslim leaders and they wonder, 'Is there more?'" But they would not ordinarily consider Christianity, which they associate with the Crusades and colonialism; they are more apt to turn to Marxism, or atheism. When they meet genuine Christians, however, they are drawn to them. In one instance, he believes, "the way we treated our children was what drew friends to be interested in Christ."

North Africans generally gave the family a warm welcome (in contrast to their sojourn in Europe). But the situation also had unpleasant and oppressive aspects, especially for Jeanie Little. While her husband had desired since his teens to live among Muslims, she did not find it so congenial. "It's not easy being a woman there," she says. "They have to be careful. Like remembering never to make eye contact with a man on the street, or even with unknown shopkeepers." The women she found very friendly—sometimes too much so.

People see such a life as adventurous and glamorous, she says, but that was not the reality for her. Her visiting mother had difficulty understanding why they would choose to live in such a country, and feared for their safety. She believes she was able to handle it only because God supplied grace: "Coming to terms with how God works in your life—that's what North Africa means to me."

For the converts, of course, things could be tougher still, since their families and friends regarded a decision for Christ as a major betrayal. "Some people were put out of their homes, or written out of wills," Don Little says. "We needed to be there to help them and provide them with a community."

Each time they returned to Canada for a visit they rethought their decision, the Littles say, and it was quite clear God wanted them there. But the children—three of them in the end—were approaching their teen years. "The children were increasingly isolated there," says their father of the family's 1998 decision to return to Canada. They now live in Ontario, and Don works as director of Arab World Ministries Canada (AWM), which still takes him to North Africa and the Middle East. Two of the children talk of returning as adults.

"After you adjust to another culture," says Don Little, "your ideas are always different—you never completely belong to any culture." Once the children are grown, he and Jeanie Little think they could return to Africa. For now, though, their role is to support AWM's overseas workers—especially in the current situation. "One woman just flew back there," Don says. "We generally don't run away in a crisis, which builds true oneness with our neighbours in these countries. Some of our people are in danger, but they're staying."

Copyright of *The Report Newsmagazine (Alberta Edition)*, 10/22/2001, Vol. 28 Issue 20, p. 6

1. How were the Littles allowed to live in Northern Africa as "missionaries"? North African governments allow Westerners to privately practice their Christian faith, although they are not allowed to witness publicly.

2. Since proselytizing in Northern Africa is illegal, how did the Littles share the Gospel? Don Little worked as a teacher and by developing relationships with his students was able to engage in conversations about religion. He also would respond to questions from people he met, like shopkeepers.

3. Why are young Northern Africans disillusioned with Islam? Why are they hesitant to consider Christianity? They associate Islam with a poor economy and political corruption. They are hesitant to consider Christianity because they associate it with the Crusades and colonialism.

4. What does Don Little believe drew Muslims to Christ? They saw that the Littles were genuine Christians with strong family values (in the way they treated their children).

5. What aspect of Northern African life was difficult for Jeanie Little? Women cannot make eye contact with unknown men or shopkeepers.

6. How did the Littles' family react to their move to Northern Africa? How did the families and friends of Muslim converts react to their conversions? Jeanie Little's mother could not understand why they would choose to live in Northern Africa, and she was afraid for their safety. Families and friends of Muslim converts saw them as traitors, driving them from their homes and writing them out of their wills.

7. How are the Littles still serving the Lord from Canada? They help to support missionaries that are still in Northern Africa.

SKILL: Analysis

CHAPTER REVIEW

Using the information that you learned from reading and studying this chapter, answer the following questions. Try to answer as many as you can before looking in the textbook.

1. List the countries of the Sahel, from west to east. _Mauritania, Mali, Niger, Chad_

2. Name the coral reef located south of the Sinai Peninsula. _Ras Muhammad Reef_

3. Name the nomadic people who account for the majority of Mauritania's population and who at one time engaged in the slave trade. _Moors_

4. What natural process provides fresh water for the Maghreb? _orographic rainfall from the Atlas Mountains_

5. What is the primary occupation of the population of the Sahel? _subsistence farming_

6. What is the wealthiest country in Africa? _Libya_

7. What is the most important body of water in the Sahel? _Lake Chad_

8. In which country was the world's highest temperature recorded? _Libya_

9. Which mountain range is made up of dormant volcanoes? _Tibesti Mountains_

10. What geographic feature as large as the state of New Jersey may be the future location of a new hydroelectric project? _Qattara Depression in Egypt_

11. Which two countries of the Sahel have had the least Arab influence in their history? _Mali, Niger_

12. List the two causes of the shrinkage of the body of water in question 7. _irrigation, reduced rainfall_

13. If you were to travel from north to south in Algeria, what three distinct geographic regions would you pass through? _mild Mediterranean coast, the Tell, the Saharan plateau_

14. Which modern Sahel country was once part of three empires? _Mali_

15. What process ended the yearly flooding of the Nile? _construction of dams, especially the Aswan High Dam_

16. Which covers most of the Sahara, regs or ergs? _regs_

17. How does Algeria's government fund industry and education? _uses income from petroleum and natural gas_

18. Which North African country is the world's leading exporter of phosphates? _Morocco_

19. Which country of the Sahel has the fewest paved roads? _Chad_

20. How much larger is Tunisia's population than Libya's? _twice as large_

21. Political reform now allows what in Egyptian government for the first time? ___multi-candidate presidential___ ___elections___

22. Name the primary cities of the east and west coasts of the Gulf of Sidra. ___East—Banghazi; west—Tripoli___

23. Name the mountain traditionally acknowledged as Mount Sinai. What does its name mean? ___Jebel Musa; Mount of Moses___

24. What grows in the desert and provides food for camel riders? ___date palms___

25. What products were carried north on ancient camel routes? What products were carried south? ___gold, ivory, slaves; salt, cloth, dates___

26. Of what type of government is Muammar Qaddafi the head? ___military dictatorship___

27. List the three largest cities in North Africa. ___Cairo, Alexandria, Casablanca___

28. List four important agricultural products of the Maghreb. ___(any four) olives, wheat, tomatoes, citrus fruits, wine___

29. What term describes dried-up shallow lakes that leave behind mineral deposits? ___chotts___

30. What is the world's longest river? ___the Nile___

31. From what industry does Cairo get most of its income? ___tourism___

32. What is the name of the land bridge between Africa and Asia? ___Isthmus of Suez___

33. What is the most barren desert region in the Sahara? ___Libyan Desert___

SKILL: Recognition

CULTURAL GEOGRAPHY

MAP OF THE EASTERN MEDITERRANEAN

Locate and label on the map the following places and features.

Turkey (and capital)	Bosporus
Iran	Pontic Mountains
Jordan River	Cyprus (and capital)
Greece	Dardanelles
Iraq	Taurus Mountains
Dead Sea	Syria (and capital)
Bulgaria	Aegean Sea
Saudi Arabia	Tigris River
Red Sea	Lebanon (and capital)
Georgia	Mediterranean Sea
Egypt	Euphrates River
Gulf of Aqaba	Israel (and capital)
Armenia	Gaza Strip
Black Sea	Istanbul
Suez Canal	Jordan (and capital)
Azerbaijan	Sinai Peninsula

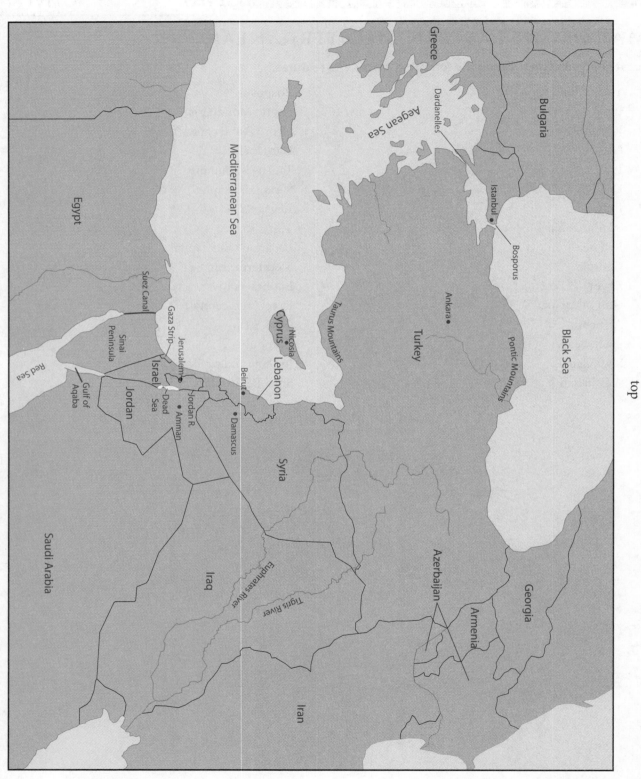

THE HOLY LAND IN BIBLE TIMES

Using your Bible and a map (or a Bible atlas), identify the places described in the following statements. Write the answers in the blanks and label the places on the map on the back.

1. The heavily fortified city near the Jordan River that literally fell to Israel (Josh. 6:1, 20) __Jericho__

2. Where Saul—later called Paul—met Ananias after his conversion and received instruction (Acts 9:8, 10) __Damascus__

3. Where Elijah faced the prophets of Baal in a showdown (1 Kings 18:19) __Mt. Carmel__

4. Two cities that marked the northern and southern extent of the kingdom of Israel (Judg. 20:1)
   __Dan and Beersheba__

5. Where David was born and anointed king and where Jesus was born (1 Sam. 16:1, 13; Matt. 2:1)
   __Bethlehem__

6. Where Jesus grew to adulthood (Luke 2:51–52) __Nazareth__

7. The nation that arose from the descendants of Lot and one of his daughters (Gen. 19:36–37) __Moab__

8. The working territory of Peter, Andrew, James, and John at the time Jesus called them to be His disciples (Matt. 4:18–22) __Sea of Galilee__

9. Mountain that marked the northern extent of Israel's conquest of the Promised Land (Josh. 12:1)
   __Mt. Hermon__

10. A "crowning city" renowned for its honorable merchant princes (Isa. 23:8) __Tyre__

11. A Philistine city where Samson showed his strength (Judg. 16:1–3) __Gaza__

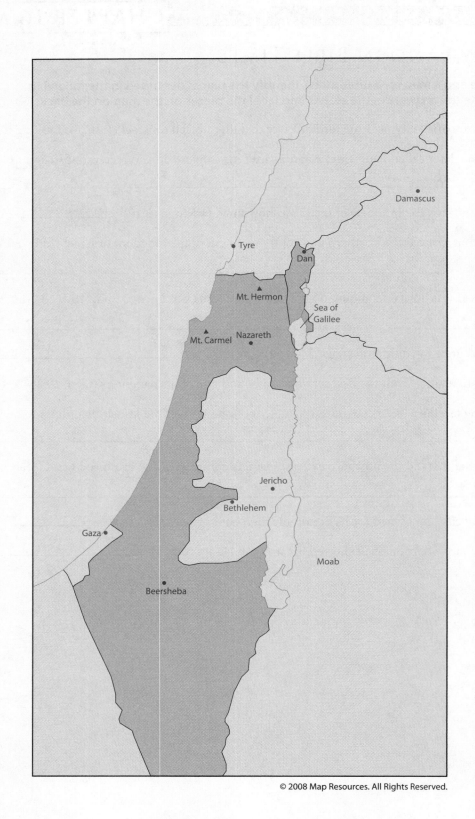

Damascus

Tyre

Dan

Mt. Hermon

Sea of
Galilee

Mt. Carmel Nazareth

Jericho

Bethlehem

Gaza

Moab

Beersheba

SKILLS: Bible Study, Maps

CULTURAL GEOGRAPHY

Name _____

THE JEWISH AND MUSLIM CALENDARS

Both Jews and Muslims have their own systems of reckoning dates. Read the text about each religion and study the corresponding table. Then answer the questions that follow.

THE JEWISH CALENDAR

The Jewish calendar is lunisolar, meaning that months are set up to follow the cycles of the moon and years to follow the revolutions of the earth around the sun. The problem with such a system is that twelve lunar months (each with twenty-nine or thirty days) fall short of a full revolution of the sun by eleven days. To correct this problem, Jews add an extra month of thirty days seven times every nineteen years. Consequently, some of their years are shorter than those of the Christian calendar and some are longer.

The beginning of the Jewish year occurs around our month of September. The first day of the new year may be set back a day or two to ensure that certain Jewish holy days do not fall on the wrong days of the week.

The Jewish calendar does not base its numbering of years on the birth of Christ (i.e., they are not designated as AD or BC). Instead, it starts with the supposed date of Creation (3761 BC by the Christian calendar). Years are followed by AM, meaning anno mundi, "year of the world."

Jewish month	Date of holy day	Selected holy day
Tishri	1–2 10	Rosh Hashanah (New Year) Yom Kippur (Day of Atonement)
Heshvan		
Kislev	25	Beginning of Hanukkah
Tevet	2 or 3	End of Hanukkah
Shevat		
Adar (First and Second Adar in leap years)	13 14–15	Fast of Esther Purim
Nisan	15–22	Passover
Iyar	5	Israel Independence Day
Sivan	6–7	Feast of Weeks
Tammuz	17	Fast (Mishna)
Av	9	Fast (Mishna)
Elul		

1. What is the problem with the way the Jewish calendar is organized? <u>Months are arranged by the moon</u>
   <u>and years by the sun. A solar year is eleven days longer than twelve lunar months.</u>

2. How is this problem corrected? <u>An extra month of thirty days is added seven times every nineteen years.</u>
   _____

3. What event begins the Jewish numbering of years? <u>the supposed date of Creation, 3761 BC by our calendar</u>

4. Assuming that Jewish and Christian calendars contain roughly the same number of years, what would be the Christian equivalent of the Jewish year 5735 AM? __AD 1974__

5. Which of the selected holy days on the table were instituted in the Old Testament, and which are extrabiblical (i.e., originated outside of the Bible)? __from the Old Testament: Fast of Esther (Est. 4:16; 9:29–31),__ __Purim (Est. 9:20–22, 27–28), Passover (Exod. 12:3–20), and the Feast of Weeks (Deut. 16:10, 16); extrabiblical: Rosh__ __Hashanah, Yom Kippur, Hanukkah, Israel Independence Day, Fast (Mishna)__

Muslim Calendar

The Muslim calendar is based entirely on the cycles of the moon. The Muslim year has twelve months that alternate between twenty-nine and thirty days. Each year typically has 354 days. Because the calendar is never corrected to match the solar year, seasons do not always occur in the same months.

Muslims start their year with the Hegira, or the flight of Muhammad from Mecca to Medina (AD 622 by the Christian calendar). The month of Ramadan is the Muslims' holy month. Faithful Muslims fast each day of Ramadan from sunrise to sunset.

Muslim month	Number of days
Muharram	30
Safar	29
Rabīʿ I	30
Rabīʿ II	29
Jumādā I	30
Jumādā II	29
Rajab	30
Shaʿbān	29
Ramadān	30
Shawwāl	29
Dhū al-Qaʿdah	30
Dhū al-Hijjah	29

1. What is the basis for the Muslim calendar? __the lunar cycles__

2. How does the situation in question 1 affect the seasons in a Muslim country? __Seasons do not occur__ __in the same months every year.__

3. What is the event that begins the Muslim numbering of years? __the Hegira, the flight of Muhammad__ __from Mecca to Medina__

4. If the Muslim New Year began on January 1 of the Christian calendar this year, how many years would pass before the next time it occurred around January 1? (Remember how many days the 354-day Muslim calendar loses each year compared to the 365-day Christian calendar.) __at least thirty-three years__

5. The first year of the Muslim calendar starts with the Christian date of July 16, 622. If you were using the present Christian calendar, what would be the date for the start of the first Ramadan? __March 9, 623__

CHAPTER REVIEW

Read the following statements and write the correct answers in the blanks.

1. Who is called the "Father of Modern Turkey"? ___Kemal Atatürk___

2. What did the Greeks call the strait that is now referred to as the Dardanelles? ___the Hellespont___

3. What is Turkey's corner of the Balkan Peninsula called? ___Thrace___

4. What is the largest city in the Middle East? ___Istanbul, Turkey___

5. After the Roman Empire collapsed in the west, what was the remaining eastern segment called?
   ___the Byzantine Empire___

6. Which Eastern Mediterranean country contains the sites of the seven key churches of Revelation?
   ___Turkey___

7. Which city is thought to be the oldest continuously inhabited city in the world? ___Damascus, Syria___

8. Which Muslim faction formed around the testimony of an eleventh-century Egyptian ruler, Al-Hakim, who claimed to be God? ___the Druze___

9. Which island country is made up of 78 percent Greek Orthodox Christians? ___Cyprus___

10. What do both Jews and Christians call Palestine? ___the Holy Land___

11. After the fall of the Ottoman Empire, which European country was given Palestine to rule as a mandate?
    ___Great Britain___

12. Which group of modernist Jews views Judaism as a social identity rather than as a religion?
    ___the Reconstructionists___

13. What single factor distinguishes the various branches of Judaism? ___the degree of their devotion to tradition___

14. The Palestinians are descendants of which biblical people group? ___the Philistines___

15. Which Middle Eastern figure received the Nobel Peace Prize in recognition of negotiations he undertook as leader of the Palestine Liberation Organization? ___Yasir Arafat___

16. What term is used for dry streambeds in the Eastern Mediterranean that fill up with water after rainstorms? ___wadis___

17. What elevated area did Israel capture from Syria during the Six-Day War? ___the Golan Heights___

18. What term means a large mound that forms as new cities are built over the ruins of earlier cities?
    ___tell___

19. What area on the edge of the Jordan River did Israel capture from Jordan during the Six-Day War?
the West Bank

20. Which country established the first true democracy in the Middle East? Israel

21. What term means a Jewish community in which the residents share everything in common, including the work? kibbutz

22. What is Israel's legislature called? the Knesset

23. What peninsula did Israel capture from Egypt during the Six-Day War? the Sinai Peninsula

24. Which body of water in the Middle East is near the sites of the ancient cities of Sodom and Gomorrah and provides a source for mineral mining? the Dead Sea

25. What is one of the three most feared Palestinian terrorist groups operating against Israel today?
Hamas, Hezbollah, or the Islamic Jihad

SKILL: Comprehension

CULTURAL GEOGRAPHY

Name _____

CHAPTER 17 ACTIVITY 1

SURVEY OF ISLAM

The religion of Islam is in the news now more than ever before. This chapter includes a variety of information about Islam, which is one of three great monotheistic (one god) religions (the other two being Judaism and Christianity). Give the following basic facts about Islam and then evaluate Islam from Scripture.

1. founder _Muhammad_

2. holy book _Koran_

3. requirement to become a Muslim _Repeat the declaration, "There is no God but Allah, and Muhammad is His Messenger."_

4. Five Pillars of Islam _Declare that there is no God but Allah; pray five times a day; give alms to the poor; fast during the month of Ramadan; make a pilgrimage to Mecca at least once in life_

5. most holy place _Kaaba at the Great Mosque in Mecca (Muhammad's birthplace)_

6. second most holy place _Prophet's Mosque (over Muhammad's tomb) in Medina_

7. first day on the Muslim calendar _1 Anno Hegirae (July 16, 622), the day Muhammad fled to Medina_

8. month of fasting during daylight hours and feasting at night _Ramadan_

9. Islamic worship building _mosque_

10. religious police _mutawa_

11. black cloak that strict Muslim women wear _abaaya_

12. Islamic pilgrimage _hajj_

13. ancient religious law of Islam _sharia_

14. highest title of honor of a Shiite Muslim _Ayatollah_

15. the two main rival Muslim groups and their key doctrinal differences _Sunni—orthodox, conservative followers of the caliphs (the appointed successors to Muhammad); Shiite—honor the imam (the hereditary successor of Muhammad who claims to be a divine manifestation qualified to interpret the holy writings)_

16. minor Islamic religion begun in Persia by renegades _Baha'ism_

17. minor Islamic religion begun in Persia and followed by peace-loving mystics who believe nothing exists except God _Sufism_

For each of the following Scripture passages, summarize first the similarity between Islam and Christianity and then the difference.

18. Deuteronomy 6:4–5 _Both are monotheistic, but the triune God of Christianity is not the same as Allah, and Christianity requires genuine faith, not just a declaration._

© 2008 BJU Press. Reproduction prohibited.

129

19. Matthew 6:1–4

Both encourage giving, but Christianity does not require it as a tax and demands that it be done in secret, not publicly.

20. Matthew 6:5–8

Both emphasize regular prayer, but Christianity does not view praying as a good work done at preset times with preset words; it is to be done in secret and not with vain repetitions.

ISLAM—NOT A PEACEFUL RELIGION

Ergun and Emir Caner are the sons of a Muslim *mwazien*, or scholar. Their family immigrated to the United States and settled in Columbus, Ohio. Their father, Acar Mehmet Caner, was their hero when they were growing up. He was also a devout Muslim who reared his sons in the mosque in Columbus, where he helped found the Islamic Foundation and sometimes did the call to prayer. When a high school friend invited the Caner brothers to a revival service and they came to know the Lord Jesus Christ as their Savior, their father disowned them. As difficult as that loss was, the brothers both went on to college and seminary, where they prepared themselves for a life of service to the Lord. They are in demand as expert commentators on Islam. Read the following excerpts from their book that show that Islam, despite what some people say, is *not* a peaceful religion. Then answer the questions at the end.

On February 23, 1998, five Islamic caliphates signed a fatwa declaring war against the United States. Representing five radical factions, these men united to call the Muslim world to common cause against the perceived enemy of Islam. The . . . text reads [in part]:

> [I]n compliance with Allah's order, we issue the following fatwa to all Muslims. *The ruling to kill the Americans and their allies—civilians and military—is an individual duty for every Muslim who can do it in any country in which it is possible to do it*, in order to liberate the al-Aqsa Mosque and the holy mosque from their grip, and in order for their armies to move out of all the lands of Islam, defeated and unable to threaten any Muslim. This is in accordance with the words of Almighty Allah, "and fight the pagans all together as they fight you all together," and "fight them until there is no more tumult or oppression, and there prevail justice and faith in Allah." This is in addition to the words of Almighty Allah "And why should you not fight in the cause of Allah and of those who, being weak, are ill-treated and oppressed—women and children, whose cry is 'Allah rescue us from this town, whose people are oppressors; and raise for us from thee one who believes in Allah and wishes to be rewarded to comply with Allah's order to kill the Americans and plunder their money wherever and whenever they find it. We also call on Muslim ulema, leaders, youths, and soldiers to launch the raid on Satan's U.S. troops and the devil's supporters allying with them, and to displace those who are behind them so that they may learn a lesson.

[Among the five men who signed this fatwa were Osama bin Laden and Ayman al-Zawahiri, both of whom are now sought in connection with the September 11, 2001, terrorist attacks on America.]

⌒

Thousands of persons lost their lives on September 11, 2001, as the United States saw the first manifestation of this declared fatwa—the World Trade Center towers were reduced to burning rubble. Were the men who flew planes into the towers and into the Pentagon acting out the wild ranting of a cultic leader who has [perverted] the peaceful religion of Islam? Or did they offer their lives because they believed orthodox Islamic doctrine? The authors of this book assert that Islam does in fact have an essential and indispensable tenet of militaristic conquest. The terrorists were not some fringe group that changed the Qur'an to suit political ends. They understood the Qur'an quite well and followed the teaching of Jihad to the letter.

In both the Qur'an and the Hadith, the infidel (kafir) must be converted or conquered. Muslims who die in the struggle against infidels (jihad) will immediately be translated to the highest level of paradise. Much of this doctrine draws on admonitions and injunctions in the Hadith, but strong Qur'anic foundations exist for holy war.

The Qur'an, supposedly from the very mouth of Allah, takes a dim view of the nonbeliever. Strictly speaking, jihad means a continuing *warfare* against them. Despite the explanations of Islamic apologists after the terrorist attacks, jihad does not primarily refer to a "struggle of personal piety." Jihad is combat on the fronts of politics, warfare, and culture. Muhammad exemplified this principle when he authorized the slaughter of thousands of men throughout the Arabian Peninsula in the name of Allah. If jihad is only a personal internal struggle, the Prophet misled the people through his actions and words as recorded in the Hadith. In the end, he was the personification of a militaristic theologian, which the Hadith accurately illustrates. In surah 2:190, Allah says, "Fight [jihad] in the cause of Allah those who fight [ajihad] you." The definition of this struggle includes the possibility of violence:

> And slay them wherever you catch them, and turn them out from where they have turned you out, for tumult and oppression are worse than slaughter. (surah 2:191)

The apparent contradiction of conquering the oppressors so all through oppression have faith in Allah can be understood with a proper interpretation of jihad. Military warfare is an absolute necessity if Allah is to be honored and worshiped.

The very presence of the infidel stirs turmoil and requires Islam to win victory: "And fight them on until there is no more tumult or oppression, and let there prevail justice and faith in Allah; but if they cease, let there be no hostility except to those who practice oppression" (surrah 2:193).

The current Muslim apologists who stress the concept of intellectual debate in this warfare must hasten to surah 2:216: "Fighting is prescribed for you, and you dislike it. But it is possible that you dislike a thing which is good for you, and that you love a thing which is bad for you. But Allah knows, and you know not." It is impossible to translate the word *fighting* in this text to mean anything but the traditional combat sense.

The Hadith also interprets jihad as a "fight, struggle, or battle." Bukhari's very first volume notes, "Allah's Apostle was asked, 'What is the best deed?' He replied, 'To believe in Allah and His Apostle (Muhammad).' The questioner then asked, 'What is the next (in goodness)?' He replied, 'To participate in Jihad in Allah's cause'"(surah 2:25). In hadith 3.46.724, which is narrated by Abu Huraira, Muhammad said, "A pious slave gets a double reward," and Abu Huraira added, "By Him in Whose Hands my soul is but for Jihad [holy battles], Hajj, and my duty to serve my mother, I would have loved to die as a slave." Thus, death is seemingly a possible end of such jihad.

1. What qualifies the Caner brothers to speak authoritatively about Islam? <u>They were reared as devout Muslims,</u>
   <u>their father was a Muslim scholar and an active leader in the religion, and they know and quote authoritatively</u>
   <u>from the Qur'an. They are also trained Christian scholars, one an expert in church history and the other in theology.</u>

2. What is the meaning of *jihad*? <u>warfare, a military struggle against all non-Muslims, both military and civilian</u>

3. Against which specific nation—and its allies—is this particular fatwa directed? <u>the United States</u>

4. To what do the Caners point as proof that the terrorists were not merely a fringe group of Muslims?
   <u>The terrorists understood well the Qur'an's militant tenets of jihad "to the letter." The Caners point out from the</u>
   <u>Qur'an and the Hadith the teachings that prompted the attacks.</u>

5. What should be the Christian's response to such religious fanaticism? The nation's response?
   <u>Answers will vary. Consider having an extended class discussion of the various ways of responding.</u>

SKILLS: Analysis, Original Sources

MAP OF THE PERSIAN GULF

Locate and label on the map the following places and features.

Saudi Arabia (and capital)	Tigris River
Syria	Qatar (and capital)
Gulf of Aqaba	Afghanistan
Yemen (and capital)	Euphrates River
Israel	Bahrain
Red Sea	Pakistan
Oman (and capital)	Caspian Sea
Lebanon	Jordan
Gulf of Aden	Egypt
Iraq (and capital)	Mecca
Turkey	Medina
Arabian Sea	Basra
Iran (and capital)	Kirkuk
Armenia	Mediterranean Sea
Persian Gulf	Jiddah
Kuwait (and capital)	Sudan
Azerbaijan	Eritrea
Gulf of Oman	Ethiopia
United Arab Emirates (and capital)	Djibouti
Turkmenistan	Somalia

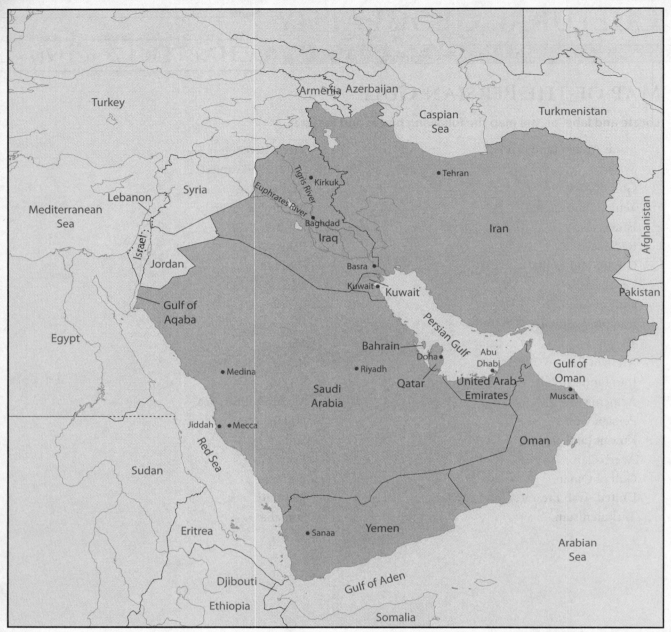

Turkey

Armenia Azerbaijan

Caspian
Sea

Turkmenistan

Mediterranean
Sea

Lebanon

Syria

Tigris River • Kirkuk

Euphrates River

Israel

Jordan

• Tehran

Iran

Afghanistan

• Baghdad

Iraq

Pakistan

• Basra

Egypt

Gulf of
Aqaba

Kuwait

Kuwait

Persian Gulf

Bahrain

• Medina

Saudi
Arabia

• Riyadh

Doha

Qatar

Abu
Dhabi

United Arab
Emirates

Gulf of
Oman

• Muscat

Red Sea

Sudan

• Jiddah • Mecca

Oman

Eritrea

Yemen

Arabian
Sea

• Sanaa

Djibouti

Gulf of Aden

Ethiopia

Somalia

SKILL: Maps

FINDING TREASURE IN THE DESERT

You have discovered a diary in a box of books that you bought at a local flea market. It contains a lot of information, but to understand the diary entries, you must use your trusty geography textbook and perhaps a dictionary. Using the chapter on the Persian Gulf region, particularly the relief map, provide the name of the person, place, or thing described in each numbered diary entry.

1. I started my vacation in the city that was Muhammad's birthplace. __Mecca__

2. Traveled due west to a city on the Red Sea. __Jiddah__

3. Took passage on a boat going south. Passed through Bab el Mandeb and stopped at the city that gives its name to the gulf between the Red Sea and the Arabian Sea. __Aden__

4. Do not buy any of the shrub leaves chewed as a narcotic! __Khat__

5. Continued by ship northeastward into the gulf between the Arabian Sea and the Persian Gulf. __Gulf of Oman__

6. Saw the ruler of Oman. __sultan__

7. Visited Qatar and observed the complicated process of removing salt from saltwater. __desalination__

8. Spent a day in the Persian Gulf island country famous for its natural springs and oil refinery. __Bahrain__

9. Landed at Ad Dammam and continued inland to the capital of Saudi Arabia. __Riyadh__

10. Saw a photograph of the first king of Saudi Arabia, who united the desert tribes early in the twentieth century. __Ibn-Saud__

11. Spent an evening outside the city, enjoying the traditional hospitality of the desert nomads. __Bedouins__

12. With some fear and only after taking the precaution of hiring armed security guards, proceeded by car north to the "land between the rivers." __Mesopotamia__

13. With the help of a multinational coalition, the Iraqi people are struggling to rebuild their country after suffering the terrors of a brutish dictator. __Saddam Hussein__

14. Stopped among the Shiites living in the marshy area at the confluence of the Tigris and Euphrates rivers. __Shatt al Arab__

15. Caught a boat going upriver to the exotic capital, the setting of the *Thousand and One Nights*. __Baghdad__

16. Rented a jeep to see the ruins of the capital of the ancient Assyrian Empire in northern Iraq where Jonah preached. _Nineveh_____

17. Spent the night among the ruggedly independent minority Iraqis in northeast Iraq just south of the Turkish border. _Kurds_____

18. Crossed the border into Iran and traveled through the mountain range where the Persian Empire began.
    _Zagros Mountains_____

19. Stopped briefly in the largest city among the Persian Gulf countries. _Tehran_____

20. Everywhere are murals and pictures of the highest official among Shiite Muslims.
    _Ayatollah_____

MAP: THE CAUCASUS AND CENTRAL ASIA

Using your textbook, locate and label on the map the following places and features. Then answer the questions that follow the map.

Georgia (and capital)	Kazakhstan (and capital)	Kyrgyzstan (and capital)
Black Sea	Persian Gulf	Kyzyl-Kum Desert
Almaty	China	Turkey
Armenia (and capital)	Turkmenistan (and capital)	Tajikistan (and capital)
Caspian Sea	Caspian Depression	Steppes
Hindu Kush	Russia	Pakistan
Azerbaijan (and capital)	Uzbekistan (and capital)	Afghanistan (and capital)
Aral Sea	Kara Kum Desert	
Kandahar	Iran	

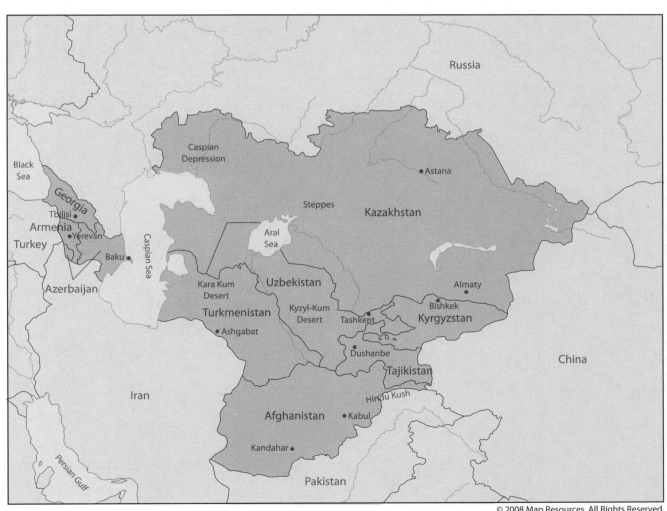

© 2008 Map Resources. All Rights Reserved.

1. What two militant Muslim countries that have concerned the United States since September 11, 2001, border Afghanistan? __Iran and Pakistan__

2. Which countries share borders with western China? __Kazakhstan, Kyrgyzstan, and Tajikistan__

3. Which countries in this region are separated from the others by the Caspian Sea?
   __Georgia, Armenia, and Azerbaijan__

4. What body of water do Kazakhstan and Uzbekistan share? __Aral Sea__

⌖ Which countries in this region share the same parallel of latitude as Philadelphia, Pennsylvania?
   __Kyrgyzstan, Uzbekistan, Turkmenistan, Azerbaijan, and Armenia__

SKILL: Maps

ROOTS OF RAGE: MILITANT ISLAM IN CENTRAL ASIA

BY EDWARD W. WALKER

The following selection was delivered in a panel discussion shortly after the terrorist attacks on the United States on September 11, 2001. Read the selection carefully, perhaps marking the most important points as you read. Then answer the questions that follow.

Let me begin by correcting an impression that I may have given in choosing the phrase "Roots of Rage" in my title today. I did not mean to suggest that Central Asians are, in fact, deeply enraged, hostile to their governments, radically anti-Western or pro-Taliban, or sympathetic to fundamentalist or militant Islam in general. On the contrary, polling data and anecdotal evidence suggest that overwhelming majorities are deeply fearful that the conflict in Afghanistan and Islamic militancy will destabilize their countries. Large majorities also appear to support their governments (with the exception of Tajikistan) despite the fact that none are particularly liberal or democratic—and, in the cases of Uzbekistan and Turkmenistan, are very repressive. While most see Russia as their most important source of external support, most also have generally favorable attitudes towards the United States and the West. As for Islam, significant majorities describe themselves as believers, but large majorities also feel that secular, not Islamic, law should govern and that Islamic parties should be banned. . . .

[T]he first point I want to make is that Central Asia is not Afghanistan. With the exception of Tajikistan, governments in the region have managed to preserve order, and society is politically demobilized and for the most part unarmed (again with the exception of Tajikistan). Above all, Central Asians value personal security, internal order, and material well being, and they will support governments that can provide those valued goods at a time when all are seen as being at great risk.

Nevertheless, Central Asian officials are deeply concerned about a perceived threat from militant Islamic movements, which they claim are products of external meddling. They accordingly refer to all Islamic radicals as "Wahhabis," a reference to the Islamic puritanical movement of the early eighteenth century that was adopted by the Saudi royal family and is Saudi Arabia's state religion today.

What I want to do . . . is try to assess whether these fears are justified and consider whether there really is a significant risk that militant Islam will find fertile soil in Central Asia.

First, however, let me say just a few words on terminology. I make two types of distinctions. The first is between "traditionalist" Islam and "fundamentalist" Islam. . . . Traditionalists are Muslims who support forms of Islam traditionally practiced in most parts of the Islamic world—that is, an Islam that accommodates practices, beliefs, laws, and social institutions not specifically prescribed by the Koran or the sayings and actions of the Prophet (the sunna). Fundamentalists, on the other hand, advocate a literal interpretation of the Koran and sunna, oppose accommodation to tradition or to changing social conditions, and espouse a return to an idealized vision of Islam as practiced at the time of Muhammad and/or the caliphates. . . .

Second, I distinguish between moderate, radical, and militant forms of Islam. By moderate Islam I basically mean tolerant Islam—that is, an Islam that is willing to accommodate both other religions as well as other forms of Islam itself. Radical Islam is the opposite—that is, Islam that is intolerant of "heretical" or non-Islamic beliefs and practices. Militant Islam, finally, is any form of Islam that advocates the use of violence in an effort to impose a particular form of Islam on others.

1. Why does the author insist early in his presentation that "Central Asia is not Afghanistan"?

   He wants the readers to understand that whereas Afghanistan was a hotbed of Islamic extremism and therefore in a

   state of perpetual agitation that prevented a growing economy and alienated other countries, the Central Asian

   countries were neither extreme in their Islam nor unstable or threatening to other countries of the world.

2. Which Central Asian country does he present as the sole exception to the region's order and stability?

   Tajikistan

3. Explain the distinction that the author makes between "traditional" Islam and "fundamentalist" or militant

   Islam. "Traditional" Islam embraces the historic position of the religion, rejects violence, accommodates

   both other forms of Islam and other religions, and is practiced in most of the Islamic world. "Fundamentalist" or

   militant Islam, on the other hand, is radical, intolerant of both "heretical" Muslims and all other non-Islamic religious

   views, and is willing to use violence to force its way upon everyone.

Islam arrived in the region that we know today as Central Asia . . . at the hands of Arab invaders at the beginning of the seventh century. It was embraced only gradually and variously, however, becoming the majority religion around the ninth century. By the tenth century, Central Asia had become one of the great centers of Islamic learning and culture, particularly the great Silk Road cities of Bukhara and Samarkand.

The vast majority of Central Asians are Sunni Muslims. . . . The standard argument is that Sunni Islam ultimately prevailed over Shia Islam in the region because it was better able to accommodate local practices and traditions. . . . Shia Islam became the dominant form of Islam only in Iran and across the Caspian Sea, in what is now Azerbaijan, but it is also practiced by the Khazaras of Afghanistan, the Ismailis of the Pamir region of Tajikistan and Afghanistan, as well as minority groups among certain Central Asian nationalities, such as the Turkmen.

The speed and degree to which Islam was embraced by the peoples of the region varied. In general, formal Islam was accepted more readily by the sedentary peoples of the region—particularly ancestors of today's Uzbeks and Tajiks. The region's nomadic peoples—ancestors of today's Turkmen, Kazakhs, and Kyrgyz—converted more slowly and retained more pre-Islamic beliefs and practices in the culture. Likewise, formal and orthodox Islam was more prevalent in urban than in rural areas.

Russian colonization in the nineteenth century was driven primarily by geopolitical, not religious, concerns, and as a result, Russian colonial administrators, who already had centuries of experience accommodating Muslim peoples in the empire, were for the most part willing to allow local peoples to practice Islam in peace. The Soviets, in contrast, launched a full-scale assault on Islamic institutions and practices in the mid-1920s, a campaign that intensified dramatically during Stalin's "revolution from above" and the purges of the late 1920s and 1930s. The great majority of mosques were destroyed as a result, and most members of the Islamic clergy were imprisoned or shot. Nevertheless, Islamic beliefs and practices of everyday life survived, while World War II brought a softening of the campaign against organized religion.

Eventually, an accommodation of sorts was reached between the regime and Islam. While the clergy was formally prohibited from proselytizing, the church was legalized. While the official clergy was deeply penetrated by the political police and important appointments were vetted [examined and approved or rejected] by Communist Party

140

organs, the official clergy was also given a substantial measure of autonomy. . . . At the same time, Central Asians, like Muslims elsewhere in the former Soviet Union, adapted Islamic beliefs and practices to Soviet conditions. . . .

Islam thus remained an important part of everyday practice and identity in Soviet Central Asia. So-called "parallel" Islam (as opposed to the official Islam overseen by . . . the Communist Party) was not, however, necessarily political or hostile to the regime. Even less was it fundamentalist. A great many Central Asians smoked tobacco, drank alcohol, and prayed intermittently at best (although few would eat pork), while women almost never covered their faces in public, let alone wore the full burqas that we [saw] in Afghanistan [under the Taliban]. . . . Women also had more-or-less equal access to education and employment. In general, better-educated urban residents tended to be more sovietized and secular than residents of rural or highland areas.

With the launching of the Gorbachev reforms, the region began to undergo an "Islamic revival." The number of Central Asians making the [pilgrimage] to Mecca increased dramatically, and many new mosques were built, much of it with funding from Islamic governments, charitable organizations, and wealthy individuals abroad. The number of imams and mullahs, and the number of students studying in Islamic schools both in the region and abroad, also increased dramatically.

Nevertheless, both elites and society in Central Asia remained politically conservative throughout the Gorbachev period, suspicious in general of Gorbachev's liberalizing reforms and very opposed to the breakup of the USSR. Independence for them was for the most part an unwelcome surprise.

In the decade since, Central Asia's Islamic revival has continued, and the great majority of the traditionally Muslim peoples of the region today identify themselves as believers. Nevertheless, all five states are formally secular, and only Tajikistan has legalized Islamic parties or allowed an Islamic party to participate in government. There is, however, considerable variation in the way that Islam is practiced in the five Central Asian successor states, as well as in the way that different regimes have reacted to politicized Islam.

4. When did Islam come to the countries of Central Asia? <u>in the seventh century</u>

5. Which people were the most reluctant to accept Islam and why? <u>the nomadic peoples; probably because</u> <u>they moved around more than others and were reluctant to surrender their centuries-old traditions in favor of</u> <u>something foreign</u>

6. To which of the two major branches of Islam do most Central Asians belong? <u>Sunni Islam</u>

7. How has Russia interacted with Islam in Central Asia over the centuries? <u>At first, the Russians</u> <u>accommodated the Muslims into the Russian Empire, but the Communists under Stalin repressed Islam until World</u> <u>War II, when they relaxed their opposition because they needed help to defeat Hitler. The Soviet secret police</u> <u>heavily infiltrated the Islamic clergy, but they still allowed them a degree of autonomy. The Muslims opposed the</u> <u>liberalization and eventual breakup of the Soviet Empire under Gorbachev.</u>

↩

Of the five Central Asian states [Afghanistan, Turkmenistan, Tajikistan, Uzbekistan, Kazakhstan, and Kyrgyzstan], the one that is the least directly affected by turmoil in Afghanistan and that is least concerned about destabilization by Islamic militants is

Kazakhstan. . . . [T]he two most important for regional stability are Uzbekistan and, to a lesser extent, Tajikistan. The Tajik civil war, which killed some 50,000 people, completely devastated the Tajik economy. Its population is also now the most armed and militarized in the region, and it has an extremely weak government that is unable to exercise any writ over large parts of Tajik territory. More Tajiks than any other nationality identify themselves as Muslim believers. There are also many Tajiks in northern Afghanistan, and Tajiks make up the core of the fighting forces of the Northern Alliance, which I should note is comprised only of parties that describe themselves as "Islamist."

❧

To date, Uzbekistan has . . . been the most cooperative Central Asian government in the U.S.-led campaign against the Taliban. Tashkent has apparently agreed to allow the U.S. to use its territory not only for humanitarian assistance but for offensive operations as well, in exchange for which the U.S. is stepping up economic assistance. More importantly, Washington has apparently offered the Uzbeks a rather vague security guarantee.

❧

[T]he Uzbek government has . . . been extremely aggressive in repressing [unapproved] Islamic groups. . . . It targets people who make public their sympathies with non-official Islam, forcibly cutting men's beards, harassing people who wear Islamic costume, arresting unofficial mullahs, and closing down [unapproved] mosques and Islamic schools. . . . The Uzbek government, like the Soviet government before it, vigilantly monitors the activities . . . to the point that it frequently gives the official clergy instructions on what to say or not say in sermons.

❧

Let me conclude with a few brief comments on the roots of Islamic militancy in Central Asia. Certainly both internal and external factors are important. External influences include the safe-haven provided to militants by the Taliban; access to terrorists and guerilla training camps in Afghanistan; funding from wealthy individuals and charitable organizations sympathetic to militant Islam; and the provision of weapons and supplies. However, most important, in my opinion, is the fact that Islamic radicals abroad offer up an extremely effective mobilizing ideology of resistance to a region that is deeply troubled and where communism and socialism have been discredited by 70 years of Soviet power; where nationalism has been undermined by the multi-ethnic nature of society and by numerous competing sub-national and supra-national identities; and by the apparent inability of liberalism or democracy to provide answers to the region's profound problems. Moreover, militant Islam has an extraordinarily effective, decentralized, and autonomous propaganda apparatus available to it in the form of often well-funded mosques and madrassas led by militantly anti-Western and orthodox mullahs and imams, an apparatus that benefits from the fact that in most cases both Islamic and non-Islamic governments are reluctant to intrude into spiritual affairs.

While external factors look more significant in the wake of September 11 and what we've learned since about al-Qaeda, internal factors are at least as important. Population pressures, land scarcity, depletion of water resources, environmental degradation, widespread corruption, drug smuggling and consumption, growing inequality, and extremely high unemployment have given Central Asians much to be disgruntled about. The social base of militant Islam in Central Asia, as elsewhere, are young unemployed males, both rural and urban, poor and middle class, who feel that their life opportunities are minimal. Moreover, in most of Central Asia, as in much of the Islamic world, opportunities for articulating grievances are minimal.

On the other hand, it [is] important to reiterate that, as of yet at least, militant Islam has relatively few supporters, . . . and there are powerful obstacles to its popularization in the region. The form of Islam traditionally practiced in Central Asia is neither puritanical nor fundamentalist. Fundamentalist Islam, not to speak of militant Islam, is opposed not only by the great majority of political and economic elites but also by the traditional Muslim establishment, which views it as a threat to its influence and position. . . . Even more importantly, fundamentalism has to overcome the many national, ethnic, clan, and regional lines of cleavages in the region. Indeed, only in Uzbekistan is religion the most salient political cleavage today. In Kyrgyzstan, in contrast, it is ethnicity, while in Tajikistan it is regionalism. . . . And finally, and perhaps most importantly, unlike Afghanistan and Chechnya, the region has managed to avoid, with the partial exception of Tajikistan, a complete breakdown of internal order, civil war, and the arming of the civilian population.

(Excerpt from the online article "Roots of Rage: Militant Islam in Central Asia" by Edward W. Walker from the *CCAsP Newsletter,* Winter 2001-2. Used by permission of the author.)

8. Which Central Asian country is least directly affected by the war in Afghanistan and least concerned about the dangers of militant Muslims? Kazakhstan

9. Which Central Asian country has been the most cooperative with the U.S.-led coalition fighting global Islamic terrorism, and what has it gained in return? Uzbekistan; it has received more economic assistance from the United States.

10. List the external and the internal factors that affect Islamic militancy in Central Asia.
External—safe-haven for Taliban militants; access to terrorist training camps in Afghanistan; financial support of wealthy outsiders (individuals and organizations) who are sympathetic to militant Islam; provision of supplies and weapons to militants. Internal—population growth, land scarcity, depletion of water supplies, environmental problems, government corruption, drug smuggling and use, economic inequality, high unemployment.

11. What other factors present greater problems for Central Asian countries than militant Islam?
divisions based on national, ethnic, clan, and regional factors

COMPARING AND CONTRASTING THE COUNTRIES

Using the Fast Facts at the beginning of Chapter 18 and your chapter readings, complete the following table and then answer the questions comparing and contrasting the countries of the Caucasus and Central Asia. In the first four columns, give each country's rank from 1 (the leader) to 9 (the lowest).

Country	Area (sq. mi.)	Pop. (M)	Pop. density (per sq. mi.)	Per capita GDP	Religion	Major resources/industries
AFGHANISTAN	2	1	6	9	Muslim	Afghans, rugs, jewelry; lapis lazuli; opium; wheat, barley, corn, cotton; sheep, goats, wool
ARMENIA	9	9	1	3	Orthodox	Barley, wheat, potatoes; copper, bauxite
AZERBAIJAN	7	4	2	4	Muslim	Cotton, grain, tea, silk; rugs, shawls; chemicals; fish, salt; oil, natural gas
GEORGIA	8	8	3	5	Orthodox	Hazelnuts, tea, grapes, tobacco, wheat, citrus fruits; services
KAZAKHSTAN	1	3	9	1	Muslim	Sheep, cattle; oil, chromite, lead, copper, uranium; fruit
KYRGYZSTAN	5	6	7	7	Muslim	Yaks (for milk and meat), sheep, cattle; wheat, fruits, vegetables; textiles; food processing
TAJIKISTAN	6	5	5	8	Muslim	Electrical power production
TURKMENISTAN	3	7	8	2	Muslim	Petroleum, natural gas
UZBEKISTAN	4	2	4	6	Muslim	Cotton, uranium

1. Which two countries have the lowest per capita GDP? _Afghanistan and Tajikistan_

2. Which country is called the "giant" of Central Asia and why? _Kazakhstan; because it is the largest in area_ _and has the highest per capita GDP_

3. Which country's capital city was moved following the fall of the Soviet Empire? _Kazakhstan_

4. What is happening to the Aral Sea and why? _It is shrinking because the Soviets in 1956 built the Kara Kum_ _Canal and began to divert water from the rivers that feed it elsewhere to raise cotton._

5. Which country was home for the Taliban until a U.S.-led military coalition overthrew them in the war against terrorism? _Afghanistan_

THE TRAVELS OF MARCO POLO IN CENTRAL ASIA

Marco Polo traveled through Asia during the thirteenth century and recorded his adventures in *The Travels of Marco Polo*. His thrilling account helped to spark the great Age of Exploration, which forever changed the world. Read the following excerpts from his book; then answer the questions.

OF THE CITY OF KAMADIN AND ITS RUINS; ALSO TOUCHING THE KARAUNAH ROBBERS

After you have ridden downhill two days, you find yourself in a vast plain, and at the beginning thereof there is a city called Kamadin [near the Zagros Mountains in western Iran], which formerly was a great and noble place, but now is of little consequence, for the Tartars [warlike tribes from Central Asia] in their incursions have several times ravaged it. The plain whereof I speak is a very hot region.

In this plain there are a number of villages and towns which have lofty walls of mud, made as a defense against the bandits, who are very numerous, and are called Karaunahs. This name is given them because they are the sons of Indian mothers by Tartar fathers. And you must know that when these Karaunahs wish to make a plundering incursion, they have certain devilish enchantments whereby they do bring darkness over the face of day, insomuch that you can scarcely discern your comrade riding beside you; and this darkness they will cause to extend over a space of seven days' journey. The old men who they take they butcher; the young men and the women they sell for slaves in other countries; thus the whole land is ruined and has become well nigh a desert.

Marco himself was all but caught by their bands in such a darkness as that I have told you of; but, as it pleased God, he got off and threw himself into a village that was hard by, called Conosalmi. However he lost his whole company except seven persons who escaped along with him. The rest were caught, and some of them sold, some put to death.

OF THE WEARISOME AND DESERT ROAD THAT HAS NOW TO BE TRAVELED

On departing from the city of Kerman [a city in southern Iran] you find the road for seven days most wearisome; and I will tell you how this is. The first three days you meet with no water, or next to none. And what little you do meet with is bitter green stuff, so salty that no one can drink it. Hence it is necessary to carry water for the people to last these three days; as for the cattle, they must needs drink of the bad water I have mentioned, as there is no help for it, and their great thirst makes them do so. But it scours them to such a degree that sometimes they die of it. In all those three days you meet with no human habitation; it is all desert [the Dasht-E-Lut in Iran], and the extremity of drought. Even of wild beasts there are none, for there is nothing for them to eat.

OF AN ASCENT FOR THREE DAYS, LEADING TO THE SUMMIT OF A HIGH MOUNTAIN

When you ride three days northeast of Wakhan [in Central Asia], always among mountains, you get to such a height that it is said to be the highest place in the world! And when you have got to this height you find a great lake between two mountains, and out of it a fine river runs through a plain clothed with the finest pastures in the world; insomuch that a lean beast there will fatten to your heart's content in ten days.

The region [of the Pamir Mountains in southeast Tajikistan] is so lofty and cold that you do not even see any birds flying. And I must notice also that because of this great cold, fire does not burn so brightly, nor give out so much heat as usual, nor does it cook food so effectually.

1. An important part of understanding original sources is the ability to discern facts from exaggeration. What incident from the preceding excerpts shows that Marco Polo included some "tall tales" in his writings? Which parts of that incident might be true? <u>His report of bandits with devilish enchantments</u> <u>is farfetched; bandits might have attacked travelers and taken slaves, perhaps attacking only at dusk or when the sky</u> <u>was overcast during storms.</u>

2. What do we know today as the highest place in the world? Was Polo actually at the world's highest spot? <u>Mt. Everest; no</u>

3. The effects mentioned in the last paragraph of the last excerpt are the typical results of high altitude on cooking. Lower air pressure enables water to boil at a lower temperature. How would this cause food to cook less "effectually"? <u>It would take longer to cook food since the water was boiling at a lower temperature.</u>

4. What hardships did Marco Polo face during his travels? <u>losing some of his men to bandits, heat and lack</u> <u>of drinking water in the desert, cold in the mountains, weak fire for cooking food</u>

5. In which area through which Marco Polo traveled have the allied nations been fighting Islamic terrorists? <u>the Hindu Kush or Pamir Mountains of northeastern Afghanistan and southeastern Tajikistan</u>

SKILLS: Original Sources, Synthesis

CULTURAL GEOGRAPHY

Name _____

MAP OF SOUTH ASIA

Using your textbook or an atlas, locate and label the following natural and political features on the map of South Asia.

India	Bangladesh	Bhutan	Maldives
China	Arabian Sea	Indian Ocean	Brahmaputra River
Himalayas	Western Ghats	Great Indian Desert	New Delhi
Dhaka	Male	Chennai	Mumbai
Pakistan	Nepal	Sri Lanka	Afghanistan
Myanmar	Bay of Bengal	Ganges River	Indus River
Vindhya Mts.	Eastern Ghats	Islamabad	Kathmandu
Colombo	Chittagong	Kolkata	Thimphu

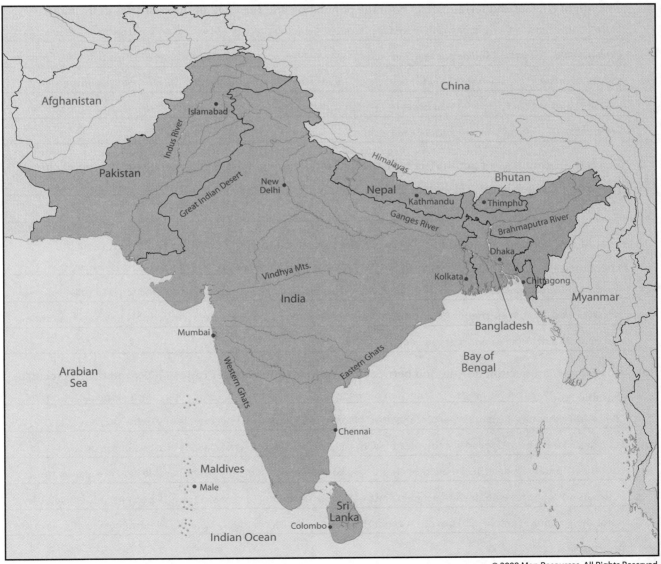

CULTURAL GEOGRAPHY

Name _____

COMPARING COUNTRIES

Using the following table and the map in your textbook, respond to the questions below to draw conclusions about the various countries of South Asia.

Country	Area (sq. mi.)	Arable Land (%)	Pop. (M)	Pop. Density (sq. mi.)	Per Capita GDP ($US)	Life Span
Bangladesh	51,703	62	144.32	2,850	2,100	62.08
Bhutan	18,147	3	2.23	126	1,400	54.39
India	2,973,190	54	1,080.26	954	3,400	64.35
Maldives	116	13	0.35	3,099	3,900	64.06
Nepal	52,819	22	27.68	536	1,500	59.80
Pakistan	300,664	28	162.42	551	2,400	63.00
Sri Lanka	25,332	14	20.07	792	4,300	73.17

1. How might climate and terrain affect both the population and the GDP of the countries in the table?

    More people tend to live in areas with moderate climates, avoiding both extreme heat and extreme cold, especially

    extreme cold. They also tend to prefer living in areas where the land is flat or slightly hilly, which encourages farming;

    they tend to avoid areas where the land is extremely steep, rugged, and rocky. In South Asia, more people live in the

    lowlands and conduct activities that provide a higher GDP; few live in the mountains, where it is difficult to sustain

    activities that contribute to a high per capita GDP.

2. Which three countries of South Asia have the highest per capita GDP, and generally what kind of climate and terrain do they have? Sri Lanka, Maldives, and India; they have a warm, moist climate and terrain that is amenable to farming and industry.

3. What, if any, connection do you find between the various countries' per capita GDPs and their life expectancies? The countries with the lowest per capita GDPs (Bhutan, Nepal, and Bangladesh), also have the

    shortest life expectancies (54.39, 59.80, and 62.08, respectively). A likely factor in this connection is that the relative

    poverty of the people and nations limits the quality and quantity of medical care, standards of health and sanitation,

    and general nutritional support of the people.

4. What, if any, connection do you find between the various countries' per capita GDPs and their percentage of arable land? There is no clear connection between these two statistical categories in these particular countries.

    The country that has the largest percentage of arable land (Bangladesh, 62 percent) is one of the poorest

    countries in the world. Conversely, the country with the least amount of arable land is also one of the poorest

    countries (Bhutan, 3 percent). On the other hand, two countries with some of the least arable land are among the

    South Asian countries with the highest per capita GDPs (Maldives and Sri Lanka, 13 and 14 percent, respectively). It

    is not the amount of arable land but rather what the people do with what they have that determines a country's

    productivity.

SKILLS: Charts, Maps

HINDUISM—IN ITS OWN WORDS

Read the following introductory text and then the subsequent selections from Hindu writings. Then, using those excerpts and your Bible, answer the questions at the end.

INTRODUCTION

Go into any secular bookstore and you will find a large selection of books about the New Age, many of those books on the topic of Hinduism. Increasing numbers of Westerners are seeking to find peace through Hindu practices and ways of thinking. If you live in a city that has a large secular university, no doubt you will encounter Hindus attending there in pursuit of a Western education. For this reason, it is good for a Christian to know Hindu beliefs and sacred writings. Most importantly, however, the Christian should know the truth of the gospel so well that he or she will be able to discern the errors of foreign religious teachings.

You should not be surprised to learn that a Hindu will think it is okay for you to be a Christian—but that it is just as appropriate for him or her to be a Hindu because both paths lead to the same end. (The current emphasis on toleration and multiculturalism makes it especially easy for one to fall into this trap.) A Christian must emphasize that Christ is the *only* way, truth, and life. This exclusive claim is what makes Christianity unpopular in today's world.

Hinduism has several books of scripture. The earliest documents are known as the *Vedas* ("knowledge"), or the *Sruti* ("what is heard or revealed"). The *Vedas* are considered to be revelation from God, and they provide the fundamental teachings of Hinduism. All other Hindu scriptures are called *Smriti* ("what is remembered"). These secondary scriptures are a collection of traditions that explain and illustrate the teachings of the *Sruti*. Many Hindus do not know their own scriptures well because their religion is based primarily on oral traditions, personal feelings, works, and the teachings of their prophets, gurus, and other holy men.

The *Upanishads* are part of the *Vedas* and are philosophical essays that explain the teachings in the *Vedas*. Some are single chapters; others are divided into parts, chapters, and sections (verses). For example, the reference II. v. 4 indicates part two, chapter five, and verse four.

Although the *Bhagavad Gita* was written much later than the *Vedas*, modern Hindus usually include it in the *Sruti*. This small book, consisting of eighteen chapters, is the most popular of all Hindu scriptures. Whereas the Upanishads are philosophical, the *Gita* is practical. The *Gita* presents a dialogue between Krishna (an incarnation of Vishnu, one of the three most important Hindu gods) and the Hindu warrior Arjuna while they are on a battlefield, about to engage in war with Arjuna's relatives.

BRAHMAN

[Arjuna said:] "O my Lord, O supreme Person, what is Brahman? What are fruitive activities? What is the Atman, and what is the creative energy of Brahman? Explain the nature of this relative world, and of the individual man. Who is God who presides over action in this body, and how does He dwell here? How are you revealed at the hour of death to those whose consciousness is united with you?"

[Krishna said:] "Brahman is the indestructible, the Supreme, which is imperishable, and independent of any cause but Itself. When we consider Brahman as lodged within the individual being, we call Him the Atman ["Self"]. And action pertaining to the development of these material bodies is called *karma*, or fruitive activities.

". . . [W]hoever, at the time of death, gives up his body and departs, thinking of me alone, then he will be united with me; of that there is no doubt. Whatever a man remembers at the last, when he is leaving the body, will be realized by him in the hereafter; because that will be what his mind has most constantly dwelt on, during this life."

"He who meditates on the Supreme Person with his thought attuned by constant practice and not wandering after anything else, he reaches the Person, Supreme and Divine.

"Great souls who find me have found the highest perfection. They are no longer reborn into this condition of transience and pain." *Bhagavad Gita* 8:1–8, 21

KARMA

"One who executes his duties according to my injunctions and who follows this teaching faithfully becomes free from the bondage of fruitive actions. But those who, out of envy, disregard these teachings and do not practice them regularly, are to be considered bereft of all knowledge, befooled, and doomed to ignorance and bondage." *Bhagavad Gita* 3:26, 21–32

"Ignorant fools, regarding sacrifices and humanitarian works as the highest, do not know any higher good. Having enjoyed their reward on the heights of heaven, gained by good works, they enter again this world or a lower one.

"But those wise men of tranquil minds who live in the forest on alms, practicing penances appropriate to their stations of life and contemplating such deities as Brahman, depart, freed from impurities, by the Path of the Sun, to the place where that immortal Person dwells whose nature is imperishable." *Mundaka Upanishad I.* ii. 9–11

REINCARNATION

"As the soul passes in this body through childhood, youth and age, even so is its taking on of another body. The sage is not perplexed by this.

"That which pervades the entire body is indestructible. No one is able to destroy the imperishable soul.

"Just as a person casts off worn-out garments and puts on others that are new, even so does the embodied soul cat off worn-out bodies and take on others that are new." *Bhagavad Gita* 2:12–13, 17, 22

‿

1. According to the preceding excerpts, what is Brahman? the Atman? Brahman is a soul who is over all and in all; Atman is Brahman in the individual man. [Hinduism varies on its belief in God. Some Hindus believe in one single god; others believe in many gods. The Hindu scriptures are just as contradictory.]

2. According to Hinduism, what determines one's state after death? what the dying person is thinking about at the time of his or her death

3. According to Hinduism, how does one free himself or herself from bad karma? by working with a spirit of devotion, not for rewards

4. According to Hinduism, how is one freed from impurities? by meditating on gods and practicing penance

5. According to the Bible, what determines one's state after death, and what does the Bible say about perfection? One's state after death is determined by the decision he or she has made concerning Jesus Christ. Those who reject Him face eternity in hell; those who accept Him as personal Lord and Savior spend eternity in heaven with Him. They will attain perfection only when they reach heaven's glories and receive a glorified body.

THE CONQUEST OF EVEREST BY SIR JOHN HUNT

In the spring of 1953, Englishman Sir John Hunt led an expedition to conquer Mt. Everest. The expedition included people from several nations. Sir Edmund Hillary of New Zealand and Tenzing Norgay, a Sherpa guide, reached the summit on May 29, 1953. Read the following account. (First, Hunt discusses the reasons for climbing Mt. Everest. Then, Hillary describes the final leg of his climb. The final section gives Hunt's reflections.) Then answer the questions.

REASONS FOR CLIMBING MT. EVEREST

To those looking for a material objective, there is no satisfactory answer, for there was indeed no desire for, nor expectation of, any material reward.

Nor is the question answered simply by a passion for climbing mountains.

Yet to solve a problem which has long resisted the skill and persistence of others is an irresistible magnet in every sphere of human activity. . . . The possibility of entering the unknown; the simple fact that it was the highest point on the world's surface—these things goaded us on.

MAY 29—HILLARY'S ACCOUNT (INCLUDED IN HUNT'S BOOK)

At 4 A.M. it was very still. . . . We started up our cooker and . . . drank large quantities of lemon juice and sugar, and followed this with our last can of sardines on biscuits. I dragged our oxygen sets into the tent, cleaned the ice off them and then completely rechecked and tested them. . . . Over our down clothing we donned our windproofs and onto our hands we pulled three pairs of gloves—silk, woolen, and windproof.

At 6:30 A.M. we crawled out of our tent into the snow, hoisted our thirty pounds of oxygen gear onto our backs, connected up our masks and turned on the valves to bring life-giving oxygen into our lungs. A few good deep breaths and we were ready to go. . . . The ridge was now all bathed in sunlight and we could see our first objective, the south summit, far above us. . . .

The soft unstable snow made a route on top of the ridge both difficult and dangerous. . . . After several hundred feet of this rather trying ridge, we came to a tiny hollow and found there the oxygen bottles left on the earlier attempt by Evans and Bourdillon [members of the expedition who had made an attempt a few days before]. I scraped the ice off the gauges and was greatly relieved to find that they still contained several hundred liters of oxygen—sufficient to get us down to the South Col [camp at the South "Pass"] if used very sparingly. With the comforting thought of these oxygen bottles behind us, I continued making the trail. . . . The snow conditions . . . were, we felt, distinctly dangerous, but as no alternative route seemed available, we persisted in our strenuous and uncomfortable efforts to beat a trail up it. . . .

The weather for Everest seemed practically perfect. Insulated as we were in all our down clothing and windproofs, we suffered no discomfort from cold or wind. However, on one occasion I removed my sunglasses to examine more closely a difficult section of the ridge but was very soon blinded by the fine snow driven by the bitter wind and hastily replaced them. . . .

After an hour's steady going we reached the foot of . . . a rock step some forty feet high. . . . On its east side was another great cornice [overhanging mass of snow or ice along a ridge, formed by wind] and running up the full forty feet of the step was a narrow crack between the cornice and the rock. Leaving Tenzing to belay [secure to a projection with a rope] me . . . , I jammed my way into this crack, then kicking backwards with my crampons [spikes attached to boots for use on hard snow or ice] I sank their spikes deep into the frozen snow behind me and levered myself off the ground. Taking advantage of every little rock hold and all the force of knee, shoulder, and arms I could muster, I literally cramponed backwards up the crack, with a fervent prayer that the cornice would remain attached to the rock. Despite the considerable effort involved, my progress although slow was steady, and . . . I inched my way upward until I could finally reach over the top of the rock and drag myself out of the crack onto a wide ledge. For a few moments I lay regaining my breath. . . . [Then] I took a firm stance on the ledge and signaled to Tenzing to come on up. . . .

I went on cutting steps [using an ice ax to cut holes in the snow to step into] on the narrow strip of snow. The ridge curved away to the right and we had no idea where the top was. As I cut around the back of one hump, another higher one would swing into view. Time was passing and the ridge seemed never-ending. . . . I was beginning to tire a little now. I had been cutting steps continuously for two hours, . . . I wondered rather dully just how long we could keep it up. . . . A few more whacks of the ice ax in the firm snow and we stood on top.

My initial feelings were of relief—relief that there were no more steps to cut—no more ridges to traverse and no more humps to tantalize us with hopes of success. I looked at Tenzing and . . . there was no disguising his infectious grin of pure delight as he looked all around him. We shook hands and then Tenzing threw his arm around my shoulders and we thumped each other on the back. . . . It was 11:30 A.M. The ridge had taken us two and a half hours, but it seemed like a lifetime. . . .

I checked our oxygen once again and worked out our endurance. We would have to move fast in order to reach our life-saving reserve below the south summit. After fifteen minutes we turned to go. . . .

HUNT'S REFLECTIONS

How was it that we succeeded . . . when so many others before us had failed to do so? . . . We of the 1953 Everest Expedition are proud to share the glory with our predecessors. . . .

Next in order of events I would place sound, thorough, meticulously detailed planning. [W]e were able not only to foresee our needs in every detail—guided by previous experience provided by others, we judged aright—but to have constantly before us a clear program to carry out at every stage. . . .

Above all else, I should like to stress our unity as a party. This was undoubtedly the biggest single factor in the final result, for the ascent of Everest, perhaps more than most human ventures, demanded a very high degree of selfless co-operation; no amount of equipment or food could have compensated for any weakness in this respect. . . .

Was it worthwhile? For us who took part in the venture, it was so beyond doubt. . . .

The story of the ascent of Everest is one of teamwork. If there is a deeper and more lasting message behind our venture than the mere ephemeral sensation of a physical feat, I believe this to be the value of comradeship and the many virtues which combine to create it.

1. What reasons did Hunt give for climbing Mt. Everest? _to do something no one had been able to do, to explore the unknown, and to conquer the highest point on earth_

2. How long were Hillary and Tenzing at the top of Mt. Everest? Why weren't they there longer? _Only fifteen minutes; they had to get to their reserve oxygen supply before their main supply ran out._

3. What reasons did Hunt give for his team's success? _Previous expeditions had paved the way, teaching them valuable lessons; their effort was well organized; the team had great unity._

4. Someone has said that the conquest of Mt. Everest was the "greatest single adventure of the twentieth century." Do you agree or disagree, and why? _Answers will vary. Reaching the South Pole was another feat that took planning, organization, courage, and endurance; but Hunt's expedition had to go *up* as well as *far*. Reaching the moon might be an even greater accomplishment, or descending into the Mariana Trench._

CHAPTER REVIEW

Answer as many of the following questions as you can without using your textbook. Then go back and use your textbook to answer the ones you cannot remember.

1. Name the seven countries that make up South Asia. _India, Pakistan, Bangladesh, Bhutan, Nepal,_ _Maldives, Sri Lanka_

2. Which of those countries used to belong to India and was later divided to form two independent countries? _Pakistan; it was divided to form Pakistan and Bangladesh_

3. What is the name given to the winds that bring rains to South Asia? _monsoons_

4. What three rivers were central to the development of India and remain important features of modern India? _the Ganges, Indus, and Brahmaputra rivers_

5. What are the two major religions of India? _Hinduism and Islam_

6. What name is given to the belief that living creatures, including humans, go through a series of lives in different forms? _reincarnation_

7. Which minority religion in India teaches that people should not harm any living creature and therefore its adherents wear masks over their mouths to avoid accidentally breathing in flies? _Jainism_

8. What are the names of the two mountain ranges that border the Indian peninsula? _the Eastern and Western Ghats_

9. What is the name of the interior plains of India? _the Deccan_

10. Which South Asian country is at the center of the war on terrorism? What conflict does that fact create for the leader of that country? _Pakistan; the leader, Musharraf, is trying to help the West against the terrorists, but his country has an overwhelmingly Muslim population._

11. Which South Asian country is home to the world's highest mountain, and what is that mountain? _Nepal; Mt. Everest_

12. Almost all of which country is made up of the delta of the Ganges and Brahmaputra rivers? _Bangladesh_

13. What is the name of the famed Nepalese mountain climbers and guides? _Sherpas_

14. What is the name of the other famed Nepalese with world renown for their fighting expertise? _Gurkhas_

15. What is the name of the large island off the southeastern coast of India? _Sri Lanka_

16. What is the name of the 475-mile-long chain of islands off India's southwestern coast?

    the Maldives

17. What is the monetary unit of India? rupee

18. How do the Himalayas influence the climate of South Asia? They block much of the cold northern air
    from entering the South Asian countries and keep the monsoon rains in the subcontinent.

19. Where did an early civilization develop in modern Pakistan? Mohenjo-Daro

20. Who led nonviolent protests in India and is considered the Father of the Nation? Mahatma Gandhi

21. What is another name for the Great Indian Desert? Thar

22. What area is disputed by Pakistan and India? Kashmir

23. What is the name of the only pass through the Hindu Kush Mountains between Pakistan and Afghanistan?

    Khyber Pass

24. According to the student text, page 487, what is the poorest nation in South Asia? Bangladesh

25. What three bodies of water are the bounds of three sides of the Indian subcontinent?

    Bay of Bengal, Arabian Sea, Indian Ocean

SKILL: Recognition

MAP OF CHINA AND VICINITY

On the following page, identify and label each of the places, regions, and geographic features listed below.

Mongolia	Thailand
Gobi Desert	Myanmar
Beijing	India
Tianjin	Nepal
Shanghai	Bangladesh
Huang He	Pakistan
Chang River	Tajikistan
Xi River	Kyrgyzstan
Hong Kong	Kazakhstan
Macau	Russia
Lhasa	North Korea
Ulaanbaatar	South Korea
Taiwan	Japan
Taipei	Sea of Japan
Xizang (Tibet)	Yellow Sea
Taklimakan Desert	East China Sea
Vietnam	South China Sea
Laos	

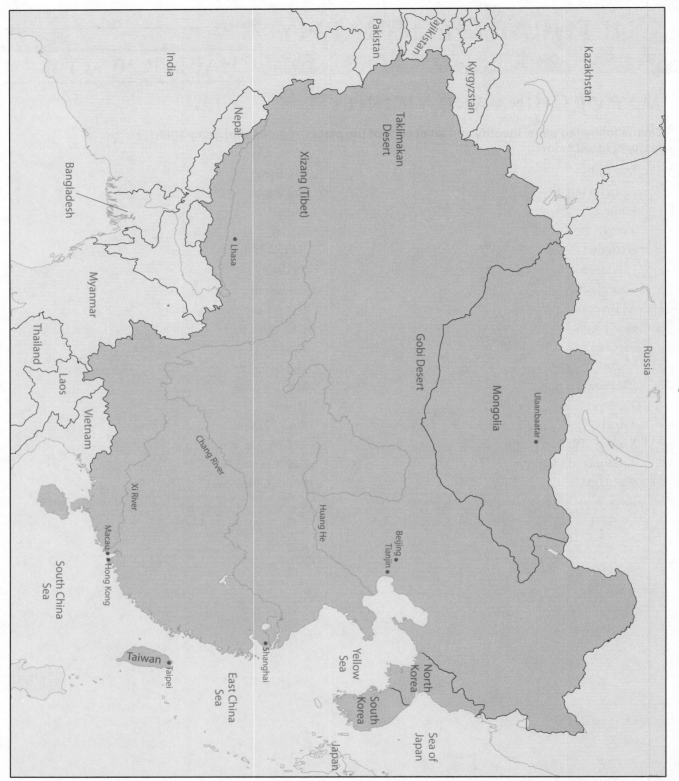

India

Pakistan

Tajikistan

Kyrgyzstan

Kazakhstan

Nepal

Bangladesh

Taklimakan
Desert

Xizang (Tibet)

•Lhasa

Myanmar

Thailand

Laos

Vietnam

Chang River

Xi River

Macau•

Hong Kong

South China
Sea

Taiwan

Taipei•

East China
Sea

Shanghai•

Gobi Desert

Mongolia

Ulaanbaatar•

Huang He

Beijing•
Tianjin•

Yellow
Sea

Japan

North
Korea

South
Korea

Sea of
Japan

Russia

THE CHURCH IN CHINA

Read the following essay about the persecution of Christian churches in China. Then answer the questions that follow the essay.

CHINA'S PERSECUTED CHURCH BY LEE DUIGON

President Bush's recent visit to China—he arrived there shortly after the State Department listed China as one of eight countries "of particular concern" for suppressing freedom of religion—once again drew attention to the tribulations of the church in the world's most populous nation.

"Our government has lodged a protest against the State Department action," Chu Maoming, press counselor at the Chinese Embassy in Washington, D.C., told Chalcedon. "The Chinese Constitution guarantees religious freedom. Our government permits all religious activities, under the rule of law. Every religious activity should be conducted according to the rule of law."

Under Chinese law, only churches licensed by the state can meet, worship, or conduct any other kind of business legally. President Bush attended services at one of only five Protestant churches in Beijing that are registered with the government. Beijing has a population of almost 15 million.

For Americans who have followed this story over the years, the more familiar picture is of Chinese Christians being beaten, dragged through the streets, and weeping as their house churches are bulldozed.

That China persecutes the church is "not true—totally groundless," Chu said. "Our government does not permit torture. The stories, the pictures, are all made up by the media."

When he was read Mr. Chu's comments, Todd Nettleton of Voice of the Martyrs laughed out loud.

"I'm sorry," he said, "but if you don't laugh at this, you have to cry. I've been to China four times, and I have a different view of the situation."

The Voice of the Martyrs, headquartered in Bartlesville, Oklahoma, is a nonprofit organization "serving the persecuted church for more than 35 years." VOM monitors anti-Christian persecution all over the world and aids victims by providing moral and material support—from Bibles to medical supplies—and rallying world opinion to speak out against it.

In the months preceding the president's visit, according to VOM, the Chinese government waged a fierce persecution of unregistered house churches all over the country—demolishing homes where believers met for worship services, confiscating church property, arresting, beating, humiliating, imprisoning, and often torturing church members and their pastors. These stories make grim reading. (For details, see the VOM Newsletter, Nov. 2005, www.persecution.com.)

"We have pictures, video clips, interviews, names, and addresses," Nettleton said. "Some of this we've collected ourselves; some of it has been smuggled out of the country. American teachers and missionaries have been arrested, too."

About 20% of China's Christians belong to the state-licensed churches, he said, with the other 80% in house churches: "All of their meetings are illegal, so they're always liable to be arrested and imprisoned."

China is of particular interest because of its size, a population of 1.3 billion. Although there are no firm statistics, Nettleton said, "I'm sure China has at least 100 million Christians. The largest house group membership in China would dwarf the largest American denomination.

"The Chinese government is very concerned. There are already probably more Christians than there are Communist party members. At the rate the church is growing, 30 years from now, China could be a mostly Christian nation."

Although Nettleton doubted that the president's visit or the State Department's public statement would have any immediate effect on China's religious policies, he said the actions of American Christians can be very valuable to the persecuted church in China.

"First, pray. That's the thing that makes the most difference," he said. "Then contact the Chinese government through the embassy. They are very concerned with what the world thinks about them."

Every letter or phone call to the embassy, he said, "generates a cable back to Beijing.

"The Chinese respond to worldwide indignation. We've had many Chinese Christians tell us that their prison sentences were shortened, or even ended right away, because of the letters and phone calls the government received from American Christians." VOM frequently identifies persecuted Christians by name so that Americans can mention them in their letters to the embassy—and in their prayers.

Why does a powerful communist country like China care about public opinion?

"They've got a lot of little green reasons for why they want to court world opinion," Nettleton said, "billions of dollars' worth of business they do with America. Because of that, they're sensitive. A persecuting country like North Korea, on the other hand, where they don't do business with America, doesn't care what we think. But China cares very much.

"All religions are persecuted in China—Christianity, Tibetan Buddhism, Falun Gong, and even Islam. If it were up to the Communist party, there'd be no religion at all in China."

But the Chinese church is growing in spite of persecution.

"We report some pretty terrible stories," Nettleton said. "You'd think the people undergoing this persecution would be depressed, or intimidated, but that's not the case. The spirit of these Christians is strong. You can't help being impressed by them.

"Persecution tends to produce a more solid Christian. Everyone who's in those churches is willing to sacrifice for their faith. They know what they're risking, and they are committed to the cause of Christ. Confronting this issue can be a challenge for American Christians. We're not used to thinking in terms of persecution."

1. How does the Chinese government explain reports of persecution of Christians there? They are all made up by the media.

2. Specifically what type of churches does the Chinese government target for persecution?
unregistered house churches

3. How many Christians are in China today? 100 million (Nettleton's estimate); 10 million (communists' estimate)

4. What can non-Chinese Christians do about the persecution of the Chinese Christians?
pray for the Chinese Christians; write or call the Chinese embassy to protest human rights abuses

5. Why are Chinese officials concerned about how other countries of the world view China?
They are afraid that a bad image might cost them money needed for further economic development.

6. What ultimately is the result of persecution of the church? The church grows stronger and bigger; individual believers are strengthened in the faith and made better Christians.

SKILL: Analysis

CHINA'S MANY MESSAGES TO QUELL UNREST

Read this article and then answer the questions that follow.

BEIJING - As Chinese leaders fret over rising peasant protests, political instability, and a decay of traditional values, the Communist Party is experimenting with multiple new messages - designed to capture the hearts and minds of ordinary people.

"It is a very intelligent strategy," says a Western historian here. "If people are nostalgic for Mao [Zedong] and old moral values, they've got Lei Feng [a model soldier lauded for selfless service]. For those who say China has lost its traditions, they promote Confucianism. For those who long for spirituality, it is Buddhism. The party is saying, 'you name it, we've got it.'"

But the disparate propaganda campaigns often seem like unrelated story lines in search of a central script. Last month, President Hu Jintao launched the "eight honors, eight disgraces"—spelling out the virtues of hard work and discipline, and the vices of cheating and selfishness. Other campaigns include engineering a "new socialist countryside," promoting old model revolutionary soldiers such as Lei Feng as "cool" for kids, and biweekly ideology sessions for party members billed as a chance to "refresh your mind."

In a fresh twist, the Party is also quietly backing campaigns that diverge from the standard political propaganda: opening a department of Confucianism at People's University, turning the late pop star Cong Fei into [a] "young pioneer" style model, holding the first Buddhist forum in modern China on April 13. And a hard-core neo-Marxist faction has been allowed to rise—contrary to a decade of greater liberalization—which helped kill a proposed law allowing private property rights at the annual People's Congress last month.

A CCTV producer says that in March a senior minister ordered yet another new campaign to be broadcast on the evening news. But he balked. There were so many other campaigns being promulgated there wasn't room in the broadcast. The Party is trying for a delicate balancing act, say experts, somewhere between the extremes of doubt and zealotry.

"It has become a consumer Communist Party . . . a party based on marketing, not Maoism," says Russell Leigh Moses, an American scholar at the Peoples University in Beijing. "[The messages] are a great experiment, a way to figure out what will take."

But is anyone listening?

For example, Beijing bus No. 117, like many in this city, has a set of flat screen TVs that show news, traffic, weather, cooking, and sports. Monday, along with shots of President Hu shaking hands with Saudi princes on his current overseas trip, there was a Discovery Channel-style 5-minute segment that memorialized a soldier who had infiltrated the enemy reactionary forces in the 1930s and became a hero for the cause of Red China. Called "Eternal Monument," the regular segment is part of a broader campaign called "Maintaining the Advanced Nature of the Party," that is spun off into various kinds of patriotic media efforts.

But the TV on Bus 117 only vaguely catches the attention of afternoon riders as they wind past the second ring road skyscrapers, past the Lama Temple, and toward the new suburbs sprouting outside the fourth ring road. Shows like "Eternal Monument" vie for time alongside pop stars, game shows, skin-cream ads, and an endless flow of "infotainment."

Passengers, like Ji Tong, a garment salesman, are aware . . . that China's leaders are trying to promote something called a "harmonious society" that will correct social ills and disparities. He advocates a broader campaign of "self-criticism" for China's party officials. But other passengers, such as a shy young man from Hunan, looking for a job in a restaurant, has [*sic*] heard of the "eight virtues and disgraces," but couldn't name one.

This year marks the 40th anniversary of the brutal Cultural Revolution, a time China closed itself to the world, and when Mao—through the Party machine—spoke to people over neighborhood loudspeakers. But gone are the days when the Party can dominate and speak with one voice by proclamation every waking moment. Daily life and "public space" continues to diversify. Chinese are busy—looking for a better job, a husband, a wife, English or music lessons for the kids, a business partner, a factory or construction site for a job.

"Mao and Deng [Xiaoping] were really good at speeches, writing articles, and getting people excited," says Yang Zhaohui, a professor of humanities at Beijing University. "They had won the war against Chiang Kai-shek. But today is a different climate. Hu and [Premier] Wen [Jiabao] are engineers. They don't have experience creating ideology."

But the No. 1 campaign deals with the economy. It goes under the term "a scientific Perspective on Development and a Harmonious Society." Essentially, this campaign builds on China's budding research and development sectors.

It highlights the pride in developing new products such as turning coal to liquid fuel, and China's AIGO brand digital cameras, MP3s, and memory discs—technology that will allow China to compete with Japanese and Korean companies. The media here offers proud, self congratulatory stories on the Shuguang 4000A supercomputer and the Zhonguancun Science and Technology Park in Beijing, which is heralded for producing its own patented products. . . .

In March, President Hu Jintao unveiled the tenets of his socialist value system:
- The honor of loving the motherland; the shame of endangering the motherland.
- The honor of serving the people; the shame of turning away from the people.
- The honor of upholding science; the shame of ignorance and illiteracy.
- The honor of industrious labor; the shame of indolence.
- The honor of togetherness and cooperation; the shame of profiting at the expense of others.
- The honor of honesty and keeping one's word; the shame of abandoning morality for profit.
- The honor of discipline and obedience; the shame of lawlessness and disorder.
- The honor of striving arduously; the shame of wallowing in luxury.

By Robert Marquand. Reproduced with permission from the April 25, 2006 issue of *The Christian Science Monitor* (www.csmonitor.com). 2006 The Christian Science Monitor. All rights reserved.

1. According to this article, is the Chinese Communist Party becoming more liberal or retaining its same hard-line stance against freedom of thought among the common people? __It is trying to give the impression__ that it is market driven and offering the people freedom of choice, but it is actually only allowing economic liberties if the people remain submissive to the typical Communist propaganda. This is evidenced by the way neo-Marxism was allowed to kill a proposed law allowing private property rights.

2. What examples of the modernization of China does the article mention? __extensive Western-style TV__ programming; flat-screen TVs on buses; Chinese-made digital cameras, MP3s, and memory discs; supercomputers; progress of the Zhonguancun Science and Technology Park in Beijing

3. What are the pros and cons of the "eight virtues and disgraces" that the Chinese are now promoting? __Pros—to at least some extent all of them are commendable traits that good citizens of any country should exemplify,__ especially Christians; Cons—when understood in the overarching context of communism (which China has never hinted at repudiating), they all subordinate the individual to the group and the state, they are all based on man's works, and they leave no place for God in man's thinking or efforts.

SKILLS: Using Resources, Analysis, Evaluation

CULTURAL GEOGRAPHY

MAP OF THE KOREAN PENINSULA AND JAPAN

Locate and label on the map the natural and political features listed below. Then answer the questions that follow.

North Korea	Pyongyang	Shikoku	Korea Strait
South Korea	Seoul	Tokyo	Yellow Sea
DMZ	Pusan	Nagasaki	East China Sea
Japan	Hokkaido	Hiroshima	
Russia	Honshu	Pacific Ocean	
China	Kyushu	Sea of Japan	

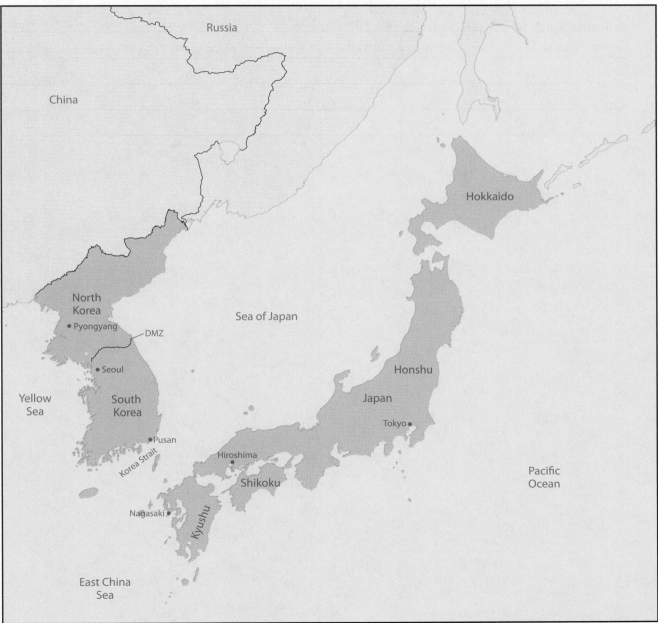

1. List the Communist countries that are Japan's neighbors. _North Korea, China_

2. Why do you think the United States insists on—and South Korea and Japan readily agree to—having military bases in South Korea and Japan? _because of the presence of and potential threat posed by the Communist regimes in North Korea and China and the uncertainty in the formerly Communist Russia_

3. Why does North Korea consider China its greatest ally? _because they both have similar forms of government, share a border, and China has continued trade and diplomatic relations with North Korea when many Western nations have severed such ties_

4. Why do you think the United States depends so much upon China, Japan, and South Korea in its efforts to influence North Korean policies? _because it does not have diplomatic relations with North Korea, whereas China does, and because China, Japan, and South Korea have a great stake in ensuring a stable, peaceful regime in North Korea_

SKILL: Maps

LETTER FROM PYONGYANG

Read the following essay about North Korea. Then answer the questions that follow.

By Anonymous

The Democratic People's Republic of Korea has a population of [more than 23] million people, but only two citizens—and one of them is dead.

. . . [N]o one in North Korea is famous except for the Kims. Led by the Great Leader, Kim Il Sung, who died in 1994, the family also includes the Dear Leader, Kim Jong Il, and the mother of all Korea, Kim Jong Suk. (Kim Jong Suk's picture crops up from time to time and place to place, but she is of little or no importance.)

So two Kims, one alive and one dead, control all aspects of life in this tiny, impoverished country, where Kim Il Sungism is the reigning ideology. Questioning that ideology brings banishment from the cities, imprisonment, or public execution.

All visits to North Korea start with an obligatory visit to Mansudae Hill and the [65-foot]-tall statue of the Great Leader. Built in 1982 to celebrate his seventieth birthday, the statue is now the focal point for all pilgrimages to Pyongyang. Each person or delegation is expected to bring flowers to lay at the feet of the giant bronze, and bowing is mandatory. On either side of the statue are massive statues of workers, peasants, and especially soldiers fighting against Japanese or U.S. soldiers in the struggle for liberation.

Two basic images of the Great Leader can be found everywhere. The standard image, displayed on all government buildings and in all homes, is the stern portrait that glares down upon the population. The new image, the "smiling portrait," was painted after Kim's death, and has become very popular.

The official portrait of the younger Kim emphasizes his seriousness while de-emphasizing his Elvis-style hair and excess weight. It hangs everywhere beside the portrait of his father, including inside railway carriages and subway cars. Hotel rooms for foreigners seem to be an exception to the ubiquity [apparent existence everywhere] of these official portraits, but staff areas are never without them. Pictures of Kim Jong Suk show her wearing the army uniform she is said to have worn during the fight against the Japanese.

The national art gallery displays numerous paintings of the Great Leader and the Dear Leader giving "on-the-spot guidance" to happy workers, peasants, and soldiers. One of the newest additions to the collection is a massive work showing the Dear Leader with his Mercedes.

There are only two public pictures in Pyongyang of people who do not belong to the Kim family—in the main square are two smallish images, one of Marx and one of Lenin.

PRESIDENT FOR ALL ETERNITY

After Kim Il Sung's death, the constitution was altered to enshrine him as the eternal president of Korea. This is why Kim Jong Il has not assumed the title of president, ruling instead as chairman of the National Defense Commission.

In keeping with Kim Il Sung's posthumous [after one's death] position as permanent president, the presidential palace has been converted to the world's largest mausoleum. His former home and office were sealed up with granite and marble, and the world's longest moving sidewalk was installed to take visitors past his body. Dead-leader-visiting junkies will be disappointed to learn that they may not get in to see Kim as easily as when they visited Lenin, Mao, or Ho Chi Minh: Only ideologically appropriate people are invited to gaze upon the . . . corpse and father of "juche." . . .

According to the official line, juche "means that the masters of the revolution and construction are the masses of the people and they are also the motive force of the revolution and construction. In other words, one is responsible for one's own destiny." More succinctly, juche refers to the idea that the state must be totally self-reliant. North Koreans abhor what they call "flunkeyism," or reliance on foreigners. In fact, no mention is ever made of the role of either the Soviet Union or the People's Republic of China in building or defending North Korea. Those countries are apparently of no importance to the past, present, or future of Korea.

Another obligatory stop is at the shrine at Mangyongdae, the birthplace of the Great Leader. Koreans are obliged to visit this place on a regular basis. But it is one of the nicer parks in Pyongyang, so many Koreans visit of their own free will. One is unlikely ever to see anything as obviously fake, however, as the alleged childhood home of the Great Leader, the "original" peasant house on the edge of a former graveyard. A wooden and thatch shack, it is beautifully kept and adorned with family photographs.

Even more completely fake is the legendary birthplace of Dear Leader Kim Jong Il, who is said to have been born in a humble log cabin at sacred Mount Paektu in the northernmost reaches of Korea during the anti-imperialist war against the Japanese. He was actually born in the Soviet Union.

Other fakes in the northern areas include slogans gouged into tree trunks. More of these carvings, said to have been made by anti-imperialist fighters led by comrade Kim Il Sung between 1925 and 1945, seem to be discovered every day. They appear amazingly fresh, free from weathering or overgrowth. When found, they are preserved behind Plexiglass [sic]. Their message: that there has always been only one true leader of all Korea, the Great Leader, who almost single-handedly defeated the Japanese Imperial Army.

Understanding the depth of yearning for international recognition comes with a visit to the International Friendship Exhibitions at the Myohyangsan Mountains. There one repository is dedicated to Kim Il Sung, and another to Kim Jong Il. Both exhibits, housed inside a mountain, contain tens of thousands of gifts—impressive ones from world leaders and silly little gifts from ordinary people. Many items look odd displayed behind glass, particularly common household goods like a working-class dining room table or small trinkets from souvenir shops around the world. The display is apparently intended to show both foreigners and Koreans that the world recognizes how important the Great and Dear Leaders are. And there is, in fact, an almost religious quality to the way the collection of relics is displayed.

LIFE IN PYONGYANG

Pyongyang is one of the quietest cities on the planet, due to the near total absence of automobiles. The population of more than [3 million] has fewer cars than any town in the West.

Unlike other Asian countries, Korea eschewed bicycles for decades. Only recently have they been allowed, and only now are they beginning to become a major mode of transportation. Most people must still walk or wait for public transport.

Pyongyang's public system consists of trolleys, electric buses, and a two-line subway. All are terribly overcrowded but somehow keep on running. For every [31,000 miles] it travels, a bus in Pyongyang has a red star painted on its side. Some buses are completely covered with red stars.

Because the public transport system is hopelessly inadequate, most Pyongyangers must walk to and from work each day. It is common to see locals walking at all hours. They often march in regimented groups to and from various activities.

The economy is in tatters with over half of industry idle—the population is much larger than the number of jobs remaining. Many Koreans spend much of their time squatting on the ground, as if they are waiting for a moment when they can spring into action. Yet there is little likelihood that their services will ever be needed, and squatting seems more like an adaptation to imposed idleness—and a symbol of loss.

THE NEXT GENERATION

What is odd about the children . . . is the way they look—or more often do not look—at an outsider. Either a foreigner is subjected to a hate-filled stare or he is invisible.

Many younger children believe their lessons—that all Westerners are imperialists who want to crush Korea. They stare with unbounded hatred at Caucasian foreigners. Many older children look right through a foreigner, as though the offending person is not even there.

A SENSE OF HISTORY

After the war in Vietnam ended in 1975, the Vietnamese eventually discarded their war mentality and moved on with developing their economy and their relations with the outside world. The Korean War ended in 1953, but North Korea lives as though the war were yesterday.

THE FUTURE

There is no threat to the regime other than the lack of food. Because the famine is largely contained in areas with completely marginalized populations, and because there is a very strong security presence at all levels, there is no danger that the hungry or disaffected will topple the government or the ruling Korean Workers Party.

The one thing that brings foreign diplomats and international organizations to North Korea is nuclear weapons, or at least the threat of nuclear weapons. Without a nuclear program North Korea would be seen as nothing more than a tiny, sparsely populated, hermit kingdom with a totalitarian regime. Although it is starving, there would be little outcry and little attention would be paid. But with a nuclear program in place, North Korea can command the attention of the world, or at least those parts of it willing to trade aid for nonproliferation.

Anonymous. "Letter from Pyongyang," *Bulletin of the Atomic Scientists* (July/August 2002), pp. 50–54, 70. Copyright © 2002 by *Bulletin of the Atomic Scientists*, Chicago IL. Reproduced by permission of Bulletin of the Atomic Scientists.

1. Although juche focuses on the people and their self-reliance and independence from foreign powers, what aspects of North Korean life show that it is actually worship of the rulers? __the various ways in which__ __the government deifies the Kims and forces people to honor and revere them, the presence of the leaders' pictures__ __everywhere, huge statues of the leaders and the forcing of the people to visit and bow to them__

2. What aspects of North Korean society reveal the economic backwardness of the country? __the relative absence of cars and even bicycles on the streets, the widespread practice of walking everywhere, the__ __obvious age and run-down condition of the buses, the famine, etc.__

3. Why do you think the children of North Korea hate foreigners so much? __That's how the government__ __has trained them to react; they know no better.__

4. What one thing makes North Korea a major player in world events? __its possible possession of nuclear__ __weapons and the threat to use (or sell) them__

CHAPTER REVIEW

Answer as many of the following questions as you can without consulting your textbook. Then go back to the questions you cannot answer and locate the correct answers in your textbook.

1–10. Name each of the countries that make up East Asia and the capital city of each.

China–Beijing; Mongolia–Ulaanbaatar; North Korea–Pyongyang; South Korea–Seoul; Japan–Tokyo

_____

_____

11. Which autonomous island province does China claim but has taken no steps to subdue?

Taiwan

12. Which city of China was until 1997 a British colony?   Hong Kong

13–14. What are the two major rivers of China that define the North China Plain?

Huang He and Chang

15. What is the neutral zone that separates North Korea from South Korea?   Demilitarized Zone (DMZ)

16–17. Name the first Communist dictator of North Korea and his successor.   Kim Il Sung; Kim Jong Il

18. What controversial project is being constructed on the southernmost of the two rivers in questions 13–14?   Three Gorges Dam

19. Which of the seven architectural wonders of the world is located in North China?

Great Wall

20–21. Who led the respective armies during the Chinese Civil War, which the Communists won in 1949?

Mao Zedong–Communists; Chiang Kai-shek–Nationalists

22. What term is used for North Korea's teaching—essentially state worship—that emphasizes national self-reliance and total independence of all foreign assistance?   Juche, or kimilsungism

23. Which Chinese autonomous region is called "the Roof of the World"?   Tibet

24. Which religious philosophy pervades Japanese society?   Shinto

25–28. Name the four largest islands that make up Japan.   Kyushu, Shikoku, Honshu, Hokkaido

_____

29. On which of those islands do the most people live?   Honshu

30. What is Japan's most famous mountain?   Fujiyama, or Mt. Fuji

   SKILL: Recognition

I. MAP OF SOUTHEAST ASIA

Locate and label the listed natural and political features on the following map. Then complete the section titled "Playing with Shapes."

China	Ho Chi Minh City	Kuala Lumpur
Vietnam	Thailand	Indian Ocean
Singapore	Brunei	Cambodia
Phnom Penh	Bangkok	Philippines
Myanmar	South China Sea	Manila
Malaysia	Laos	Philippine Sea
Hanoi	Indonesia	

© 2008 Map Resources. All Rights Reserved.

II. Playing with Shapes

Countries come in all shapes and sizes. There are five major classifications of countries by shape, and Southeast Asia has four of them. For each classification below, list all of the countries in this chapter that best fit the definition. For the classification that does not appear in this region, name any other country in the world that fits the description.

1. Compact (Most of the country is a single mass of land with fairly smooth borders.)

   Cambodia, Brunei

2. Elongated (Most of the country is a long, narrow mass of land.)

   Vietnam, Laos

3. Fragmented (The country is broken up into several pieces of separate land of varying sizes.)

   Malaysia, Singapore, Indonesia, Philippines

4. Perforated (The country has other small countries located entirely within its borders.)

   Examples of this rare shape include Italy and South Africa.

5. Protruded (The country is mostly compact but has an elongated tail.)

   Thailand, Myanmar

Skill: Maps

BUDDHISM

Read the following description of Buddhism and the two selections from the Buddhist sources. Then, using your Bible, answer the questions that follow.

Buddhism began as a Hindu sect around 500 BC. Siddhartha Gautama, the founder of Buddhism, was a rich young man. After seeing old, sick, and dying people, he became disenchanted with his wealth and left his wife and child to become a poor wanderer, searching for an end to man's suffering. Eventually, he decided that extreme self-affliction was no more righteous than worldly living. After long meditation, he experienced "enlightenment" and believed that he had found the way to salvation. Gautama became known as Buddha ("enlightened one") and spent the rest of his life traveling through the land telling others of his way, which he termed "the Middle Way."

His primary aim was to eliminate the cause of suffering; his sermons focus on man's effort to solve his own problems. The highest goal of Buddhism is to escape the cycle of death and rebirth and to reach Nirvana, a state of nothingness that brings complete rest and happiness. The only way to reach Nirvana is to stop desiring anything in this world; then man becomes free from attachment to the physical self and becomes enlightened. The state of Nirvana comes at the moment of enlightenment.

Buddha's sayings (*suttas*) were not written down for several hundred years. The Pali *Tipitaka*, more than twice the size of the Bible, is the holy book of Theravada Buddhism (the oldest form of Buddhism still practiced). The name of these scriptures comes from two parts: Pali, which is the dead language (related to Sanskrit) used in the writings, and *Tipitaka*, the "Three Baskets": the Basket of Discipline (rules for monks), the Basket of Discourses (Buddha's sermons), and the Basket of Further Dhamma (philosophical teachings).

Knowing the basic Buddhist beliefs will enable Christians to defend the faith and witness to Buddhists. But witnessing to Buddhists is difficult because they have a completely different perspective. For example, Buddhists are not interested in eternal life because their ultimate goal is to stop the cycle of rebirth. Buddhists do not believe in a personal God but in an impersonal Nirvana, or Emptiness. Also, a Buddhist might respond that Jesus was just a good teacher, like Buddha. Verses such as John 3:16 and 10:30, however, show that Jesus is God and has a special relationship with Him. Buddha never claimed to have a relationship with God. Whatever objections a Buddhist might have, be patient and humble as you seek to show the true way. Use a friendly, conversational manner rather than a "preachy" tone.

While some Buddhists focus on the teachings of Buddha, others worship Buddha as a god. Most Buddhists, however, share several common doctrines, which are included in Buddha's first sermon after his enlightenment, the first selection given below. In that message, Buddha lists "The Four Noble Truths" and the "Eightfold Path."

DHAMMACAKKAPAVATTANA ("SETTING THE WHEEL OF DHAMMA IN MOTION")

Thus have I heard: at one time the Lord [Buddha] dwelt at Benares [the modern city of Varanasi, India] . . . in the Deer Park. There the Lord addressed the five monks:

"These two extremes, monks, are not to be practiced by a holy man . . . self-indulgence and luxury, which is vulgar, common, ignoble, and useless; and self-torture, which is painful, ignoble, and useless. Avoiding these two extremes, the Tathagata [Buddha] has gained the enlightenment of the Middle Path, which produces insight and knowledge, and leads to calm, to higher knowledge, enlightenment, and Nirvana. And what, monks, is the Middle Path? . . . This is the noble Eightfold Way: namely, right view, right intention, right speech, right action, right livelihood, right effort, right mindfulness, right concentration. This, monks, is the Middle Path, of which the Tathagata has gained enlightenment, which produces insight and knowledge, and tends to calm, to higher knowledge, enlightenment, and Nirvana.

"Now this, monks, is the noble truth of pain: birth is painful, old age is painful, sickness is painful, death is painful, sorrow, lamentation, dejection, and despair are painful. Contact with unpleasant things is painful, not getting what one wishes is painful. . . .

"Now this, monks, is the noble truth of the origin of pain: the desire, which tends to rebirth, combined with pleasure and lust, seeking satisfaction now here, now there; namely, the desire for the gratification of the passions, the desire for a future life, or the desire for success in this present life.

"Now this, monks, is the noble truth of the destruction of pain. It is the destruction, in which no passion remains, of this very desire; the abandonment of, forsaking of, release of, and non-attachment to this desire.

"Now this knowledge and insight has arisen within me. The release of my mind is unshakable; this is my last existence; now there is no rebirth."

Sutta Pitaka, Samyutta Nikaya 56:11 [Basket of Discourses, Grouped Collection 56, sutta 11]

MAHAPARINIBBANA SUTTA ["THE LAST DAYS OF BUDDHA"]

[In this sutta, the dying Buddha addresses his cousin and closest disciple, Ananda.]

Therefore, O Ananda, be ye lamps unto yourselves. Rely on yourselves, and do not rely on external help. Hold fast to the truth as a lamp. Seek salvation alone in the truth. Look not for assistance to any one besides yourselves.

And how, Ananda, can a brother be a lamp unto himself, rely on himself only and not on any external help, holding fast to the truth as his lamp and seeking salvation in the truth alone, looking not for assistance to any one besides himself?

Herein, O Ananda, let a brother, as he dwells in the body, so regard the body that he, being strenuous, thoughtful, and mindful, may, whilst in the world, overcome the grief which arises from the body's desires. . . .

And so, also, when he thinks, or reasons, or feels, let him so regard his thought that being strenuous, thoughtful, and mindful he may, whilst in the world, overcome the grief which arises from the desire due to ideas, or to reasoning, or to feeling.

Those who, either now or after I am dead, shall be a lamp unto themselves, relying upon themselves only and not relying upon any external help, but holding fast to the truth as their lamp, and seeking their salvation in the truth alone, shall not look for assistance to any one besides themselves, it is they, Ananda, among my monks, who shall reach the very topmost height! But they must be anxious to learn.

Sutta Pitaka, Digha Nikaya ["Long Collection"] 16 [sutta number], 2:33–35 [part two, verses 33–35]

1. According to Matthew 5:6, is all desire wrong? What did Jesus teach about desire?

   No; we should desire righteousness.

2. What are the four noble truths?   1. Life is full of pain. 2. Pain is caused by desire for things of the physical world.

   3. Pain can be eliminated by destroying desire. 4. Desire can be eliminated by following the Eightfold Path.

3. According to Isaiah 64:6, why won't the Eightfold Path bring salvation? It is based completely on man's

   work and leaves God out of the plan.

4. What is wrong with being a lamp unto yourself? (See Romans 3:23.) How do Jesus's words in John 14:6

   contradict the teaching of Buddha? Man is sinful and cannot save himself; salvation is found only in Jesus.

CULTURAL GEOGRAPHY

CHAPTER REVIEW

In the two sections below, complete the matching and the short answer questions.

I.   INDOCHINA

Matching:

A. Cambodia	D. Thailand
B. Laos	E. Vietnam
C. Myanmar	

_____C_____   1.   Its major river is the Irrawaddy.

_____D_____   2.   the only Indochinese country never to be a colony of a European power

_____B_____   3.   the only landlocked country of Southeast Asia

_____A_____   4.   fell victim to the Khmer Rouge

_____E_____   5.   Once divided, it was reunited when the Communist side defeated the non-Communists.

Short Answer:

6.   It was the former name of Ho Chi Minh City. _Saigon_____

7.   where the French army was defeated, ending French control of French Indochina

  _Dien Bien Phu_____

8.   the former name of Myanmar _Burma_____

9.   the name given to the area where Myanmar, Laos, and Thailand meet _Golden Triangle_____

10.   the former name of Thailand _Siam_____

II.   MALAY ARCHIPELAGO

Matching:

A. Brunei	D. Philippines
B. Indonesia	E. Singapore
C. Malaysia	

_____B_____   1.   the largest Southeast Asian country by both area and population

_____C_____   2.   Its capital city is Kuala Lumpur.

_____A_____   3.   tiny country on the northwest coast of Borneo

_____D_____   4.   the busiest seaport in Southeast Asia

_____C_____   5.   former Spanish colony that was controlled by the United States for almost fifty years

Short Answer:

6. the world's newest country in Southeast Asia _Timor-Leste_

7. the two largest islands of the Philippines _Luzon and Mindanao_

8. shares the Malay Peninsula with Thailand _Malaysia_

9. the island hub of Indonesian civilization and the most densely populated Indonesian island

   Java

10. the name of the western half (Indonesian side) of the island of New Guinea _Irian Jaya_

SKILL: Recognition

MAP OF AUSTRALIA AND NEW ZEALAND

Using the maps in the chapter, locate and label the following places and features.

Western Australia	Gibson Desert
Darwin	Hobart
Coral Sea	Great Dividing Range
Northern Territory	Tasman Sea
Alice Springs	Canberra
Great Australian Bight	Indian Ocean
South Australia	Perth
Adelaide	Timor Sea
Great Barrier Reef	South Island
Queensland	Stewart Island
Brisbane	Auckland
Great Victoria Desert	Wellington
Sydney	Christchurch
New South Wales	Tasmania
Melbourne	North Island
Victoria	Cook Strait

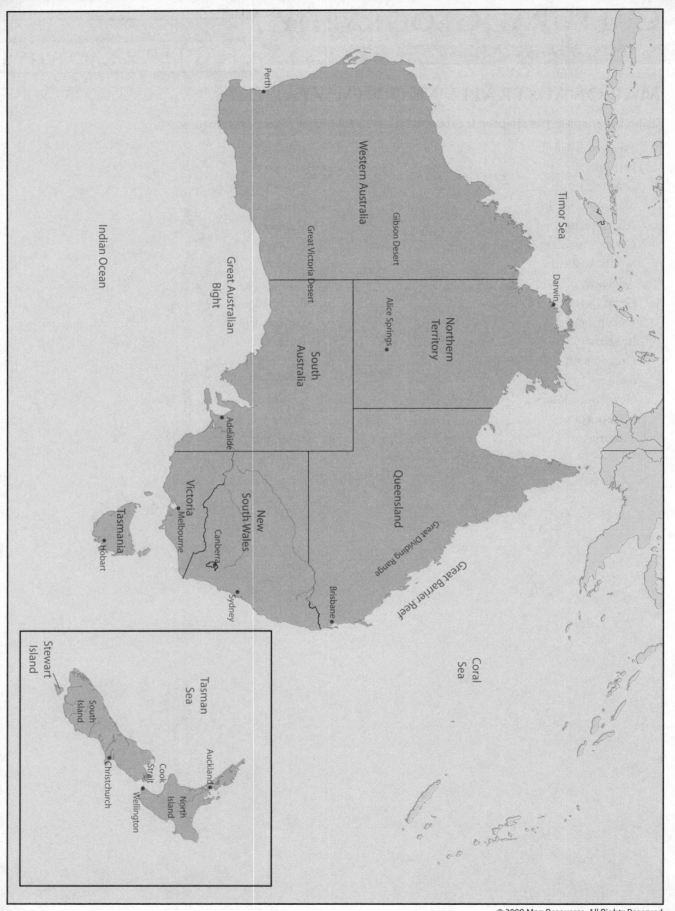

Perth

Western Australia

Gibson Desert

Timor Sea

Darwin

Great Victoria Desert

Northern Territory

Alice Springs

Indian Ocean

Great Australian Bight

South Australia

Queensland

Adelaide

Great Dividing Range

Victoria

Tasmania

Melbourne

New South Wales

Great Barrier Reef

Hobart

Canberra

Sydney

Brisbane

Coral Sea

Stewart Island

Tasman Sea

South Island

Auckland

Cook Strait

Christchurch

North Island

Wellington

THE GREAT BARRIER REEF BY NORMA MASTIN

Read the following article about Australia's Great Barrier Reef; then answer the questions about the article.

Anyone who has never snorkeled or skin-dived has missed a fascinating, colorful world of living organisms. Of course, there are many places to view the marine world, but my favorite is the Great Barrier Reef of Australia, which is one of the natural wonders of the world. It must not be considered a wall, but rather a labyrinth [maze] with periodic openings to the Eastern coast of Queensland.

It extends 1250 miles from Brisbane to New Guinea, the largest single structure ever formed by an animal. The reef varies in distance from the mainland. It is 42 miles offshore on the south end and about 4 1/2 miles on the northern edge. Many smaller cays or islands form the Great Barrier Reef and many of these also have a fringing reef. From the air, the colors of the water surrounding a small cay vary from royal blue to turquoise to green making a spectacular view of the island. The two islands I have visited most frequently are Green Island and Heron Island. Green Island is only 5 miles from Cairns, Queensland. Because of its proximity to the mainland, it has become very commercialized. Many people go out just for a day of swimming and sunning. Thirty-five years ago when I first visited Green Island there was a wonderful reef around the island, but the Crown of Thorns Starfish and several cyclones have destroyed much of the reef. Now the only attribute is a small aquarium that is very nicely run and one of the few places to escape the hordes of people.

My favorite island is Heron Island that is situated close to the outer limits of the reef, 40 miles from Mackay on the mainland. The boat ride takes 3 hours. They now have a speedier helicopter, but it is expensive. . . . No day visitors are allowed and, therefore, the island doesn't seem to be overrun with people.

There is a marine research station on the island operated by the University of Queensland, and students and scientists can stay there. . . .

One of my favorite times to visit Heron Island is mid to late October, when the sea turtles come ashore to lay their eggs. It is also nesting time for the sooty shearwaters (mutton or moaning birds), the white-capped noddy terns and the herons. During this . . . time, low tide provides the best photographic opportunities, as many organisms are exposed in the tide pools and their color is much better in shallow water. In deeper water one needs to have underwater equipment with a powerful flash and close-up lenses.

Corals grow and flourish in warm, tropical seas, ideally above a depth of 100 feet, but cannot be too close to the surface nor exposed for long periods of time during low tide. The calcareous [made of calcium, calcium carbonate, or limestone] skeletons of the corals are primarily responsible for reef building, although other organisms are also involved. Corals are very minute and have hundreds or even thousands of animals in each coral structure. Each animal is a polyp, most of which are nocturnal feeders. There are many forms of coral—staghorn, brain, mushroom, and several soft forms. One of the unusual ones is the Bubble Coral that often has a Yellow-striped Cardinal Fish near it.

Some soft corals have microscopic plant cells, *Zooxanthellae*, that live in the fleshy tissues of corals and are responsible for the dull olive or brown coloration of many corals. Other corals have beautiful coloration often coming from association with other organisms. When you see the garish colors of coral for sale at souvenir shops, they have been painted. The calcium carbonate of the coral skeleton remains white when it is dead.

Although corals are the main reef builders, many other organisms help in reef formation, such as the pink encrusting coralline algae [algae that resemble coral]. The giant clams, *Tridacna*, are the largest bivalve mollusks in the world, and are often embedded in the reef. The smaller ones may be literally strewn over a reef flat. The beautiful mantle is often exposed and varies in color, depending upon the algae living in it. . . .

[M]yriad . . . creatures live around and among the corals—some strange, some lovely, some venomous, all fascinating. Moray eels are often spotted, sometimes with a cleaner shrimp working on the moray. Sea turtles are often seen gliding along the surface of the crystal, clear water. Cone shells are beautiful, but all are carnivorous, and they are the only gastropods in the world capable of directly causing death to human beings. If picked up from the rear, they are safe. However, if handled from the anterior end, the proboscis will dart out and inject venom.

Cowry shells are renowned for their beauty, unsurpassable polish, and attractive shape. The white eggshell cowry with its black mantle exposed is one of the most striking.

Most of our west coast nudibranchs, or naked-gilled sea slugs, are quite small and are found at low tide. The Spanish Dancer is one of the largest and most spectacular nudibranchs found on the Barrier Reef. It can grow to a length of 12 inches. Instead of gliding along on its foot, it moves with a fascinating undulating movement.

In addition to sea urchins similar to ours, there are some unusual ones on the Barrier Reef. The Slate-pencil Urchin has broad spines. Diadema has extremely long, tapering needle-sharp spines, and, consequently, should not be handled. It may grow up to 12 inches across. Other echinoderms [symmetrical marine invertebrates] include some brilliantly colored sea stars or starfish, brittle stars and an unusual Basket Star. At first glance, the Basket Star doesn't resemble a starfish, as it is quite thick with no visible rays. However, when turned over, the 5 rows of tube feet are visible. The most striking sea stars are the royal blue Linckia and the bright red Enrichia.

At times, a variety of fish will be among the corals, anemones, and other reef structures. Blue-green Puller fish brighten a reef scene, as does the Moorish Idol or a school of Bat Fish. The highly ornate Butterfly-cod or Fire Fish should be carefully avoided, as its numerous venom-charged spines can cause considerable pain.

When the Great Barrier Reef is alive, many specimens are brilliantly colored and beautiful. The Beaked Coral Fish . . . adds to the beauty. The reef is so fascinating that it entices one to return again and again!

(Used by permission of the author.)

1. How great is the variety of distance of the Great Barrier Reef from the mainland?
   from 4.5 miles at the closest on the northern edge to 42 miles at the farthest on the southern end

2. Which two islands are the author's favorite areas of the reef to visit? Which of those two does she like most? Green Island and Heron Island; Heron Island

3. Why does she think that low tide is the best time to explore the reef? That time produces the best photographic opportunities because many organisms are exposed in tide pools and their colors are more vivid in shallow water.

4. What is the composition of the coral skeletons? calcium, calcium carbonate, or limestone

5. Which creature living on the reef is the only gastropod capable of directly killing human beings?
   cone shells, which, if picked up from the front, can inject a lethal venom from the proboscis

SKILL: Analysis

CULTURAL GEOGRAPHY

THE DISCOVERY OF NEW ZEALAND

Read the following account of Captain James Cook's discovery and exploration of the coast of New Zealand, and then answer the questions.

"The land on the Sea-Coast is high with steep cliffs, and back inland are very high mountains. . . . The face of the Country is of a hilly surface and appears to be cloathed with wood and Verdure."—Captain Cook's Journal, 8 October 1769

James Cook was born in Yorkshire, England, and entered the navy as an able seaman in 1755. By 1768, he had been promoted to first lieutenant and was given command of the . . . *Endeavor*, a well-constructed ship of 368 tons.

In [the] same year, Cook received instructions to set sail for the Pacific in order to study the passage of the planet Venus across the disc of the sun. [No similar event would take place for another 105 years.] The second set of instructions concerning this voyage were secret. After [observing] Venus, Cook was to search for the mysterious and elusive "southern continent"—*Terra Australis Incognita*.

On 26 August 1768, the *Endeavor* set sail from Plymouth [England], stocked with 18 months [of] supplies and with 94 men aboard. Accompanying Cook were Joseph Banks, [a] botanist; Daniel Solander, a naturalist; and Charles Green, from the Greenwich Observatory.

On 13 April 1769, the *Endeavor* laid anchor in Tahiti, where the passage of Venus was duly observed, in perfect conditions. Friendly relations were established with the Tahitians. A Tahitian chief named Tupaia, who spoke some English and who wanted to travel, joined the *Endeavor* with his boy servant when the ship left Tahiti for New Zealand and the search for the southern continent. Tupaia was an invaluable companion, advising Cook and Banks of the practices and customs of native inhabitants of other islands . . . as the *Endeavor* continued its southerly course.

On 6 October 1769, Nicholas Young, the surgeon's boy, sighted the coastline of New Zealand from the [mast] of the *Endeavor*. On 8 October, the *Endeavor* sailed into a bay and laid anchor at the entrance of a small river in Tuuranga-nui (today's Poverty Bay, near modern Gisborne). Cook named a peninsula in this bay "Young Nick's Head" after Nicholas Young.

Noticing smoke along the coast, an indication that the country was inhabited, Cook and a group of sailors headed for shore in two small boats, hoping to establish friendly relations with the natives and to take on refreshments. Four sailors were left to guard one of the boats but were surprised by the sudden appearance of four Maori brandishing weapons. When one Maori lifted a lance to hurl at the boat, he was shot by the coxswain.

Cook's party returned to the *Endeavor* and the next day came ashore once again, accompanied by Tupaia. Some Maori were gathered on the river shore, and communication was made possible as Tupaia's language was similar to that of the Maori. Gifts were presented, but the killing of the day before had left the Maori hostile. When one Maori seized a small cutlass from one of the Europeans, he was shot.

That afternoon Cook would have attempted a further landing, but heavy surf made this impossible. On noticing the appearance of two canoes, Cook planned to intercept them by surprise, with the idea of taking the occupants prisoner, offering them gifts, gaining their trust, and then setting them free.

However, the canoe occupants noticed the arrival of one of the *Endeavor*'s small boats and attacked as it approached. The Europeans, firing in self-defense, killed or wounded three or four Maori. Three other Maori who had jumped overboard were picked up by the Europeans and taken on board the *Endeavor*. They were offered gifts, food, and drink and soon overcame their fear. Communication was possible via Tupaia, and the next day the three Maori were taken back to shore, where their armed kinsmen were waiting. There was no violence on this occasion.

Cook, however, upset by the killings which had already taken place, decided to leave [the] area. He gave it the name Poverty Bay, as he had been unable to take on refreshments.

The *Endeavor* continued [sailing] to Te Matau-a-Maaui (Maaui's fish hook, or modern Hawke's Bay) on the east coast of the North Island. Cook named Hawke's Bay after Sir Edward Hawke of the Admiralty.

On 15 October, as the *Endeavor* was off the coast, a large canoe came alongside. With the help of Tupaia, Cook communicated with the Maori, who numbered about 20, and trade for fresh fish commenced. However, as Tupaia's young servant Tayeto was making his way to the canoe to accept the fish, he was grabbed by the Maori, who paddled off with their prisoner at great speed. Cook's men fired on the canoe, killing one Maori. This gave Tayeto the opportunity to leap overboard, where he was picked up by the *Endeavor*. Because of this event, Cook named the area Kidnapper's Bay.

From [t]here, the *Endeavor* continued to Cape Turnagain, [sailing along the coast of] East Cape and the Bay of Plenty. On 3 November, suitable anchorage was found at Mercury Bay—so named as ten days were spent [t]here observing the transit of Mercury. Before leaving Mercury Bay, the date and the ship's name . . . were carved into a tree, and Cook took formal possession of [the] area. Sailing farther north, the *Endeavor* arrived at the Bay of Islands.

While navigating around the northern tip of New Zealand on 13 December, the *Endeavor* ran into strong gales off Cape Marie van Diemen, forcing the ship off course. About nine miles offshore and in daylight hours, the *Endeavor* passed by the French ship *St. Jean Baptiste*, under the command of Jean François Marie de Surville, struggling to remain on course but in the opposite direction.

The *St. Jean Baptiste* was a French Indian ship on a trading mission. Its commander was looking for a bay in which to anchor in order to take on fresh water and fruit for his scurvy-ridden crew. The *St. Jean Baptiste* knew nothing of Captain James Cook and the *Endeavor*, just a short distance away. Incredibly, neither the British nor the French sighted each other.

On 17th December, the *St. Jean Baptiste* laid anchor at Doubtless Bay, in the North Island. The Bay had been given this name by Captain Cook, as on sighting it for the first time from afar, he is reported to have said, "This is doubtless a bay."

In the beginning of January 1770, as the *Endeavor* was sailing down the western coast, Mount Taranaki was sighted. Cook named it Mount Egmont after the First Lord of the Admiralty.

On the 14th January, the *Endeavor* arrived at "a very broad and deep bay or inlet." The ship was in the South Island of New Zealand, and in this inlet a perfect anchorage was found at Ship Cove. Cook named the inlet Queen Charlotte's Sound and took formal possession of [the] area. Friendly relations were established with the Maori, and trade for fish and fresh vegetables commenced.

On 6 February, the *Endeavor* made for Cook Strait while surveying the coastline of the South Island. By 13 March, the most southern point of the South Island was rounded, and the *Endeavor* commenced coasting up along the west coast. A bay which was passed as night fell was given the name Dusky Bay.

The *Endeavor* left New Zealand on 31 March 1770, after having spent two days in Admiralty Bay refitting the ship. Cook had just charted 2,400 miles of New Zealand coastline in under six months.

Cook was to return to New Zealand on two further occasions, once in 1773 in command of the *Resolution*, accompanied by Tobias Furneaux in command of the *Adventure*, and again in 1777 in command of the *Resolution*, and with Charles Clerke in command of the *Discovery*.

Taken from the website New Zealand in History. Used by permission from Robbie Whitmore.

1. How did Cook's "public" orders differ from his "secret" orders?

His public orders were strictly scientific—the observation of the course of planets, particularly the once-in-a-lifetime

passage of Venus across the sun; but his secret orders—to search for a "southern continent"—had international

implications that had potential for not only increased trade, thereby giving England a commercial edge over other

countries, but also competition from (and possibly even war with) other countries.

2. What does Cook's practices in naming places he discovered tell us about him?

He was practical, personal, and politically sensitive. He named some places based on what happened to them there

(e.g., Poverty Bay, where they could not get resupplied, and Kidnapper's Bay, where Tupaia's servant was kidnapped

by Maori). He named one peninsula in honor of the surgeon's boy who first sighted it, Young Nick's Head. Yet, Cook

also remembered to whom he was ultimately responsible, naming another place after a lord in the Admiralty

(Hawke's Bay).

3. What was the significance of the sudden appearance on the scene of the *St. Jean Baptiste*?

It was a French ship, and if the Frenchmen had seen the English ship, there may have been a confrontation and an

international incident with far-reaching trading and foreign policy implications.

4. What do you think the names of Cook's various ships and those that accompanied him—*Endeavor*, *Resolution*, *Adventure*, and *Discovery*—say about the English during the time period?

Answers will vary but might include the following: attitude of courage and bravery, characteristics that were required

of all seamen and explorers of the day; determination of the English to work hard and risk all to discover, achieve, and

prosper as a nation and an empire.

ABORIGINAL PEOPLES

One thing that Australia, New Zealand, and the United States have in common is that their histories begin with native peoples who lived there before the coming of the Europeans. In many ways, those aboriginal peoples are similar, but they also differ in many ways. Using your textbook and other resources (such as an encyclopedia), complete the following chart comparing and contrasting the indigenous people of each country.

	Aborigines	*Maoris*	*Native Americans*
COUNTRY	Australia	New Zealand	United States
ORIGINS	Southeast Asia	Polynesian islands north of New Zealand	Asia (across the Bering Sea to present-day Alaska and from there throughout North America)
MEANS OF SURVIVAL	hunting and gathering (nomads)	fishing and hunting, later farming	hunting and gathering, some farming
WEAPONS	spear and boomerang	guns from Europeans	bow and arrow, spears and clubs, tomahawk, guns from Europeans
INTERACTION WITH EUROPEANS	pushed into interior, many were killed or died of disease	fought bloody wars though outnumbered; violations of Treaty of Waitangi led to Land Wars; Europeans won and took land	pockets of fierce resistance; were settled on reservations; many were killed or died of disease
GROUP ORGANIZATION	tribes divided into bands and clans	many small, competing chieftainships	tribes divided into bands or clans and associations, sometimes joined together in confederations
RELIGION	superstitious; spirits control life and created world in Dreamtime	impersonal; spiritual force (mana) flows through people and things; those with too much force are dangerous and are declared taboo	spirit power throughout nature influences lives; Great Spirit joined by other spirits
CURRENT NATIONAL STATUS	many on reservations, but the government has returned large tracts of land	many in cities; have been integrated into European way of life	many on reservations; face significant social problems, including poverty, unemployment, alcoholism
CURRENT POPULATION	approx. 460,000	approx. 500,000	approx. 215,000,000 (includes Native Alaskans)

SKILL: Synthesis

MAP OF OCEANIA

Draw lines around the three cultural subregions of Oceania: Micronesia (blue), Melanesia (green), and Polynesia (red). Then locate and label the following places and features on the map.

Mariana Islands	French Polynesia
Papua New Guinea	Kwajalein
Samoa	Midway Islands
Marshall Islands	Tahiti
Solomon Islands	Nauru
Tuvalu	Hawaiian Islands
Guam	Pitcairn Island
Vanuatu	Kiribati
Cook Islands	American Samoa
New Caledonia	Easter Island
Fiji	

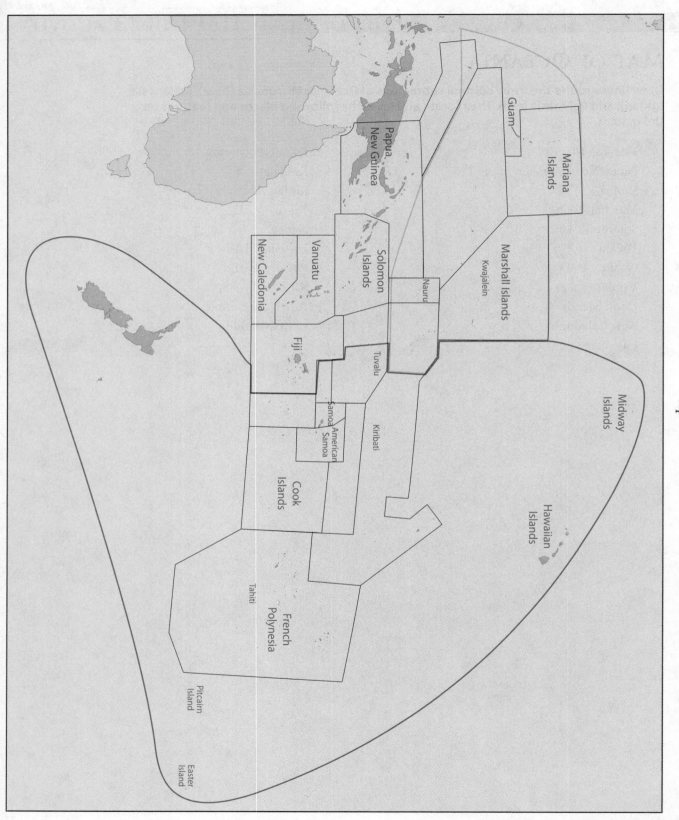

top

Papua New Guinea

Guam

Mariana Islands

Marshall Islands

Kwajalein

Nauru

New Caledonia

Vanuatu

Solomon Islands

Fiji

Tuvalu

Samoa

American Samoa

Kiribati

Midway Islands

Hawaiian Islands

Cook Islands

Tahiti

French Polynesia

Pitcairn Island

Easter Island

SKILL: Maps

CAPTAIN COOK ON EASTER ISLAND

Captain Cook's voyages to explore the Pacific Ocean helped him become the most famous British navigator. His journal of his voyages recorded his discovery of not only many new plants and animals but also the native customs of the people in the places he visited. On his first voyage, Cook explored Australia and New Zealand. On his second voyage, he stopped at Easter Island. And on his third voyage, he discovered the Sandwich Islands (later named the Hawaiian Islands). Read the following excerpts from Cook's journal entries about Easter Island, and then answer the questions.

EASTER ISLAND

MARCH 14TH, 1774. I went ashore, accompanied by some of the gentlemen, to inform myself if any refreshments or water were to be got. We landed at a sandy beach, where about 100 of the natives were collected. They gave us no disturbance at landing; on the contrary hardly one had so much as a stick in their hands. After distributing among them some medals and other trifles, they brought us sweet potatoes, plantains, and some sugar cane which they exchanged for nails and etc.; after having found a small spring or rather well made by the natives, of very brackish [containing saltwater and therefore being distasteful] water, I returned on board and anchored the ship. . . .

MARCH 15TH. [Cook sent a party to explore the island on this date. The party returned in the evening and reported their findings to Cook.] . . . They observed that this side of the island was full of gigantic statues, some placed in groups on platforms of masonry, others single, being fixed only in the earth, and that not deep; these latter are, in general, much larger than the others. They measured one which had fallen down, and found it very near twenty-seven feet long; . . . and yet this appeared considerably short of the size of one they saw standing. . . .

The stupendous stone statues erected in different places along the coast are certainly no representation of any Deity or places of worship; but most probably burial places for certain tribes or families. I myself saw a human skeleton lying in the foundation of one just covered with stones. . . .

[The masonry platforms] are built, or rather faced, with hewn stones of a very large size; and the workmanship is not inferior to the best plain piece of masonry we have in England. They use no sort of cement; yet the joints are exceedingly close, and the stones morticed and tenanted one into another in a very artful manner. . . .

The statues, or at least many of them, are erected on these platforms, which serve as foundations. . . . The workmanship is rude, but not bad; nor are the features of the face ill-formed, the nose and chin in particular; but the ears are long beyond proportion; and as to the bodies, there is hardly anything like a human figure about them. . . .

We could hardly conceive how a nation of people like these, wholly unacquainted with any mechanical power, could raise such stupendous figures, and afterwards place the large cylindric stones upon their heads. The only method I can conceive is by raising the upper end by little and little, supporting it by stones as it is raised, and building about it till they got it erect; thus, a sort of mount or scaffolding would be made, upon which they might roll the cylinder, and place it upon the head of the statue, and then the stones might be removed from about it. . . . But let them have been made and set up by this or any other method, they must have been a work of immense time, and sufficiently show the ingenuity and perseverance of the age in which they were built; for the present inhabitants have most certainly had no hand in them, as they do not even repair the foundations of those which are going to decay.

MARCH 16TH. I sent a boat ashore to purchase such refreshments as the natives might have brought to the waterside. Not one of them had so much as a stick or a weapon of any sort in their hands. After distributing a few trinkets amongst them, we made signs for something to eat, on which they brought down a few potatoes, plantains, and sugar cane and exchanged for nails, looking-glasses and pieces of cloth. We presently discovered that they were as expert thieves and as tricking in their exchanges as any people we had yet met with. It was with some difficulty that we could keep the hats on our heads, but it was hardly possible to keep anything in our pockets, not even what themselves had sold us; for they would watch every opportunity to snatch it from us, so that we sometimes bought the same thing two or three times over, and after all did not get it.

1. Look up *plantain* in a dictionary. What is it, and why was it common? A fruit similar to a banana; it grew well in the Polynesian climate.

2. What reason does Cook give for the statues' existence on Easter Island? What are some other possibilities? He believed they were burial places. They might also have been idols, or they might have been placed around the island to scare away would-be intruders if they were superstitious.

3. Why did Cook believe that the statues had been built by a previous generation, not the current inhabitants? Many of the statues had fallen down, and the natives did not seem interested in repairing the foundations, which were decaying.

4. What complaint does Cook record against the natives on Easter Island? He said that they were "expert thieves" and master manipulators when it came to trading (buying and selling).

5. Why do you think the natives were so eager to trade "potatoes, plantains, and sugar cane" for "nails, looking-glasses and pieces of cloth"? The natives had the named crops in abundance, but they did not have the items for which they traded those crops.

CHAPTER REVIEW

Match each of the definitions on the left with the appropriate term on the right. Put the letter of the answer in the blank to the left of each definition.

_____F_____ 1. Dried coconut meat

_____A_____ 2. Exposure of one group to and acceptance of the values and lifestyle of a foreign group

_____H_____ 3. "Black Islands"

_____E_____ 4. People who worship a human individual or group who has brought them material riches

_____C_____ 5. A potato-like root that is a popular food in Melanesia

_____D_____ 6. Latin for "Scotland"

_____B_____ 7. A ring of coral on the submerged cone of a volcano

_____J_____ 8. "Many islands"

_____G_____ 9. Framed house with a thatched roof and open sides that can be enclosed by lowering coconut leaf blinds

_____I_____ 10. "Small islands"

A. acculturation

B. atoll

C. taro

D. Caledonia

E. cargo cult

F. copra

G. fale

H. Melanesia

I. Micronesia

J. Polynesia

Match the descriptive phrases on the left with the appropriate place on the right. Put the letter of the answer in the blank to the left of each description.

_____D_____ 11. Largest of the Solomon Islands; site of heavy fighting in World War II

_____C_____ 12. "The crossroads of the South Pacific"

_____A_____ 13. Scuba diving site among World War II shipwrecks

_____E_____ 14. The largest of the Mariana Islands

_____G_____ 15. The largest atoll in the world

_____H_____ 16. The third-smallest country in the world

_____F_____ 17. Formerly called the Gilbert Islands

_____J_____ 18. The last remaining kingdom in the Pacific

_____I_____ 19. The place the HMS *Bounty* was sent to gather breadfruit

_____B_____ 20. Island famous for its mysterious stone heads called maoi

A. Chuuk

B. Easter Island

C. Fiji

D. Guadalcanal

E. Guam

F. Kiribati

G. Kwajalein

H. Nauru

I. Tahiti

J. Tonga

Match the person on the left with the thing for which he is noted in this chapter.

___F___ 21. Captain William Bligh

___D___ 22. Captain James Cook

___A___ 23. Ferdinand Magellan

___C___ 24. Alvaro de Mendana

___G___ 25. Jacob Raggeveen

___B___ 26. Earl of Sandwich

___E___ 27. King George Tupou I

A. Named the Pacific Ocean

B. Original name of Hawaiian Islands was in his honor

C. Discovered the Solomon Islands

D. Named the New Hebrides

E. Tonga chief who converted to Methodism

F. Captain of the HMS *Bounty* who survived a mutiny in the South Pacific

G. Discovered Easter Island

SKILL: Recognition

THE JOURNALS OF AMUNDSEN AND SCOTT

In 1911, both Roald Amundsen of Norway and Robert Scott of Great Britain set out on separate expeditions to the South Pole. Amundsen originally had been on his way to the North Pole, but he decided to head to Antarctica when he learned that someone else had already reached the North Pole. About the same time, Scott decided to make the same attempt. It became a race between the two explorers, each of whom knew of the other's attempt, to see which could reach the South Pole first. Read the following excerpts from Amundsen's book *The South Pole* **and Scott's personal journal. Then answer the questions at the end.**

ROALD AMUNDSEN: *THE SOUTH POLE*

NEAR THE POLE

[**December 9, 1911**] Every step we now took in advance brought us rapidly nearer the goal. . . . None of us would admit that he was nervous, but I am inclined to think that we all had a little touch of that malady. What should we see when we got there? A vast, endless plain, that no eye had yet seen and no foot yet trodden; or—No, it was an impossibility; with the speed at which we had traveled, we must reach the goal first, there could be no doubt about that. And yet—and yet—Wherever there is the smallest loophole, doubt creeps in and gnaws and gnaws and never leaves a poor wretch in peace.

AT THE POLE

[**December 14, 1911**] At three in the afternoon a simultaneous "Halt" rang out from the drivers. They had carefully examined their sledge meters, and they all showed the full distance—our Pole by reckoning. The goal was reached, the journey ended. I cannot say—though I know it would sound much more effective—that the object of my life was attained. That would be romancing rather too barefacedly. I had better be honest and admit straight out that I have never known any man to be placed in such a diametrically opposite position to the goal of his desires as I was at that moment. The regions around the North Pole—well, yes, the North Pole itself—had attracted me from childhood, and here I was at the South Pole. Can anything more topsy-turvy be imagined? . . .

After we had halted we collected and congratulated each other. We had good grounds for mutual respect in what had been achieved, and I think that was just the feeling that was expressed in the firm and powerful grasps of the fist that were exchanged. After this we proceeded to the greatest and most solemn act of the whole journey—the planting of our [Norwegian] flag. Pride and affection shone in the five pairs of eyes that gazed upon the flag, as it unfurled itself with a sharp crack, and waved over the Pole. I had determined that the act of planting it—the historic event—should be equally divided among us all. It was not for one man to do this; it was for all who had staked their lives in the struggle and held together through thick and thin. This was the only way in which I could show my gratitude to my comrades in this desolate spot. I could see that they understood and accepted it in the spirit in which it was offered. Five weatherbeaten, frostbitten fists they were that grasped the pole, raised the waving flag in the air, and planted it as the first at the geographical South Pole.

DEPARTURE

[**December 17, 1911**] We began our preparations for departure. First we set up the little tent we had brought with us in case we should be compelled to divide into two parties. . . . Inside the tent, in a little bag, I left a letter, addressed to H.M. [His Majesty] the King, giving information of what we had accomplished. The way home was a long one, and so many things might happen to make it impossible for us to give an account of our expedition. Besides this letter, I wrote a short epistle to Captain Scott, who, I assumed, would be the first to find the tent.

[Amundsen's well-planned and well-executed expedition made it safely back from the South Pole.]

THE JOURNALS OF ROBERT FALCON SCOTT

Night, January 15 [1912].—It is wonderful to think that two long marches would land us at the Pole. We left our depot today with nine days' provisions, so that it ought to be a certain thing now, and the only appalling possibility the sight of the Norwegian flag forestalling ours. . . . Only 27 miles from the Pole. We *ought* to do it now.

Tuesday, January 16.—Camp 68. Height 9760. T. [temperature] –23.5°. The worst has happened, or nearly the worst. . . . About the second hour of the march Bowers' sharp eyes detected what he thought was a cairn [a pile of stones built as a marker]; he was uneasy about it, but argued that it must be a sastruga [a long ridge of snow formed by the wind]. Half an hour later he detected a black speck ahead. Soon we knew that this could not be a natural snow feature. We marched on, found that it was a black flag tied to a sledge bearer; near by the remains of a camp; sledge tracks and ski tracks going and coming and the clear trace of dogs' paws—many dogs. This told us the whole story. The Norwegians have forestalled us and are first at the Pole. It is a terrible disappointment, and I am very sorry for my loyal companions. Many thoughts come and much discussion have we had. To-morrow we must march on to the Pole and then hasten home with all the speed we can compass. All the daydreams must go; it will be a wearisome return. . . .

Wednesday, January 17.—Camp 69. T. –22° at start. Night –21°. The Pole. Yes, but under very different circumstances from those expected. We have had a horrible day—add to our disappointment a head wind 4 to 5, with a temperature –22°, and companions laboring on with cold feet and hands. . . . This is an awful place and terrible enough for us to have labored to it without the reward of priority. Well, it is something to have got here. . . . Now for the run home and a desperate struggle. I wonder if we can do it.

Thursday morning, January 18.—[Scott and his men discover the tent left by Amundsen.] . . . In the tent we find a record of five Norwegians having been here. . . . The tent is fine—a small compact affair supported by a single bamboo. A note from Amundsen, which I keep, asks me to forward a letter to King Haakon [of Norway]! . . .

Sights at lunch gave us ½ to ¾ of a mile from the Pole, so we call it the Pole Camp. (Temp. Lunch –21°.) We built a cairn, put up our poor slighted Union Jack, and photographed ourselves—mighty cold work all of it. . . .

Well, we have turned our back now on the goal of our ambition and must face our 800 miles of solid dragging—and good-bye to most of the daydreams!

Monday, March 19.—Today we started in the usual dragging manner. Sledge dreadfully heavy. [It was filled with heavy geological specimens that the men collected along the way.] We are 15½ miles from the depot and ought to get there in three days. What progress! We have two days' food, but barely a day's fuel. All our feet are getting bad—Wilson's best, my right foot worse, left all right. There is no chance to nurse one's feet till we can get hot food into us. Amputation is the least I can hope for now, but will the trouble spread? That is the serious question. The weather doesn't give us a chance—the wind from N. N.W. and –40° temp. today.

Wednesday, March 21.—Got within 11 miles of depot Monday night; had to lie up all yesterday in a severe blizzard. Today forlorn hope, Wilson and Bowers going to depot for fuel.

[March] 22 and 23.—Blizzard bad as ever—Wilson and Bowers unable to start—tomorrow last chance—no fuel and only one or two of food left—must be near the end. Have decided it shall be natural—we shall march for the depot with or without our effects and die in our tracks.

[In November, a relief expedition found Scott, Wilson, and Bowers dead in their tent. The searchers also found Scott's diary, letters he had written, and thirty-five pounds of geological specimens the party had pulled on the sledge.]

1. What fears did both expeditions share? _being beaten to the Pole by the other team; not making it_

   back from the Pole alive

2. What hardships did both parties face? _extreme cold, frostbite, blizzards, strong winds, lack of communication_

   with the rest of the world (especially in an emergency)

3. Contrast the reactions of the two teams upon their arrival at the Pole. _Amundsen's team congratulated each_

   other and felt pride in and affection for their nation's flag and were grateful for each other's contributions to their

   accomplishment; Scott's team revealed no joy, only disappointment, doubts about getting back alive, and the

   awfulness of the cold weather.

4. Why would Amundsen leave a letter for Scott to deliver to King Haakon of Norway?

   In case Amundsen did not make it back alive to tell of his achievement, Scott might get back alive and deliver the

   letter to the Norwegian king.

5. Why did Scott have problems with the sledge? _It was hard to pull over difficult terrain, and it was filled with_

   heavy geological specimens. His journey would have been much easier, and perhaps he and his teammates would

   have survived, if they had been willing to unload some or all of them.

6. Why did Scott and his team not survive to make it back to their last depot?

   They were weak, frostbitten, low on food, and out of fuel; and a blizzard kept them from traveling the final miles to

   the depot.

7. What difference can you detect in the overall attitudes of Amundsen and Scott that might have had an

   effect on their respective expeditions? _Amundsen always seems to have had a positive, can-do attitude even_

   when the going was rough; Scott, on the other hand, seems to have had a generally negative attitude that might have

   affected the outcome of his expedition and the morale of his teammates.

CULTURAL GEOGRAPHY

MAP OF ANTARCTICA

Locate and label on the map each of the following places and features.

South Pole (mark with a red X)	Ellsworth Mountains	Ross Island
Antarctic Peninsula	South Pacific Ocean	Transantarctic Mountains
Indian Ocean	East Antarctica	South Atlantic Ocean
West Antarctica	Ross Sea	McMurdo Station (mark with a red dot)

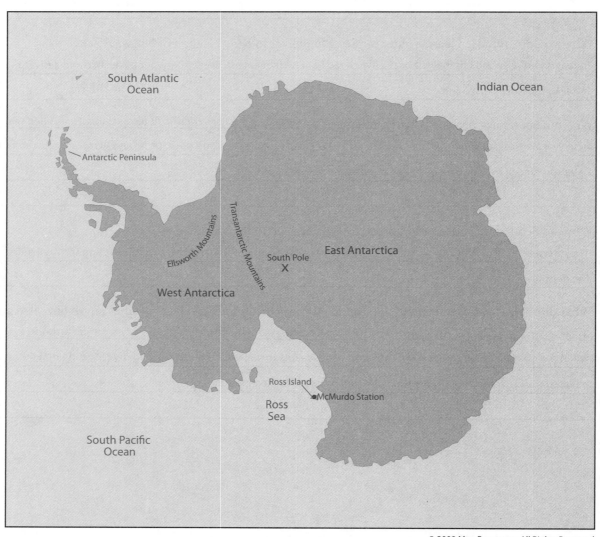

South Atlantic Ocean

Indian Ocean

Antarctic Peninsula

Ellsworth Mountains

Transantarctic Mountains

South Pole X

East Antarctica

West Antarctica

Ross Island

McMurdo Station

Ross Sea

South Pacific Ocean

SKILL: Maps

MAKING MEN INTO FISH

In the following reading selection, Jacques Cousteau—the famed diver, inventor of the Aqua-Lung self-contained underwater breathing apparatus (SCUBA), and popular documentary maker—shares the exhilaration he felt when he made the first dive using his invention. Read the selection carefully, and then answer the questions that follow.

One morning in June 1943, I went to the railway station at Bandol on the French Riviera and received a wooden case expressed from Paris. In it was a new and promising device, the result of years of struggle and dreams, an automatic compressed-air diving lung conceived by Émile Gagnan and myself. If it worked, diving could be revolutionized. I rushed it to Villa Barry where my diving comrades, Philippe Taillez and Frédéric Dumas waited.

We found an assembly of three moderate-sized cylinders of compressed air, linked to an air regulator the size of an alarm clock. From the regulator there extended two tubes, joining on a mouthpiece. With this equipment harnessed to the back, a water-tight glass mask over the eyes and nose, and rubber foot fins, we intended to make unencumbered flights in the depths of the sea.

We hurried to a sheltered cove which would conceal our activity from curious bathers and Italian occupation troops. [This is in 1943, the middle of World War II, when France was under the control of the Axis powers.] Staggering under the fifty-pound apparatus, I walked with a Charlie Chaplin waddle into the sea.

A modest canyon opened below, full of dark green weeds, black sea urchins and small flowerlike white algae. Fingerlings browsed in the scene. The land sloped down into a clear blue infinity. The sun struck so brightly I had to squint. My arms hanging down at my sides, I kicked the fins languidly [weakly, without much force] and traveled down, gaining speed, watching the beach reeling past. I stopped kicking, and the momentum carried me on a fabulous glide.

My human lungs had a new role to play, that of a sensitive ballasting system. I took normal breaths in a slow rhythm, bowed my head and swam smoothly down to thirty feet. I felt no increasing water pressure, which at that depth is twice that of the surface. The Aqua-Lung automatically fed me increased compressed air to meet the new pressure layer.

I reached the bottom in a state of transport [elation]. A school of silvery sars (goat bream), round and flat as saucers, swam in a rocky chaos. I compared myself favorably with the sars. To swim fishlike, horizontally, was the logical method in a medium eight hundred times denser than air. To halt and hang attached to nothing, no lines or air pipe to the surface, was a dream.

I thought of the helmet diver arriving where I was on his ponderous boots and struggling to walk a few yards, obsessed with his umbilici and his head imprisoned in copper. On skin dives I had seen him leaning dangerously forward to make a step, clamped in heavier pressure at the ankles than the head, a cripple in an alien land. From this day forward we would swim across miles of country no man had known, free and level, with our flesh feeling what the fish scales know.

[Excerpt "One morning in June 1943...what the fish scales know." from THE SILENT WORLD by JACQUES-YVES COUSTEAU with Frédéric Dumas. Copyright 1953 by Harper & Row, publishers, Inc. Copyright © renewed 1981 by Jacques-Yves Cousteau. Reprinted by permission of HarperCollins Publishers. Copyright © 1953 by Hamish Hamilton. Copyright © 1958 by Penguin Books. Reproduced by permission of Penguin Books Ltd.

1. Who was Cousteau's co-inventor of the Aqua-Lung? _Émile Gagnan_____

2. Why was Cousteau careful to ensure privacy when he began testing his new invention?

desire to avoid curiosity-seeking bathers and fear that nearby Axis soldiers might confiscate his invention or perhaps

even accuse him of spying or attempted sabotage

3. Why do you think Cousteau had two other divers, Philippe Taillez and Frédéric Dumas, dive with him?

to ensure safety in case anything should go wrong with the equipment or perhaps in case he encountered any

underwater hazards

4. What caused Cousteau to walk to the water in Charlie Chaplin fashion? the weight of the equipment

and the awkwardness of walking with the large fins on his feet

5. Contrast Cousteau's new Aqua-Lung and the older-style diving suit. The Aqua-Lung allowed Cousteau to

swim unencumbered by lines, tubes, or very heavy boots, helmet, and lead weights. Instead, he could swim freely

horizontally, without fear of losing his balance and falling forward, in which case he would not have been able to rise

on his own. He did not have to depend on someone on the surface to supply his air. And he could turn his head freely,

seeing all around him.

6. What are some uses of the Aqua-Lung today? rescuing people or searching for bodies underwater,

retrieving things that have been lost underwater, conducting scientific studies, engaging in strategic or

tactical national defense activities, taking underwater photographs, etc.

SKILL: Original Sources

CHAPTER REVIEW

**Match the person with the event or activity for which he is remembered in history.
(Note: One of the items has more than one answer.)**

A.	Roald Amundsen	H.	Jacques Cousteau
B.	Robert Ballard	I.	Matthew Maury
C.	William Beebe	J.	Douglas Mawson
D.	Thaddeus von Bellingshausen	K.	Jacques Piccard
E.	Carsten Borchgrevink	L.	Robert Scott
F.	James Ross Clark	M.	Ernest Shackleton
G.	James Cook	N.	Don Walsh

_____G_____ 1. Circumnavigated Antarctica in 1773 in search of a southern continent

_____D_____ 2. Sailed around Antarctica, discovering Peter I Island in the process

_____E_____ 3. First explorer to winter in Antarctica

_____F_____ 4. Made three expeditions to Antarctica; discovered several places, including McMurdo Bay

_____J_____ 5. Discovered the Shackleton Ice Shelf

_____A_____ 6. Led expedition of first humans to reach the South Pole

_____L_____ 7. Led second expedition to reach the South Pole but died on the return trip

_____M_____ 8. Led first expedition to discover the South Pole but turned back 97 miles short of it

_____H_____ 9. First person to dive beneath the ice of Antarctica

_____I_____ 10. The "Pathfinder of the Sea"; studied ocean currents

_____C_____ 11. Went below the photic zone in his bathysphere

_____H_____ 12. Inventor of the Aqua-Lung

K and N 13. Descended to the bottom of the Mariana Trench in bathyscaphe

_____B_____ 14. Discovered the wreckage of the Titanic

CAREERS IN GEOGRAPHY

Now that you have completed your textbook, you have become acquainted with information that is used in a variety of career fields under the "geography" umbrella. Following is a list of eight broad geographic fields. Beside each one, list as many specific job types as you can that might fit under the broad category. (The first one is done for you as an example.) Answers will vary.

1. Cartography, geographic information systems (GIS), remote sensing

   planners, engineers, utility companies, state agencies, construction companies, surveyors, architects, computer mappers

2. Cultural and human geography   Peace Corps volunteer, community development, map librarian, missionary

3. Economic geography   location expert, market researcher, traffic manager (shipper), route delivery manager, real estate agent/broker/appraiser

4. Environmental studies   environmental manager, forestry technician, park ranger (county, state, or national level), hazardous waste planner

5. Geographic education   elementary teacher, secondary (junior high or high school) teacher, college professor, overseas teacher

6. Physical geography and earth science   weather forecaster/meteorologist, outdoor guide, coastal zone manager, soil conservationist, agricultural extension agent, hydrologist

7. Regional geography   area specialist, international business representative, travel agent

8. Urban and/or regional planning   urban/community planner, transportation (logistics) planner, health services planner

SKILLS: Synthesis, Analysis